D0887758

MAIN STREET REVISITED

The American Land & Life Series

EDITED BY WAYNE FRANKLIN

Time, Space, and

Image Building in

Small-Town America

RICHARD V. FRANCAVIGLIA

Foreword by Wayne Franklin

University of Iowa Press

Iowa City

STREET
REVISITED

N ST. EAST, HARTFORD, MICH.

University of Iowa Press,
Iowa City 52242
Copyright © 1996 by the University of Iowa Press
All rights reserved
Printed in the United States of America
Design by Richard Hendel

Library of Congress Cataloging-in-Publication Data
Francaviglia, Richard V.
Main street revisited: time, space, and image building in
small-town America / by Richard V. Francaviglia;
foreword by Wayne Franklin.
p.   cm. — (The American land and life series)
Includes bibliographical references and index.
ISBN 0-87745-542-2 (cloth), ISBN 0-87745-543-0 (pbk.)
1. City planning — United States.   2. City planning — United States —
Maps.   3. City planning — United States — Pictorial works.
4. City and town life — United States.   I. Title.   II. Series.
HT167.F73   1996
307.76′2′0973 — dc20   95-47773
                                                              CIP

01   00   99   98   97   96   C   5   4   3   2   1
01   00   99   98   97   96   P   5   4   3   2   1

Not houses finely roofed or the stones of

walls well-builded, . . . make the city, but men able

to use their opportunity. — Alcaeus, quoted

in Aristides, *Rhodian Oration*

Dedicated to

EDWARD T. PRICE

Now Professor Emeritus, University of Oregon,

who as my major professor and writer of

important landscape studies encouraged, inspired,

and nurtured my interest in townscapes at the

University of Oregon in the late 1960s

CONTENTS

FOREWORD

By Wayne Franklin

Although the particular places we inhabit may seem resilient, unique, as far from each other in character as they are in space, we all recognize that the great majority of them repeat themes found all over the place. Like language, the human environment in fact is built from a few disarmingly simple elements. The variations on those elements produce difference without destroying intelligibility.

Richard Francaviglia is an astute student of what is intelligible in our landscape precisely because he shows how it proceeds from common sources. In *Main Street Revisited: Time, Space, and Image Building in Small-Town America*, he undertakes to explain how one of the most potent of American places has evolved over time and across space while retaining much of its essential character. He describes many actual, concrete Main Streets in the process — especially those of the Victorian town and small city — but description is not what most engages his attention. Rather, he is intrigued by the forces that caused this dominant cultural form to emerge as the axis of so many American settlements. At the crossroads of commerce and transportation, civic identity and spatial range, Main Street provided both a convenient entrepôt and a material definition of citizenship for countless communities literally across the land. It was public space structured by common activity or need and giving to the people's experience a rich body of limits and metaphors. Although it owed its origins to patterns imported from various points of departure in the Old World, it assumed in the course of American history a peculiar relation to the terms of our experience. Among all the public spaces where Americans have gathered — for good purpose or ill — few have become so evocative of the community itself as has Main Street.

Of course Main Street has undergone many crucial changes over time. The Federal-era rebuilding of the New England town that Joseph Wood has chronicled, for instance, created an illusion that the town centers of that region were survivals from the colonial age, whereas in many instances they were the fabrications of a later era, funded by new wealth and serving to solidify a new perception of a somewhat illusory past. What we now think of as Main Street itself was likewise the creature of the commercial culture of the nineteenth century. Although it has been loaded with all kinds of similarly antique meanings, the Main Street shopping district is structured around not only the imperatives of material systems (things such as proximity, concentration, the movement of goods across the counter and across town) but also, and one might say more importantly, the commercial assumptions of modern consumer culture. It is an apparatus of the modern cash/credit economy and presumes fairly high income levels, intensive levels of exchange, and a spatially focused population indoctrinated in the virtues of consumption.

Once this larger structure of values was more or less in place, the particular variations of Main Street design as Francaviglia explores them served to direct, attract, and control the interest of the populace. And they served to amuse the populace as well. In the process, Main Street ceased to be simply a place rooted in the values and activities of the people and became an idea as well. Perhaps especially as Main Street began to yield to newer material realities — from catalog marketing as instituted by the Chicago mail order retailers to the growing dominance of the automobile as a form of transport and an adjunct of "shopping" — it was burdened with new meanings. To borrow the terms of Benedict Anderson, it became a kind of imagined community, or an image of imagined community, which itself could be marketed.

This new sense of the meaning of Main Street emerged in the literature and films of the twentieth century. The key figure in its development was Walt Disney, less in his films than in his brilliant articulation of a reduced-scale archetype of the Main Street landscape at Disneyland. This symbolic landscape drew on Disney's own memories of small-town Missouri, but it was nourished as well, as Francaviglia shows, by the memories of those who worked with him on this massive "imagineering" project — especially the architect Harper Goff, whose experience in Fort Collins, Colorado, contributed much to the look and layout of the resulting amusement landscape. Disney's genius lay in his ability to tap (and shape) the fantasies of his audiences; in developing the Main Street area of Disneyland, he likewise gave concrete expression to the longing of his fellow citizens for a simpler, more cohesive sense of community than their malls and shopping strips, attenuated by the libertarian automobile, could provide. That his Main Street is the epitome of commercialism — one has to pay, after all, even to walk down it, and it is full of sites for further spending and consumption — makes it the ideal, supersaturated arche-type of the cultural landscape it seeks at the same time to cast as a good-old-days antidote to modern alienation. Ironically, Disneyland has it both ways, preaching against the present and charging the audience for the sermon.

Common landscapes acquire real power when they cease to be just actual places and become an idiom detachable from specific locations. It was probably the small-town boosters of the last century who first created a Main Street idiom and sought to make the health of local communities dependent on the brisk pace of exchange — commercial and civic — tak-ing place there. Francaviglia powerfully portrays the physical alterations of the Main Street landscape, but he shows as well this shift of terms to an-other, more complex level. It is the imagery of this ubiquitous American place that engages his attention most of all, and it is here that he makes, at last, his most important contribution. He helps us understand as few oth-ers have that Main Street — or any equivalent place we all share — exists not so much on the map of the land as in our hearts and minds. His book is a worthy guide to the lay of that territory at the same time that it sketches the other, outer landscape we all know so well that we could — and probably do — glide down it in our dreams. As with *Hard Places: Reading the Landscape of America's Historic Mining Districts*, his first book in Iowa's American Land and Life series, in *Main Street Revisited* he dissects with humor, insight, and enthusiasm a physical sector of our shared life that we take for granted precisely because it is so common. He succeeds so well in such endeavors because he understands that it is the common things in life which have the capacity to shape our experience most profoundly. He is among a handful of scholars able to look about and make sense of what too often most of us don't really see. It is this acu-ity of vision that makes all his work so valuable. Here and elsewhere, by making us see the world we live in together in crisp and significant detail, he helps us understand why we think and feel as we do about that world. In doing so, he helps strengthen our vision, refine our values, and enrich our spirits.

ACKNOWLEDGMENTS

Small-town America inspires many people in many walks of life: from townsfolk on the street willing to share impressions with me to scholars in diverse fields who write and speak about small towns. Without their help this book could never have been written.

My interest in landscapes was nurtured by Edward T. Price of the University of Oregon during the halcyon years of the late 1960s. Many graduate students, including Larry Ford, Gale Dixon, Dick Fusch, Stan Demars, and the late Aaron Gallup, shared their insights about American towns. Mike Schneerer, graduate student at the University of Minnesota, travelled extensively with me in 1971–72 in search of townscapes and inspired me to begin recording my ideas about Main Street. As an architectural design student, Ken Pavelchak at Antioch College shared many astute observations in the 1970s, as did geography student Tom Harvey. Nina Myatt and intern Scott Sanders of the Antiochiana Collection at Antioch College provided historic photographs of Yellow Springs. Barbara Bailey, careful observer of Oregon's towns, wrote an inspirational book on that subject that serves as model for detailed regional townscape study. Mary Means, formerly of the National Trust, shared many observations in the early seminal years of the national Main Street Project.

Popular culture authority Margaret King provided inspiration in the form of insightful observations about American popular culture, and local historian Trella Romine, of Caledonia, Ohio, helped by sending me photographs and information. Robert Puschendorf of the Nebraska State Historical Society provided information on the state's new Main Street Program, and Susan Roth of the Minnesota Historical Society provided historical photographs of Owatonna; Sandy Elder of the California State Historic Preservation Office located photos of the Sacramento Valley Delta town of Locke; Julian Campbell, chair of the Bloomfield, Iowa Historic Preservation Commission, and Loren Horton of the State Historical Society of Iowa in Iowa City provided important information about Iowa communities. Chandler Jackson of the University of Texas at Arlington and Merri Greenwood of Dallas located lyrics of 1970s songs about Main

Street. Katherine (Kit) Goodwin, Gerald Saxon, Marcelle Hull, and Jane Boley of UTA also provided information on Southwestern towns from the University's excellent Special Collections; David Narrett of UTA's History Department kindly shared important information about Colonial Dutch towns with me, and other members of the department, including Ken Philp, Stan Palmer, and Don Kyle, were very helpful.

My friend William (Bill) Dunaway inspired me by relating stories of growing up near the courthouse square in Decatur, Texas, and of his genealogical travels to his ancestor's home town of Shelbyville, Tennessee. Cynthia Beeman, Frances Rickard and Anise Read of the Texas Historical Commission willingly shared information on historic buildings and the Texas Main Street Program; Steve Gordon, Mary Anne Peters, Sandy Davies, Jeff Brown, and David Simmons of the Ohio Historical Society gladly assisted in the searches for information on towns in the Buckeye State. Karal Ann Marling and Andrew Lainsbury of the University of Minnesota helped find important information about the early Disney "imagineers." Rheba Massey of the Fort Collins, Colorado, Public Library's Local History Office kindly shared information and showed me historic buildings in the community. Arthur Hart of the Idaho Historical Society provided information on architectural details. Senior Secretary Darlene McAllister of the University of Texas at Arlington deserves special thanks for typing numerous drafts of the manuscript and providing editorial suggestions as the manuscript took form. Wayne Franklin never lost faith in this book and offered guidance and encouragement. These good people, and many more that I have not mentioned, deserve my sincere thanks.

INTRODUCTION

MY ADVENT IN A LITTLE TOWN OFTEN CREATED A SENSATION,

ESPECIALLY WHEN I TOOK A CHAIR AND SITTING IN IT IN THE CENTER OF A

STREET FOR AN HOUR OR MORE, TOOK A SKETCH. "WHAT IS THAT —— FOOL

DOING THERE IN A CHAIR?" WAS NOT AN UNCOMMON QUERY FROM THOSE

WITHIN MY EAR-SHOT. A KNOT GENERALLY GATHERED AROUND ME, AND

THUS WAS I PROTECTED FROM BEING RUN OVER BY SOME PASSING

VEHICLE. — HENRY HOWE, *HISTORICAL COLLECTIONS OF OHIO*

When Henry Howe wrote these humorous words more than a century ago, he spoke from more than forty years' experience as a chronicler of American townscapes. Those of us who record small towns today, camera in hand, get much the same reaction; people often ask questions such as "What do you find so interesting about this town?"

As a historian, Henry Howe instinctively knew that *all* communities possess interesting stories. Inspired by one of America's first recorders of the visual landscapes of small towns, John Warner Barber, Howe devoted his life to recording the landscapes and history of what we now call "ordinary places." Both Barber and Howe were New Englanders, and, according to Howe, Barber's 1838 *Historical Collections of Connecticut* "came upon the people like magic," for "few had ever seen pictures of places with which they were acquainted."[1] Following in Barber's footsteps, and on occasion even working with him, Henry Howe became an observer whose passion for observing, recording, and interpreting small towns remains an inspiration to the current day.

During his nearly-century-long lifetime (1816–1913), Henry Howe had ample opportunity to observe great changes in the American landscape. As recorded in Howe's many histories, America's towns reflected the development and prosperity of the country.[2] For Howe, the commercial centers of towns — what we today call "Main Street" — became the show-places of the American towns he depicted. When illustrating his histories, he most often included lithographs of Main Street as an indicator of the conditions in the community and the progress that had taken place between widely separated dates such as 1847 and 1887. Two observers of the small town recently noted, "The viability of a small town's Main Street gives a good indication of the overall health of a community."[3] Even in Howe's time, a community's Main Street was a visible manifestation of its business and political activity, its life in particular, and American life in general. Only in the relatively recent past have we separated Main Street from Wall Street. Whereas Wall Street today symbolizes large corporate transactions and Main Street symbolizes the everyday locales and the merchants and entrepreneurs who are affected by what seem to be increasingly centralized (and arbitrary) decisions, in the early nineteenth century they were one.

Although Main Street symbolized progress to Howe's generation, to us it now symbolizes the past and perhaps the alleged sanctity and security that were part of earlier, slower times. In the century and a half since Henry Howe wrote his first histories, "Main Street" has come to symbolize a place close to the people, people who have few pretenses and honest aspirations; and because it fuses images of place and time, it also symbolizes their past. Small wonder, then, that Main Street is easily romanticized and has become one of America's most cherished images. And yet, because Main Street is such a cherished icon for small-town America, it has also become a rallying point for cultural critics who see it as embodying petty concerns. Scholars — some critical and others laudatory of small towns — now realize that Main Street shows no signs of disappearing. The enduring popularity of Main Street has witnessed its becoming a part of Americans' everyday thoughts and conversations. Thus, a recent advertisement in a model builder's magazine noted, "Every town has a Main Street USA, and everyone has memories of the 'Main Street' in his or her hometown."[4] As if to exemplify the adaptability of Main Street as a concept, it is significant that WordPerfect's new "Main Street Program," as advertised in a recent issue of *Family Fun* magazine, invites the reader to "move your playroom to Main Street" with the reassuring words that "there's no better place for kids to play than on WordPerfect® Main Street."[5]

As both a place and a concept, Main Street is ubiquitous and characteristically American, which is perhaps why the immensely popular fictional American character Forrest Gump hailed from the archetypal small town of Greenbow, Alabama, with its Main Street of older red-brick commercial buildings drawing people from the surrounding rural countryside. Although America is an urban country and has been for nearly eighty years, and despite the growth of suburbs over the last fifty years, it is especially revealing that most American heroes, presidents included, have been — and continue to be — from small-town America. President Clinton's hometown of Hope, Arkansas, is but the latest example of this American phenomenon.

There are several thousand small towns in the United States, and, by definition, as many Main Streets. As the heart of the small town, Main Street serves many purposes, perhaps the most important of which is retailing — the marketing or sale of items or services to the public. As if to blur the distinctions between its economic and social functions, Main Street is usually chosen as the location of community parades, during which many people line the street and others march down it in celebration of important events. The social connection is strengthened as Main Street is also the location of government and its services. Buildings such as a city or town hall or a courthouse are an integral part of Main Street. As if to symbolize the multifaceted aspect of Main Street, the city hall may also serve as a place of entertainment — as in the case of the small, multipurpose "opera houses" that could be found in most towns with more than a thousand residents. Churches, railroad stations, grain elevators, water towers, and other important buildings and features may also be important landmarks on, or very near, Main Street; yet they are always seen in reference to the commercial buildings which line the street.

So closely does the development of Main Street parallel and reflect the life of the town that I have developed, and successfully used, a rule of thumb for towns with fewer than 12,000 people: a town's population size is closely correlated with the number of blocks of Main Street commercial architecture. Normally a block-long Main Street will characterize a community of about 500 people; a two-block-long Main Street will indicate approximately 1,000 people; four blocks about 2,000; six blocks about 4,000 to 5,000. Typically, however, Main Street will only reach a certain length (usually four blocks) before the downtown begins developing into a more squared-off or compact form — seemingly to avoid creating too long a distance to traverse. When a town is developed around a square, the formula still holds: only towns with a rather substantial population (say, 1,500 to 2,000 people) will be able to build commercial structures around all four sides of the square. This rule of thumb assumes that the built-up area reflects the population at the time the construction occurred. Therefore, in a town having a four-block Main Street and only a thousand people, many of the businesses are likely to be boarded up. Both the size and the appearance of Main Street are indicators of population change and its economic consequences.

For the purposes of this book I shall define small towns as having a population of more than about 750 and fewer than 30,000 people. These communities are large enough to have a Main Street but small enough not to take on too many characteristics of decidedly urban places. Smaller places are more likely to be hamlets; larger places are more appropriately called small cities.

When I first began writing about small-town Main Streets more than twenty years ago, I distinguished those classic *linear* Main Streets from those that exhibited *nodality* by being developed in relation to courthouse and other squares, for the linearity in the former and the centrality in the latter are indeed important design aspects.[6] Subsequent scholars have used a similar approach, considering Main Street to be linear.[7] In this book, however, I urge that Main Street be expanded to include *all* small-town commercial core areas, whether they be linear or nucleated; thus the area around a village green in the heart of a New England village (which D. W. Meinig considered to be one of America's most significant icons along with Main Street and the California suburb)[8] and the courthouse squares and plazas farther west are all included under my definition of "Main Street."

In this book, then, Main Street is used rather broadly in that it is synonymous with the downtown commercial area or district of the small town. I adopt this definition because it is helpful in understanding how real Main Streets developed into several major types of small urbanistic designs. Moreover, a broad definition enables us to better understand the contemporary incarnations of Main Street in places like theme parks, that is, Main Street as a popular icon in environments of popular culture. Whereas some writers and musicians have given Main Street decidedly urban (and sometimes rather seedy) connotations, as in songs like Bob Seeger's "Down on Main Street," the term Main Street in this book simply refers to the design and development of any small town's commercial center.

In the process of photographing and sketching Main Streets for nearly thirty years, it has become apparent to me that all Main Streets contain the seeds of urban patterns. In their historic architecture and street patterns, as well as in their placement of civic, commercial, and residential buildings, they provide glimpses into the history of American urban design. Because of their rather arrested development (that is, because they did not develop into major urban centers), many American towns possess an embryonic urban character that has been lost in our cities. Thus, small towns remain treasure troves of historic patterns, and they are best studied as small urban places.

Like all urban landscapes, Main Street consists of three major elements:

the *street* and its pattern
the *buildings* and other structures on property parcels
the *open spaces*, such as parks, squares, and greens.

In his seminal work, *Public Places: Exploring Their History*, Gerald Danzer interpreted historic "postcards of Main Street" by focussing on four major categories:

the buildings: their architecture and their functions
the vehicles on the streets
the people in the view
the street itself: its paving and its furnishings.

Thus, although Main Street is likely to convey images of buildings, Danzer's work reaffirms that streetscape is a combination of factors — building type and style, street configuration, open spaces, people, details — that convey the character of a particular place at a particular time. Since all of these elements occur in place and time, a town is never the same when viewed at different times in its history. Geography and history are inseparable in that both the location of a town (the cultural and physical setting) and the time at which it was developed help determine its character.

Place and time — two elements of extreme importance — are the defining elements of, respectively, geography and history. In interpreting Main Street, I join other authors who have sought to define the character of small towns, notably geographers John Jakle, Bob Bastian, Peirce Lewis, and Barbara Bailey and architectural historians Spiro Kostof, Richard Longstreth, and Carole Rifkind. The works of historians such as R. Lingeman and Lewis Atherton were also influential to my thinking about Main Street, but it was the works of urban-planning historian John Reps that, in retrospect, most influenced this book. In addition to academic writings, I also call upon the works of novelists when they offer insights often missed by other writers. The writings of many diverse disciplines are cited in the bibliography, and should be considered essential reading for students of America's Main Streets. Some of the sources are old but certainly not outdated, as they describe and interpret towns during important phases of their development; this literature is rich and has yet to be superseded. Recent important works on small towns are also cited. The latest, *Remembering Main Street* by Pat Ross, confirms how nostalgic we have become about Main Street. As the bibliography reveals, Main Street has been a subject of sustained interest, in both the scholarly and the popular press, since the 1920s.

In adding to the rich body of literature, I hope to offer a rather different — a considerably broader and more personal or anecdotal — approach to the study and interpretation of American Main Streets. I begin with the hypothesis that places like Main Street need to be interpreted as both real places and as expressions of collectively shared or experienced assumptions, designs, and myths. As a historical geographer, I have been fascinated by the persistence, even resurrection, of certain cultural geographic settlement types. Main Street as *archetype*[9] is one of them. By this I refer to the fact that certain specific places come to typify a whole category of places like them, so that they can serve as convenient summary statements for an entire group, or class, of places. If shown a photograph of a typical "Main Street" featuring a more or less solidly built up row of turn-of-the-century commercial buildings either fronting a square or lining the street, most Americans would easily identify it as "Main Street

USA." When asked why, many of my students cite the architecture and design features, including the characteristics of building style and height; these serve to brand the place as generically "Main Street" to them, and to many other people in all walks of life. Put quite succinctly, why and how this "Main Street" streetscape came to be — and how it became so recognizable — is the subject of this study.

This book consists of three sections. The first underscores the importance of *time* in creating place. In it, I interpret the evolution of Main Street using the most ephemeral but revealing component of Main Street: individual buildings. Through time, Main Street commercial architecture developed a distinctive personality. Like the American population itself, Main Street consists of individuals who retain their individual character while being enough like their neighbors in, say, dress and values to be identified as American. The design of Main Street invites the question, how much individuality and eccentricity will be permitted before the image breaks down? As will be seen, Main Street architecture offers very important lessons in conformity and standardization.

The second section focusses on the importance of *space* in the creation of place. In this section, the importance of street plan and property-parcel shape is interpreted as giving substance to buildings which would otherwise exist only as isolated fragments, with no order or pattern. Although a relatively limited number of street and plat patterns became institutionalized as a matrix for all Main Street development, there is, as this section reveals, a rich diversity of streetscapes, which are in part dependent on culture, economy, environment — elements which are expressed regionally. Continuing the analogy, Main Streets, like people, vary regionally in that just as accents and other traits can serve to identify *where* in America a person is from, so, too, can physical elements, such as town plans and building and streetscape details, tell us in which region of America a particular Main Street developed.

The third section of this book focusses on popular *images*, that is, the power of Main Street in our shared or collective consciousness as Americans. Regional identities notwithstanding, Main Street has come to symbolize the national American experience. On Main Street — according to the shared mythology, at least — the honest merchant, the hardworking townsfolk, and an accessible community government are all found in close proximity to one another. The streetscape reflects what seem to be time-honored traditions nurtured away from cities; again, time (the good old days) and place (nonurban if not exactly rural America) are important components of this stereotypical image.

In addressing the issue of how and why Main Street is so important to Americans today, I look sympathetically but realistically at how the powerful Main Street image developed and the methods by which it persists in the late twentieth century. This section reaffirms that life can imitate art — if by art we mean the works of filmmakers, novelists, and even the developers of theme parks. It also reaffirms the power of image building in creating the icons that become the substance of popular culture, where images are as voraciously "consumed" as products.

Ultimately, this book is about the material culture or artifactual evidence that decision makers — architects, town platters, and image makers — have left us as their legacy. Where possible, I have provided background information on these people that will permit the reader to better understand and appreciate their role in the process of townscape creation. As seen through the lives of the people who created them, Main Streets are, above all, creations that symbolize both individual and collective human energy, aspirations, and dreams. The reader is reminded that although material culture is being studied and interpreted (that is, Main Street as artifact), it is always *people* who create and sustain both the material objects and the resultant images of place.

This human drama of creation and interpretation always occurs in time, space, and place: all three are interrelated, and intersect, in both real Main Streets and those of popular culture. To help the reader to better understand the themes that characterize the design and evolution of American Main Streets, I have identified sixteen axioms — concepts or generalizations that seem to hold true for the depth of time and breadth of space that have witnessed Main Street's growth, from colonial times to the present and from coast to coast. Readers will judge for themselves whether I have succeeded in providing new insights about, and a new appreciation of, Main Street. I hope that the people who create, sustain, and enjoy Main Street will understand that I share their intuitive appreciation of Main Street as a vital part of the American experience. Thus, quite aside from any philosophical expectations, if this book stimulates readers to look more closely at and appreciate Main Street, then it will have served the purpose for which it was written.

MAIN STREET REVISITED

MAIN ST. EAST, HARTFORD, MICH.

1: TIME AND MAIN STREET

The Origins and Evolution of an Image

THE PLACES WE HAVE KNOWN DO NOT BELONG ONLY TO THE LITTLE

WORLD OF SPACE ON WHICH WE MAP THEM FOR OUR OWN CONVENIENCE.

NONE OF THEM WAS EVER MORE THAN A THIN SLICE, HELD BETWEEN THE

CONTIGUOUS IMPRESSIONS THAT COMPOSED OUR LIFE AT THAT TIME; THE

MEMORY OF A PARTICULAR IMAGE IS BUT REGRET FOR A PARTICULAR

MOMENT; AND HOUSES, ROADS, AVENUES ARE AS FUGITIVE,

ALAS, AS THE YEARS. — MARCEL PROUST, *SWANN'S WAY*

ain Street, like all places, has developed its personality and identity through time. As it is now commonly understood, the term "Main Street" signifies the built-up commercial area, or downtown, of small communities. Geographers and planners know it as the "Central Business District" (or CBD); economists call it the "commercial core"; writers portray it as the "heart" of the town. For more than two centuries, writers and travellers have commented on the look or appearance of towns, and in particular the downtown, where civic and commercial buildings fronted on important streets. A century and a half ago, James Fenimore Cooper understood the importance of Main Street when he wrote that "everywhere a country presents its best face towards its thoroughfares."[1]

In the later nineteenth century, Americans learned about their towns from the many illustrated newspapers and atlases that flourished during the Victorian era. Issues of the popular periodicals, including *Frank Leslie's Illustrated Newspaper*, often contained beautiful lithographs, woodcuts, and steel engravings of small-town scenes; typically, Main Street was prominent among them (fig. 1). The art and science of photog-

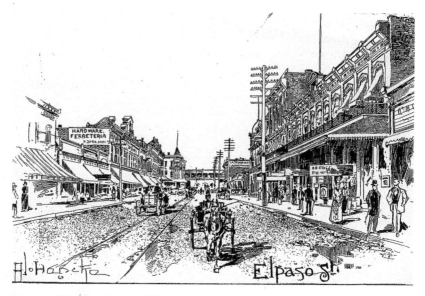

Figure 1. *The Main Street of El Paso, Texas, 1890, as it appeared in* Frank Leslie's Illustrated Newspaper, *reveals a corridor of activity — the street — framed by commercial buildings. Although El Paso was urbanizing rapidly at this time and would later become a city of 600,000 people, the street at the time conveyed the atmosphere of a bustling Victorian-era town of about 10,000 people.* Frank Leslie's Illustrated Newspaper, *Texas edition, 1890; courtesy Special Collections, the University of Texas at Arlington Libraries.*

raphy flourished in the late nineteenth century, and most towns were recorded for posterity by local or itinerant photographers. Among the most popular of subjects was a Main Street filled with activity: market day, parades, and other festivals were often immortalized as the photographer recorded the scene and then emerged from the darkroom with a record of Main Street at its busiest (fig. 2). During the golden years of the American postcard (1890–1920), when people communicated on the reverse side of photographic images of everyday scenes, Main Street was a common vignette (fig. 3).

As depicted in the many photograph and postcard collections that preserve these images, Main Street is always recognizable by the buildings that line it; most are rather elaborately detailed and formal, distinctive enough in style to command our attention and interest. Architecturally, Main Street is characterized by a repetition of individual buildings that have faces or "personalities" determined by their massing, window and

Figure 2. *The drama on the Main Street of Rufus, in eastern Oregon, was recorded as locals posed and horses and wagons crowded the wide thoroughfare to deliver sacked grain to the railroad about 1880. Trees have been planted on Main Street to soften the impact of the barren central Oregon prairie. This magnificent photographic image preserved the events — and the appearance of the streetscape — for posterity. W. A. Raymond, Bettmann Archive.*

door openings, rooflines, and other elements cited by architectural historians. Some of these buildings may convey an impression of "Main Street" more readily than others, for in reality most Main Streets consist not of one type or style of buildings but of several styles that were developed through time. Although most of the buildings on Main Street are usually

MAIN ST. EAST, HARTFORD, MICH,

Figure 3. *A postcard of Main Street East, Hartford, Michigan, ca. 1900, reveals a familiar landscape: a street defined by rows of highly detailed Victorian commercial buildings. The trees mark the end of the commercial district and the beginning of residences. Thousands of postcard scenes helped immortalize otherwise typical and anonymous small towns. Postcard originally published by Will P. Canaan Company, Grand Rapids, Michigan; author's collection.*

less than three stories in height (resulting in a streetscape with a relatively low profile), they may take different forms: Some may be simple, some complex, some narrow, some wide. Some may have towers or turrets, others simple rooflines. Any streetscape like Main Street ultimately consists of individual buildings, despite the fact that they may form the connected commercial assemblages (that is, be joined wall to wall to form a row of buildings) that are commonplace along small-town America's Main Streets.

ARCHITECTURAL STYLES AND MAIN STREET DEVELOPMENT

How did American Main Streets come to possess the distinctive profile and visual character that make them so immediately recognizable? The answer lies in the application of architecture (building design and technology) to solve a common problem: creating and situating a building so that it maximizes the travelling public's access to it. By looking closely at the Main Street of a particular town through time, one can read or interpret how the architecture developed to serve the community's needs. Doing so involves an understanding that certain features or elements of buildings, such as basic floor plan, roof type, and detailing, may change through time. Architects and architectural historians use the term "style" to refer to how these traits or elements are configured. They speak of a building having a certain massing, a type of roof, and a type of window detailing as fitting into a certain style. Thus, they would call most of the buildings facing Main Street in the postcard view of Hartford, Michigan (fig. 3), "Victorian Italianate Commercial Style" in that the buildings have trim typical of the Victorian period (mid to late nineteenth century), derived from architecture originally found in Italy, and the shape of the buildings expresses their commercial function. Typically, architectural styles are named after either place (e.g., "Greek Revival"), time periods (such as the "Federal" from ca. 1775–1820 in recognition of the early years of the United States), or people (usually architects, such as "Sullivanesque" after the American architect Louis Sullivan). By nature, styles are somewhat arbitrary or subjective, but architectural historians usually agree on the major styles, which have become widely accepted in the literature. Style is especially helpful — in most cases — in determining the general time period of construction.

Architectural style is one of the indicators of change and stability on Main Street. In certain cases, enough of a Main Street's earliest architecture, as determined by the architectural style of the building, may remain for the student to trace the street's development backward in time to when Main Street first became the commercial center of town. In many cases, however, not all of the Main Street's architectural legacy remains, for demolition and rebuilding have occurred, and therefore a picture of how the town looked at any particular point in time (say 1800 or 1950) will have to be "reconstructed" using historical descriptions, photographs, or sketches.

When observing Main Street at a particular point in time, either in the present or a century ago, we must ask the question, How *typical*, or representative, is this Main Street compared to other Main Streets elsewhere? Using accepted stylistic definitions, it becomes apparent that only a finite number of architectural styles are, or have been, found on a typical Main Street since its inception. That explains why the Main Street of Hartford, Michigan, looks quite similar to other Main Streets of the same period.

1. End chimney	15. Base	29. Semicircular arch	43. Modillion
2. Eave	16. Multiple-arched storefront	30. Central pavilion	44. Dentil
3. Lintel window head	17. Brackets	31. Mansard roof	45. Masonry round arch
4. 9 over 6 sash	18. Hood mold	32. Dormer	46. Projecting eave
5. Sidelight	19. Plate glass	33. Quoins	47. Window enframement
6. Elliptical arch	20. Tower	34. Turret	48. Chicago window
7. Pedimented gable	21. Lunettes	35. Finial	49. Spandrel
8. Tympanum	22. Stone banding	36. Bay window	50. Pier
9. Raking cornice	23. String course	37. Transom window	51. Parapet
10. Entablature	24. Buttress	38. Belt course	52. Roman arch
11. Metopes	25. Gothic arched openings	39. Pediment	53. Keystone
12. Triglyph	26. Gabled entry	40. Console	54. Ionic order column
13. Doric order column	27. Conical turret	41. Pilaster	
14. Capital	28. Decorative brickwork	42. Cornice	

Illustration by John Wells for Historic Landmarks Foundation of Indiana

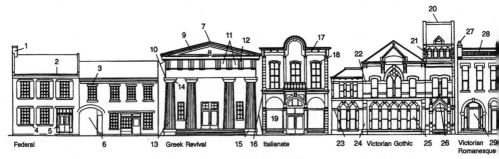

Figure 4. *A composite diagram of commercial architecture styles common from about 1820 to 1915 in Indiana reveals that styles change through time, with older styles (left) yielding to more modern styles (right). Historic Landmarks Foundation of Indiana, Indianapolis, 1978.*

Because styles may be developed/adopted and remain popular for only a decade or two, and because only one or two styles may be popular at any one time, the typical Main Street during its entire period of development may feature only a dozen (or perhaps two dozen) architectural styles.

Once we know how to identify these architectural styles, it becomes relatively easy to "read" (that is, interpret) how a Main Street has evolved. Recognizing that architectural styles change through time, the Historic Landmarks Foundation of Indiana compiled a *composite* graphic featuring actual examples of particular commercial buildings of identifiable styles placed side by side for comparative purposes (fig. 4). This hypothetical streetscape illustration offers an interesting look at how building styles on Main Street have changed through time, for it is a graph: beginning at the left of the illustration in about the year 1820 and moving to the 1920s at

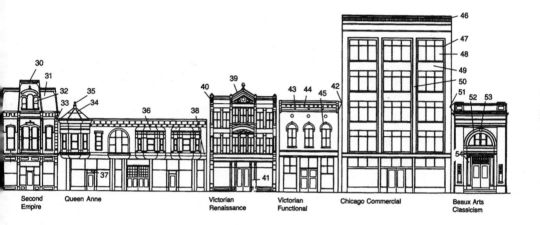

the right, this illustration shows, quite dramatically, how buildings in the same place (i.e., community) can change through time as styles are initially accepted, and then fall from favor as other styles supersede them. The reader's attention is directed to the key identifying architectural styles and elements, for many terms, such as pediments and pilasters, will be used to describe and interpret the architecture on Main Street.

Although this illustration is hypothetical, it is possible that one could find a Main Street possessing most, if not all, of these building types. Such a town would have developed over a long period of time with a modestly expanding economy. In reality, of course, most towns experience considerably more change, which is always reflected in the architecture on Main Street. Thus, towns that develop more in one period will have more examples of the architectural styles common at that time. The way in which change is manifested through time on Main Street is the focus of this section, but rather than study the Main Street of any particular American community, I will refer to figure 4 repeatedly, as it serves as a good composite model of how Main Street changes through time as new architectural styles are adopted to serve the changing needs of the merchant and consumer. I will also use photographs of actual buildings on American Main Streets, as well as the beautiful line drawings by the architectural historians at the Historic American Building Survey (HABS), to illustrate this section.

ARCHITECTURE AS BUILDING BLOCKS

The buildings in a townscape usually change in form and function through time, that is, they may be called upon to serve specific needs in one era but be adapted to new uses in another. Although it is tempting to think about commercial buildings on Main Street as being a distinct type of building, separate from, say, residential or institutional, in the past there was less of a distinction. A house, for example, might have been adapted to serve as an inn or a hotel if the business or trade (as measured in the number of travellers who passed by it) warranted its conversion into a commercial building. Interestingly, many earlier hostelries were called "houses" (such as the "American House" in 1840s Medina, Ohio), and in French *hôtel* means large house, or town mansion, as well as a "hotel" as we commonly understand the term.

Viewed as a group of individual but interrelated buildings, even the most mundane Main Street can tell very interesting stories about the drama between residential forces and commercial forces that may shape the streetscape through time. In many cases, especially where hamlets developed into small towns, the roots of Main Street commercial architecture can be traced back to residential architectural roots, that is, to residences that were built *before* commercial architecture was well differentiated. As Main Street commerce flourished, many of these buildings were adapted to serve commercial functions and altered accordingly. Thus, the earliest buildings in the Indiana Landmarks Foundation's composite illustration (that is, those on the left) originally served as houses, while later buildings (those on the right) served more exclusively as commercial buildings. Throughout its existence, the typical small-town Main Street has always provided residential options, and the upper floors of buildings often served as apartments or as the residences of merchants.

In some cases, buildings that served solely as residences on Main Street (that is, were houses) may survive into the present. As time progresses, what was once a house may later be flanked by buildings expressly built to serve commercial uses. Early historic photographs of Main Street often reveal a streetscape consisting of both houses and commercial buildings. The purely residential buildings, however, are usually set back several feet from the sidewalk (that is, they often have, or had, front yards) while the façades of commercial buildings abut the sidewalk so that a shopper walks directly from the sidewalk into the shop.

Interpreted carefully, architecture offers important clues to how Main Street evolves. If the residential architectural roots are important in "reading" even commercial streetscapes, then what diagnostic traits can one use to differentiate residential architecture from commercial architecture? In Anglo America, typically, houses have different floor plans, and different roof lines, from commercial buildings. Also, houses usually occupy a smaller portion of their building lots than do commercial buildings, which tend to fill lots. Depending on the style of architecture, the floor plan of a house may be a simple rectangle or a T or L plan; house roof lines may parallel the street or run perpendicular to it; sometimes a gable end will face the street, but the roof is almost always very visible. Commercial buildings, on the other hand, often have simple rectangular floor plans, and parapets and false fronts that hide or conceal the roofs. These commercial buildings project a very different image: their façades are bolder, more detailed, and they define the line of the sidewalk. In other words, the commercial buildings are more urban in appearance compared to their next-door residential neighbors, which could also be found in rural settings.

This differentiation becomes quite apparent as a town grows and downtown trade prospers. The early stages of this transition may be seen across the United States, especially in those small towns that have failed to become major marketing centers but instead remained in their early embryonic state as hamlets and villages. These places that progress and time have bypassed are good places to observe the origins of commercial architecture. Interestingly, although American rural vernacular residential architecture has been very well studied,[2] small-town commercial architecture itself has not. Nevertheless, because so many building types were used in both rural and town settings, those seminal architectural studies of American vernacular/folk housing in rural areas are crucial in helping students of townscapes better understand the architectural heritage of the small communities. Those vernacular traditions, which were readily carried from place to place without the need for formal plans, were easily replicated on the frontier as people sought commercial opportunities offered in places that found themselves on a developing network of roads.

ETHNICITY AND THE EARLY
ARCHITECTURAL ROOTS OF MAIN STREET

The architectural roots of American small-town architecture are very deep and very prolific. Three major types of buildings have influenced or shaped the architecture of Main Street: residential, civic, and commercial. In frontier America's two major cultural traditions — one from northwestern Europe and one from the Hispanic area of Mexico by way of Arizona and Texas — architectural patterns can be traced to source areas, or "culture hearths." Based on a half century of field-oriented scholarship, folklorists and geographers know that several important hearths could be identified as early as the eighteenth century.

The Eastern Seaboard Hearths

Ultimately, the architectural roots of Main Streets in the eastern United States reach back in time and space to Europe. Town and architectural patterns can be traced to their source countries, such as France, England, and the Netherlands, where they were well-developed by the 1600s. Soon after they arrived in the New World, the French began to create communities in parts of what are today the northeastern and central United States, especially river-oriented communities such as Detroit, Mobile, and New Orleans. Their imprint can still be seen in certain communities such as St. Charles and St. Geneviève, Missouri, where the river is a major focus. In what was originally New Amsterdam and what a historian has called "Holland on the Hudson,"[3] the Dutch brought their distinctive architecture and town planning by the mid 1600s. Here, in what is today New York and New Jersey, traces of their material culture can still be seen in early road and street patterns and in the architecture of historic houses. The Dutch style of building up the gabled fronts of buildings with distinct masonry detailing resulted in what appears to be the earliest use of the commercial false front in the Americas (fig. 5). The Germans, too, brought both urban and rural/village building types that became part of

Figure 5. *Considerable Dutch influence is revealed in this watercolor painting of Al-bany, N.Y., by James Eights in 1850 showing North Pearl Street, West Side, from Maiden Lane North, as it was in 1814. Courtesy Albany Institute of History and Art.*

their townscapes in southeastern Pennsylvania by the mid 1700s, and their influence spread to locations farther west, such as the Amana communi-ties/colonies in southeastern Iowa, the farming community of Westphalia, Missouri, and the German communities in Texas (including New Braun-fels and Fredericksburg) by the early to mid-nineteenth century.[4]

It was the British, however, who appear to have had the greatest impact in shaping the appearance of American communities on the eastern seaboard. In parts of northern Europe, but especially in the British Isles, one type of town that appears to be a prototype for American communi-ties consists of a series of formerly individual houses with rooflines paral-leling the street; these were joined together to form a continuously built-up commercial streetscape that actually consisted of individual buildings. The British called this arrangement a "row" of buildings and the term still holds; when joined at their chimney walls they form a continuous row that completely lines the street. These buildings are both residential and commercial, for shop owners live above their first- (or "ground"-) floor shops. Because commerce was a major element in the economy of these communities, their buildings are constructed along major roads or thoroughfares and often front directly onto the street or sidewalks, that is, are not set back from the street as were those rural homes built in the countryside.

The Anglo-American area known as the original Thirteen Colonies until the American Revolution was thus rich in architecture that would form the early building blocks of Main Streets in the region. Here, in the eastern United States, three major culture hearths developed by the eighteenth century,[5] and several major house forms or types helped influence commercial architecture in the small towns of the new nation. In New England, large, two-and-a-half-story houses with massive central chimneys were common, and geographers have simply called them "New England large" houses. These can still be seen in communities such as Guilford, Connecticut, and in villages in Rhode Island and Massachusetts. They were used for both houses and commercial buildings in early New England towns and villages and can be considered basic building blocks of the streetscapes there.

Other house types were common elsewhere in the early Republic. One of the more common house types of the period 1775–1825, especially in the middle-Atlantic culture hearth in the vicinity of Philadelphia, is the central-hall type (called an I-style house if only one room deep, and a "four over four" if two rooms deep). Like the "New England large" home, this simple house type often may have a symmetrical façade but always has a gabled roof whose ridge line runs parallel to the street (fig. 6). Typically, detailing on these houses was done in what is called the Federal Style, because it was during the Federal period (ca. 1780–1820) that many were built. In the Federal Style, lintels above doors and windows are simple, and hints of classical trim may be seen in formal doorways flanked by rows of small sidelight windows. Each gable end of these functional houses often features a substantial chimney; sometimes these end chimneys are "twinned" to form a brace of chimneys at each end of the building. The gable end of the building often has few or no windows, in which case it can be constructed immediately adjacent to another building like it to form a continuous row of structures joined by what are then called common walls. When a parapet rises above the roofline, as is often the case when these buildings are connected into a line or row, the raised ma-

Figure 6. *A central-hall or I-style house as a building block of Main Street (the National Road) in St. Clairsville, Ohio (left center). Note that the building's ridge pole or roofline parallels the street and that the arrangement of windows and doors is divisible into five "bays" or vertical lines. Note, too, that similar buildings placed close together help to define the street. 1986 photo by the author.*

sonry end wall can help retard the spread of fire from one building to another. Thus, parapeted gable ends serve both an aesthetic and a practical purpose as settlement density increases. A variety of vernacular houses whose roofline runs parallel to the street, and which thus can be joined at the end walls to become a row, are common on the eastern seaboard. These adaptable vernacular buildings could be arranged to suit particular local needs as commercial areas developed.

Although central-hall houses originated in northern Europe and the British Isles, they were commonplace in America by the late 1700s. Their formalized, symmetrical façades derived from formal classical architecture and showed that their owners had reached a certain status as prosperous merchants or farmers. Historical geographers note that the central-hall house type was introduced into the mid-Atlantic culture hearth of the eastern United States (which was centered in southeastern Pennsylvania) from northern Europe and the British Isles, and that it spread westward

into western Pennsylvania, Ohio, and out into the middle west and Upland South by the early to mid-nineteenth century. The Main Streets
of towns on the National Road like Clear Spring, Maryland, and St.
Clairsville, Ohio, are among the best examples of the builder's art of the
early nineteenth century — and excellent reminders of the importance of
road subsidies and improvements in shaping early American streetscapes.
Consider, for example, the townscape of Centerville, Indiana, a town also
located on the fabled National Road. Here, the Federal style buildings
lined up "end to end" to create a characteristic early Main Street. As seen
in the Indiana Landmarks Foundation's diagram of commercial architecture (fig. 4), these Federal Style buildings form the first readily identifiable
building block of commercial streetscapes in what was, in the 1810s and
early 1820s, the far western frontier.

CLASSICAL TEMPLE-FRONTED
BUILDINGS REACH MAIN STREET

Rows of relatively undifferentiated Federal Style commercial buildings
could be seen lining Main Street in many towns by the early 1800s, but
after about 1825 streetscapes were often punctuated by newer styles that
introduced visual variety to the streetscape. Although buildings with gable
ends facing the street had been common in both residential and early
commercial architecture, in the early nineteenth century the Greek Revival brought a dramatic, and elegant, architectural treatment to gable-
end façades on Main Street. With its classical columns and its triangular
tympanum or pediment atop an ornamented frieze, the Greek Revival
structure became a very powerful design element in the streetscape.
Greek Revival buildings might often be free standing, as in perhaps a
bank or even a tavern, but they could also be integrated into the streetscape of Main Street when designed as commercial buildings (see fig. 4).

More formal in style, and certainly more likely to draw attention than
simpler Federal Style buildings, the temple-fronted Greek Revival style
can be traced directly to temples of antiquity rather than to the vernacular
houses of the common folk. Formal, classically styled buildings were favored among wealthy landowners and merchants in England and on the
eastern seaboard. As material culture, they were ostentatious in that they
made statements about the wealth and status of their owners. Architectural historian Roger Kennedy has demonstrated that the Greek Revival

style was associated with wealthy entrepreneurs.[6] These merchants and entrepreneurs could afford to employ architects to replicate grand elements of Palladian (Roman) and Greek design in the newly developing countryside of the American Republic. Although the Greek Revival is synonymous in the popular mind with the "plantation style" in the deep South, it actually flourished in many small communities in the New England and Middle Atlantic culture hearths.

Inasmuch as classical revival styled buildings with prominent gabled fronts were both Roman and Greek in their inspiration and design, they followed closely the proportions of classical design formulas and brought geometry, symmetry, and formality to the American landscape. Classically Palladian (and later Greek Revival) styled buildings make a strong statement in the landscape and a strong impression on the observer. Their front elevations, gabled and facing the road or street, commanded attention through the use of vertical design elements. By imitation, the characteristic formal pediment — oftentimes with the replication of columns — provided a sense of classical architectural drama in even the most ordinary streetscapes of America. Compared to the Federal style buildings that became commonplace in the eastern culture hearths by the early nineteenth century, the earlier Palladian (late 1700s to early 1800s) and later Greek Revival (ca. 1820–1855) styles were far more impressive, and soon became quite popular for civic and institutional buildings. As ingredients in the townscape, they drew the viewer's eye toward a prominent architectural element, the façade (fig. 7). Significantly, these high-style buildings were derived from the Mediterranean classical world, which had a rich urbanistic building tradition that could be traced back at least 2,500 years. During the early years of the nation — or Republic, as trend-setting architect Thomas Jefferson called it — the classical world's republics seemed a prototype of the young democracy. Thus, at the very time that towns on the American frontier were being named Rome, Corinth, Carthage, and Syracuse, temple-fronted classical buildings inspired by those places of classical antiquity rose to face American Main Streets. These high-style buildings were a testimony to the power of fashion, for they were easily distinguished from the simpler vernacular buildings of the common folk. On Main Street, Greek Revival Style buildings were popular as banks, land offices, and stores, for they helped to generate a sense of confidence in their enterprises.

Figure 7. *In the Greek and Roman Revival styles, the gable temple-front was usually oriented toward the street, and even buildings that no longer featured columns possessed formal elements of classical trim, such as pedimented gables and elaborate round and square headed (capped) windows. This striking drawing from the Historic American Buildings Survey shows the Southport (Connecticut) Savings Bank, which was constructed in 1854. Courtesy HABS, U.S. Department of the Interior.*

Despite their impressiveness, however, grand free-standing temple-like buildings do not always make good neighbors, urbanistically speaking. One might expect certain problems when two or more Greek Revival buildings were built very close side by side, for their roofs will drain off to the sides of the building, damaging walls and leaving standing water between the two structures if the buildings and their sites are not carefully drained. Also, because they were built rather close together but had no solid walls between them to prevent the spread of fire, such buildings could be consumed rapidly as fire spread down the block with no barriers, such as parapet walls, to deter it. Despite certain shortcomings, however, the Greek Revival Style was popular for commercial buildings from the 1830s to the 1860s, lending a distinctive look to many Main Streets during the period. Because the Greek Revival remained popular into the 1860s, it characterized Main Streets that developed in the far westward expansion. This included Main Streets of numerous western mining areas, such as California's Gold Rush country and the early Oregon, Idaho, Nevada, and Colorado mining frontiers (fig. 8); it was also seen in the thriving agricultural villages and towns settled by Anglo-Americans in the far West by the 1840s and 1850s. Main Streets in Oregon's Willamette Valley and California's coastal valleys, as well as those in the valleys of the Intermountain West settled by the Mormons, featured Greek Revival style buildings.

THE BIRTH OF COMMERCIAL ARCHITECTURE

As noted above, when architectural historians search for the roots of American commercial architecture, they find it both in the "public" buildings of the classical world and in the common vernacular architecture of the countryside. Because American entrepreneurs (including property owners and merchants) often shaped their buildings to meet changing needs, it is instructive to trace how they transformed what were originally residential building forms into commercial structures. As revealed in the journals and correspondence of individuals, as well as the more formal publications (such as early historical atlases, in which buildings were often pictured), houses might be adapted to serve commercial needs by the changing of windows and door openings. A look at the residence and store of John Perkins from the 1875 county atlas of Athens County, Ohio, for example, shows that with a few simple changes — the addition of a garden window, and changes in the location of door open-

Figure 8. *Greek Revival was a popular style selected for Main Street commercial architecture in the West as the style spread there by the 1850s and 1860s. When developed as
commercial buildings, the columns were often simply incorporated into the first-floor
façade, between the window openings of shops, or as columns supporting a porch that
covered the sidewalk. Genoa, Nevada, ca. 1870, featured several such buildings (center
and left), along with many whose false fronts disguised their gable fronts. Courtesy
Nevada Historical Society.*

ings — a house could be modified into a commercial building (fig. 9). In
a pattern practiced for centuries in Europe, the Perkins store was on the
first floor, while the Perkins family lived upstairs — a compact, pragmatic
solution.

Architectural historian Richard Longstreth describes the development
of the "two-part commercial block" (which features a lower floor devoted
to retailing and an upper story occupied by residences, usually of the
owner or merchant) as essential to the development of America's Main
Street architecture.[7] These buildings began to appear on Main Street during the frontier era of the late eighteenth and early nineteenth centuries.
Historic illustrations of Main Streets reveal that the two-part commercial
block was definitely in existence as early as 1815, about the time that the
characteristic row houses began to appear in eastern cities such as Philadelphia and Baltimore.

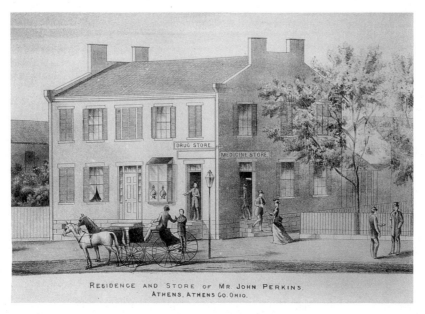

RESIDENCE AND STORE OF MR. JOHN PERKINS.
ATHENS, ATHENS Co. OHIO.

Figure 9. *The Perkins residence and store in Athens, Ohio, reveals that a Federal Style home could serve as a commercial building with a few architectural changes, including the addition of a prominent doorway (right) and a garden window to call attention to merchandise sold in the store.* Illustrated Atlas of Athens County, Ohio, 1875.

Thus, by 1840 Main Street began to be recognized by its distinctive buildings: two-part commercial block buildings with parapet walls that rose above the roofline and in effect "capped" the façade became common. They featured commercial fronts, with larger shop windows on the ground-level floor (as a way of advertising one's wares and services) and smaller, simpler windows on the second story of the façade. These buildings were readily identified as "business houses" along Main Street by their style alone; their parapets offered some protection from the spread of fire and gave the buildings a blockier look that conformed to an urbanizing streetscape. Nevertheless, despite the use of such treatments, Main Street could still be interpreted as a group of individual buildings whose residential roots were often cleverly hidden by an urban front or façade. An early photo of Oswego, New York, taken about 1850, reveals that individual buildings with rooflines paralleling the street have become, in effect, Main Street row buildings by the mid-nineteenth century (fig. 10). Note that balustrades at the top of the façades give them a finished and detailed look.

Figure 10. A *Main Street scene in Oswego, New York, about 1850, shows a streetscape that consists of numerous individual buildings arranged much like the row houses that had become popular in eastern cities in the early 1800s. Courtesy Onondaga Historical Association, Syracuse, New York.*

South by Southwest

As if to confirm the first axiom of Main Street development — *Main Street commercial architecture evolves from residential and/or vernacular as well as more formal and public building forms* — the historic Main Streets of what is today the American Southwest also reflect a varied and complex heritage. From Florida to Texas to California, the Spanish or Mexican "borderlands" area of cultural influence produced very different buildings by the eighteenth century. The Spanish built in a wealth of styles, including gabled roofs that may have featured thatch or tile roofing materials. In the Southwest especially, the Spanish often utilized adobe or masonry for construction. One building type in particular — an essentially rectangular or cubic form that had no gables, but rather a flat roof hidden behind parapets that rose about a foot above the roofline — was common there by the late 1700s and early 1800s. Architectural historians consider these "cubic" buildings to form the roots of both rural and urban architecture in the region. J. B. Jackson observed this relationship more than thirty-five years ago when he surmised that "first comes the house."[8] When seen

Figure 11. *A linear townscape of adobe buildings reveals that individual structures take on the collective appearance of streetscape as they are joined together at their end walls. Most of these buildings date from the late nineteenth century and reflect a Hispanic building tradition. Tularosa, New Mexico; 1981 photo by the author.*

standing by themselves, as in a rural setting, these vernacular buildings appear as simple cubic forms; most feature very simple window detailing and the characteristic *viga* beams and *canales* that are typical of architecture in this region during the Spanish Colonial and early Mexican period.

In the town setting, these characteristic cubic adobe structures are very easily placed side by side with other buildings to form a row of buildings, in effect creating a linear streetscape (fig. 11). This type of regional commercial street was seen throughout New Mexico, southern Texas, and southern Arizona by the early 1800s. Because load-bearing restrictions on adobe are severe, however, these buildings are usually not more than one story, and rarely more than two stories, in height, in contrast to fired-brick structures of the northern Europeans and Anglos that could be built three stories high with little or no fear of collapse.

Although adobe buildings in the southwest may appear "timeless," they are actually rather fugitive or transitory because they are susceptible to damage by moisture, which can penetrate the roofline or undermine the structure at the base of the wall.[9] Nevertheless, as one of America's vernacular building traditions, the use of adobe has persisted in the region. It can be traced to two cultural traditions: the Native American Pueblo Indians, who "puddled" adobe by applying it in wet blobs and sculpted it to shape before it dried in the sun, and the Spanish, who built using the sun-dried bricks made of mud and straw common in the old world, especially North Africa and the Middle East (*adobar* is, in fact, a Latinized version of the Arabic word *al-tub*). The widespread use of adobe helps to explain the ease with which travellers could identify Indian and Mexican towns, which seemed to rise from the earth itself and, in many cases, have a color much like it.

The Hispanic adobe tradition in this region was preceded by an earlier indigenous Native American tradition of building in cubic architectural forms. In northern Sonora, Mexico (Casas Grandes), and northern New Mexico (Taos), these cubic, flat-roofed buildings (some featuring the use of stucco and bright pastel building colors) were commented upon by the Spanish as part of a rich vernacular urbanistic building tradition to which the Spanish added their own distinctive building forms.[10] Like the tradition of colonial Anglo-American vernacular building along the east coast that extended into western frontiers by about 1800, the Hispanic architectural tradition was extended, by cultural diffusion, northward by the late 1700s into areas that we today call "the Southwest," but which was *el norte* (or the northern frontier) to the Spanish and Mexicans.[11]

The Spanish building traditions superseded native architecture in some places and blended with it in others, such as the missions and churches of Sonora, Arizona,[12] and New Mexico. The regional architectural styles seen today in northern Mexico and many other parts of the Southwest were well developed by the late 1700s, for they are featured in sketches and lithographs of the time. These buildings give the townscape a distinctive look, and yet may vary in their appearance: they may be either adobe-colored, whitewashed, or brightly colored — especially from approximately three feet down toward the foundation line. Simple porches with Spanish Colonial-era trim were often added to shade people from the rays of the sun, but these adobe buildings are usually striking in their simplicity. As noted above, gabled roof structures featuring thatch, tile, or even shake roofing could also be found in the areas settled by the Spanish. They were seen in rural and town settings, such as Laredo and San Antonio, Texas; Cordova, New Mexico; and San Juan Bautista, California. These gabled-roofed buildings usually feature the substantial masonry or adobe walls, and the relatively small window openings, that are a hallmark of Colonial New Spain. As classical trim became popular in the early to mid-nineteenth century, it, too, could be seen on Southwestern buildings — where it lent an interesting contrast to otherwise vernacular building forms.

The Southwest is an area that possesses rich Hispanic architectural and urban design traditions, and yet is most interesting for the mixing of *combinations* (called *mestizaje*) of Hispanic and Anglo-American traits and patterns. On Main Street, Anglo-American entrepreneurs used indigenous materials and traditions when it suited their needs. For the most part, however, the prevailing needs of expanding commercialism were met by creating larger window openings and more commodious door openings; these enabled people to move in and out of the buildings freely and enabled light to enter the storefront. By the 1850s, Anglo influences developed in the east had begun to transform Southwestern streetscapes.

Using both Hispanic and Anglo building techniques, Southwestern Main Streets achieved a distinctive form. The familiar process of adapting individual buildings to urban settings by joining them at their side or end walls was also practiced here, and this increased the density of the downtown. Although it was possible to identify individual buildings, they were now clearly parts of an integrated, urbanistic whole. Regardless of location, then, the second axiom of early Main Street development is: *A series of individual structures, many of them originally residences, become "townscape" by being placed side by side, or end to end, to maximize the use of valuable space in commercial sections of communities.* This dynamic affects the buildings in a number of ways. Side walls are obscured and façades become prominent; details may be modified and stylized; nevertheless, the basic building form is still detectable by architectural historians who consider the individual buildings to be so many pieces of an intriguing, and increasingly complex, puzzle as communities develop commercial cores.

THE VICTORIAN ERA: COMMERCIAL ARCHITECTURE COMES OF AGE

By the mid-1840s to early 1850s, streetscapes from coast to coast were beginning to take on a distinctive look as larger windows were added to building fronts, in effect opening up the lower stories of the façades into a series of large "bulk windows" in which merchandise could be displayed. According to architectural historian Antoinette Lee:

> In the transition of the residential-styled, multi-purpose building to the specialized retail establishment, "bulk windows" marked the initial step in this process. These windows first appeared in the early 19th century and were lighted up at night. A growing number of these display windows, clustered in a specialized commercial area, encouraged the practice of window-shopping, an important impetus to retail business.[13]

Technology worked hand-in-hand with architecture: Plate glass helped to revolutionize Main Street because it enabled designers to open up the façade at street level and create accessible storefronts for enterprises that were flourishing in American urban centers by the mid-nineteenth century. Thus, an 1864 issue of the *Arizona Miner* could claim that "the store on the east end of the Plaza, erected and occupied by Mr. Rogers, the representative of Gray & Co. of La Paz [Arizona], (is) a neat and well finished building having quite the appearance of a city establishment."[14] Old photographs reveal it to have large glass windows that permitted the merchants to display their wares very effectively.

The urban commercial storefront, as influenced by technology, appeared at a crucial time, for it helped dictate the "urban" look of American Main Streets that developed in the mid-nineteenth century (fig. 12). The urban storefront's development reflected an appreciation of Italianate and other classical architectural styles that continued to grip American architecture into the second half of the nineteenth century. This architectural fascination was in part related to changes in mobility in the early to mid-Victorian era, for steamships now made travel to Europe far more convenient than it had been just fifty years before, and many American architects travelled to Europe to study classical buildings in Italian cities firsthand; moreover, many prosperous American merchants and entrepreneurs could now travel abroad for study and general enlightenment. Thus, the buildings that were once seen only in paintings now could be seen first-hand, and replicated in American cities and towns.

The mid-nineteenth century, then, marks something of a watershed on Main Street. Whereas many earlier (pre-1850) buildings on Main Street were vernacular in design and a few reflected high styling, things changed

FARMERS' & MERCHANTS' BANK
of SHENANDOAH, PAGE CO., IOWA, T.H. READ, Prest.

Figure 12. *Easily constructed on narrow commercial lots facing Main Street, Victorian Italianate style façades helped convey an air of prosperity. The cast-iron façade of the Farmers and Merchants Bank in Shenandoah, Iowa, is typical in that it consists of three parts: a store front with large plate-glass windows, detailed upper-story windows, and an ornate pediment or cornice. A. T. Andreas' Illustrated Historical Atlas of the State of Iowa; courtesy State Historical Society of Iowa.*

rapidly when trained architects entered the picture. Most new buildings on Main Street were now more likely to be formal in style and more standardized in construction, for these high-style fads or trends were promoted in journals and magazines that became commonplace after about 1870. By the mid-nineteenth century, Victorian Italianate and Gothic styling influenced all types of buildings — residential, institutional, and commercial. Victorian styles superseded earlier styles such as the Greek Revival by the late 1860s, and the 1870s witnessed the nearly complete acceptance of Victorian styling for commercial architecture as seen in the Historic Landmarks Foundation of Indiana's graphic referred to earlier (fig. 4). It is this wholesale acceptance of Italianate commercial style architecture that gives Main Street such a recognizable identity by the late nineteenth century.

One of the distinguishing elements of the Italianate commercial style of building is its ostensibly flat roof; the viewer at street level cannot determine the type or pitch of roof because it is hidden behind a parapet wall. In some cases, a hipped roof is present, but in many cases, the roof is nearly flat, sloping gently to the rear of the building, so that water is conveyed off the roof by downspouts after being channeled through scuppers. Flat roofs of this type are usually made of tightly seamed metal, covered with thick tar to avoid leaks in the event that the water backs up or stands on the roof. In their rectangularity and design, Victorian Main Street commercial architecture was essentially urban: its "footprint" had to be long and narrow to fit commercial lots; it was modular, that is, had to be built with regard to the structures located on the adjacent narrow lots on either side of it. These buildings were often called "blocks" even though they might occupy only one lot on the block. The term epitomizes their modular individual quality as components of streetscape.

Like its urban counterparts elsewhere, Victorian commercial architecture emphasized the building's façade. These façades were often highly detailed, and their windows were separated by columns that created the impression of a colonnade when several similar buildings were constructed side by side (fig. 13). The replication, or "rhythm," of columns on the first floor might be accentuated by smaller but highly detailed windows on the second and third floors, and Victorian commercial buildings were often capped by heavily detailed or bracketed cornices that crowned the front parapet of the building. Thus, because architects no longer needed to be concerned about ornamenting the sides of the buildings, which were not usually seen by passers-by, they lavished attention on the façade. Of course, where a building lot remained empty next door, it provided a perfect opportunity to use the building's flanks for advertising: during this period, advertising signs proliferated, and they always served

Figure 13. *Victorian-era façades were often highly embellished with Italianate details. When placed side by side, the façades created the impression of an arcaded or colonnaded streetscape, as seen in this 1875 view of the Merchant's Block in Cedar Rapids, Iowa, which appeared in a contemporary atlas.* A. T. Andreas' Illustrated Atlas of the State of Iowa; *courtesy State Historical Society of Iowa.*

the purpose of luring prospective customers into the front door of a commercial enterprise.

This leads to the third axiom of Main Street development: *The façade of the building becomes more important than any other elevation because it faces Main Street.* In fact, as buildings are brought together to form streetscape, the façade is often the *only* elevation that will be seen by the observer under normal viewing. Thus, one often sees the façade of a building finished in fine brick while the remainder may be of more readily available (cheaper) lower-quality brick, or stone; hence, the local press in Prescott, Arizona, could report of John Campbell's new store in 1867 that "the three of its walls are built of stone, the front being of brick."[15] There is, of course, an underlying commercial reason why the façade becomes so dominant. As the competition for land increases on a developing Main Street, front footage becomes more valuable; consequently, as building lots narrow, and buildings become shoehorned into the property, their façades become the most valuable — and most visible — elements of the building. The Victorian streetscape dramatizes this relationship

Figure 14. *A Victorian mansard roof crowns a hotel in the mining town of Philipsburg, Montana. French (Parisian) in origin, the mansard roof brought an urban element into a streetscape in the 1870s. 1994 photo by the author.*

between commerce and architecture, but it is always operative on Main Streets in any era.

Speculators and builders spent more money on the façades of their buildings than on any other elevation, and the widespread acceptance of European classical architecture that transformed America's nineteenth-century landscape can be interpreted as a statement that entrepreneurs were seeking to create a sense of permanence and confidence. After all, the European prototypes of buildings on Main Street had stood the test of time in urban areas of great antiquity, such as Rome, Venice, Amsterdam, and Paris. These European styles seemed ideally suited to solving essentially urbanistic design problems at a time when American towns were growing rapidly, that is, urbanizing. One of those imported design solutions that worked very effectively — the mansard roof (fig. 14) — became common in residential, commercial, and institutional architecture by the mid-nineteenth century. Said to be the result of an urban concern in France — the taxation of buildings by the number of floors or stories — the mansard roof in effect creates a nearly full usable floor in what would otherwise have been "wasted" attic space. Mansard roofs sloped steeply, and were often interrupted by gabled dormer windows that permitted light to enter; thus, they created yet another opportunity for detailing the building's streetscape elevation. Mansard roofs helped to create an urban atmosphere in the small-town Main Street. As if to affirm the connection with France, mansard roofs are an integral element of what is called the "Second Empire" style that flourished on courthouses, schools, and other public and private buildings during the period 1865–1895.

Borrowing heavily from European design elements that could be imitated in cast iron and other imitative materials, commercial architecture flourished in the late nineteenth century. Although elaborate Victorian trim was seen on buildings as early as the 1840s, it became very common after the Civil War when the machines that had driven the Civil War were transformed into the machines that celebrated a boom in economic activity; foundries and other industries that had created guns and the artifacts of war were now turned toward making metal trim, such as iron columns, that could be used for building façades. The Victorian period became a time of standardization, and many foundries stamped out, or cast, iron façades and columns that could be assembled into buildings in what we speak of today as "modular" fashion.

Cast iron helped to revolutionize American architecture. It could be created in diverse forms, and yet was strong enough to support masonry. Advocates of its early use were ecstatic. In 1852, the editors of the *Philadelphia Public Ledger* marvelled at the speed in which a few workmen could transform the streetscape using cast-iron components. "In a few days at most — a building, which would endure for ages, will be seen standing erect, in dignity and beauty." [16] Architectural historian Antoinette Lee noted that "the emergence of cast iron as an architectural material captured the imagination of the urban public in ways that few building materials had in the past or would in the future." [17]

As cast-iron architectural components spread throughout the country by the 1870s, the anticipation of a cast-iron building often drew the attention of the community and was often mentioned in the local press. In 1872, for example, the Fayetteville (Arkansas) *Weekly Democrat* reported that Captain Denton D. Stark "contemplates erecting a two story iron front banking building on the north side of the square." [18] Early photographs of the building reveal a Victorian Italianate style façade having three graceful arched bays and the date of its construction, 1872, prominently featured in its curving, simulated-stone pediment. This and other Victorian-era commercial buildings in Fayetteville helped transform the area around the square, which, according to local historians in Fayetteville, "began to look prosperous" in the 1870s.[19] Fayetteville was like thousands of other communities of the era: by adopting the immensely popular high-style Victorian architecture that was sweeping the country, it courted prosperity through imitation. To cite another example, the rich architectural character of downtown Bloomfield, a small town in southern Iowa, ". . . is a statement of nineteenth century confidence," and its Victorian era commercial buildings are a "product of the Industrial era."[20]

Like other Victorian ideas and material culture, architectural traditions moved west with an expanding frontier; there is evidence that they found early acceptance in urban areas, and spread somewhat more slowly to the smaller towns in the more isolated rural areas. In the Southwest, Anglo-American architectural styles, culture, and technology spread into the Hispanic culture area with amazing speed. Architectural historian Harris Sobin studied the townscape of Florence, Arizona, and described the fusion of early Hispanic architecture with Anglo traditions into the "Territorial Style" common in the period from just after the Mexican War/Gadsden Treaty (1853).[21] These transitional styles began to yield to a growing Anglo influence before the turn of the century, certainly well before statehood (1912) in New Mexico and Arizona.

A similar condition occurred in other parts of the West as Anglos dominated indigenous cultures in their sweep westward. By the 1870s, Victorian-style building façades, hipped roofs, and mansard roofs could be found throughout the region; they found their way westward into the Pacific Northwest as people travelled by sailing ship, road, or railroad from the eastern United States. As extractive industry transformed even the most isolated areas of the far and interior West, and mining towns proliferated throughout the region, from Canada to Mexico, Victorian high styles found their way to even the most remote areas of the frontier, such as the valleys of northern Idaho, the gold camps of Colorado, and the silver-mining towns of Nevada and eastern California. The railroad appears to be their main purveyor, for architectural components of cast iron could be shipped easily by rail as the networks of lines developed from the 1870s to the 1890s.

"WELSH'S HOTEL" "J.B.WELSH PROP "KINGSBURG, FRESNO CO. CAL."

Figure 15. *This lithographed scene from the Victorian era shows Welsh's Hotel in Fresno County, California, a modest Victorian residence with high style. A false-front addition (left) next door illustrates how individual buildings become streetscape when connected to serve commercial purposes.* History of Fresno County, 1882.

Main Street on the California frontier provides a fascinating glimpse of the importation of high styles and the persistence of residential architecture as a source of Main Street architecture. An 1882 *History of Fresno County* contains an illustration of Welsh's Hotel, which is actually an agglomeration of several buildings (fig. 15).[22] Welsh's Hotel is an L-shaped structure with Italianate trim in the form of rounded windows and a corbelled chimney. The false-front building at the left is detailed with Italianate brackets, and both buildings are united by porches that protect the shoppers from sun and rain. The buildings in this vignette illustrate how easily Anglo-American architecture could be transported; this building complex could as easily have been in Pennsylvania, or Indiana, as in California. People bring architectural ideas with them as they migrate, and these ideas are influenced by popular culture as communications intensify. In the nineteenth century, ideas of style were shaped, in part, by illustrated magazines that flourished with a developing economy and found their way into the hands of the common folk, including merchants on Main Street.

It was during the Victorian period that the false front became ubiquitous. A false front in effect increased the height and massing of the façade
to conceal a simple gable front.[23] Although the disguising or embellishing
of a gable end by architectural elaboration was found in Dutch buildings
in New York as early as the 1600s, the full false front — a large, flat front
wall that covers, or nearly covers, the gable end facing the street —
reached its apogee in American towns in the nineteenth century. Historic
photos show false fronts to be a major element in frontier streetscapes of
the 1850s and 1860s; they were especially common in "boom towns,"
which required finished buildings in a hurry. False fronts were often constructed of wood, and were more or less props that gave an element of
grandeur to an individual building; when constructed side by side along
Main Street, they tended to make the streetscape appear far more impressive, and rather more complete, than it actually was. False-front buildings
reaffirm that the drama on Main Street — like all dramas — is enhanced
by a good stage setting. The Victorians knew this well.

Prosperous merchants in the period 1870–1900 often ordered standard
Victorian façades from catalogs after they realized that a façade could
help bring attention to the building and lure prospective customers into
their stores. Architectural historian Arthur Hart noted that the Victorian
trim of the period was commonly based on the high style of the Italian Renaissance, but was "usually more imaginative than accurate."[24] Although
the façade might attract people to the store, its interior had to be well ap-
pointed and organized. Thus, an 1867 issue of the *Arizona Miner* could
claim that "Campbell's New Store on Montezuma Street, fronting the
Plaza, is now completely finished both inside and out, and is well stocked
with goods tastefully arranged."[25] Campbell's New Store in Prescott was,
in fact, much like other buildings constructed in towns of the era; the style
itself came to be associated with prosperity from coast to coast.

It is tempting to think that all of these Victorian commercial buildings
that sprouted along Main Street were new, but in fact a great deal of "remodelling" occurred. Whereas a building today appears to be a Victorian
structure constructed in, say, 1879, a closer look at the actual form of the
building — as determined by a review of property maps, historical atlases,
journals, reports, and other historical information — may reveal that the
building had been modernized, perhaps more than once, as architectural
fads swept the street. Thus, the Victorian façade bearing a particular date
may actually commemorate that extensive remodelling, not indicate the

Figure 16. *Henry Howe's sketches of London, Ohio (seen here in 1846), and other communities in the mid- to late 1840s reveal a simple, largely Federal style streetscape. Howe's* Historical Collections of Ohio, 1847; *courtesy Ohio Historical Society.*

first time a building appeared on the site. In fact, the *rear* elevation of a building is usually the most effective single part in helping one to determine the building's actual age and original construction technique. Unlike the façade, the rear elevation of a commercial building does not attempt to deceive the viewer with stylistic flourishes.

From whatever angle they are viewed, Victorian-era Main Streets — like Main Streets in any era — need to be seen as not simply frozen in time, but as constantly evolving. At any particular time a streetscape may be stylistically up to date, but looking at earlier historical images (photographs, sketches) often reveals some very surprising information. To better understand the impact of stylistic change on Main Street, it will be instructive to journey back in time with Henry Howe, who, as noted in the Introduction to this book, recorded streetscapes during a sixty-year career from the 1840s to just after 1900. As a young man in 1846, Henry Howe travelled throughout Ohio and other states, leaving a rich record of townscape notes, sketches, and descriptions. Howe's notes and records reveal that townscapes in the 1840s were often, stylistically speaking, in their infancy: whereas many public buildings were prominent, they and their commercial counterparts were often relatively simple. In the central part of London, Ohio, as recorded by Howe in 1846 (fig. 16), the Federal and Georgian style architecture that characterizes most communities that developed within the first half century of the founding of the Republic is everywhere evident. London's streetscape in the late 1840s is rather

Figure 17. *Howe's view of London, Ohio, based on a C. C. Hale photo of 1887, records that the streetscape became more Victorian as high-style architecture featuring detailed brackets and window and door trim found its place along the Main Street. Howe's* Historical Collections of Ohio, *1907; courtesy Ohio Historical Society.*

simple — there are fences and simple brick and clapboard buildings with rather restrained — by later standards at least — turrets and steeples. Advertising is relatively simple and appears in the form of signage placed against the buildings. Note, too, that the conveyances are simple horses and wagons, and one features a rider on horseback as well as a family walking along the sidewalk, or "boardwalk," as it would have been called at that time.[26]

By 1889, however, London had matured considerably. It has a much more substantial urban character in Howe's later illustration (fig. 17). The community blossomed during the four-decade period between Howe's first sketch of 1847 and the photo-inspired lithograph of 1889. Perhaps the most important development was the arrival of the railroad, which assured the community's growth and development. The architectural fads that swept the rest of the country also affected London. In the years immediately following the Civil War, Victorian architecture reached its peak in popularity, as is evident in the later illustration. The new Madison County Courthouse is done in a high-style Victorian classical motif, as opposed to the earlier steepled Colonial or early Georgian courthouse, which was demolished to make way for the new one in the 1870s; note, too, the proliferation of Victorian Italianate commercial buildings on the Main Street. As rendered by Howe, the later scene appears more prosperous and animated: in keeping with the prosperity implied by the new buildings, horses and buggies make their way along the busy Main Street, and trees now soften the streetscape.

In these drawings and in many historical photographs, Main Street seems to flower in the later nineteenth century. With the exception of an occasional economic panic (e.g., 1873) that might slow growth, the years following the Civil War were indeed relatively prosperous for the American small town. The architectural personality that small-town Main Streets developed at this time has had a powerful effect on our current perceptions, or, as an editor of a popular magazine noted: "It is from the period just before and after the turn of the century that many of our Anytown USA impressions come."[27] There is much truth in this statement. The period from the 1870s to just after the turn of the century has such a strong effect in the popular mind because many Main Streets were built up as virtually intact assemblages of buildings (what architectural historians call *tout ensembles*) during this era. As earlier buildings were remodeled to match new construction, American small town streetscapes took on a very stylized, and highly standardized, appearance by the 1880s. This is true from coast to coast and from the Canadian border to the Mexican border. Viewed in context, then, the Victorian-era commercial storefront should be recognized as the first truly national building form in the history of American architecture. Although its design roots are traceable to Europe, in the hands of American entrepreneurs it became a characteristically American form: attractive, affordable, easily constructed, easily installed and, most importantly, standardized.

The buildings on Main Street reflect a standardization that became a fact of life in the American small town in the latter half of the nineteenth century. It was a standardization that swept the country as standardized time zones were developed, electricity was harnessed, the telephone was invented, and the cash register and typewriter were perfected. A host of other technological innovations radically changed commercial life and permitted ideas and patterns to be copied and spread from place to place. All of these had the cumulative effect of the United States developing what geographer Hildegard Binder Johnson called "a national landscape" in the late nineteenth century.[28] Main Streets developed during this period bore a look of urban prosperity, for they were indeed smaller versions of their urban counterparts. Orderliness, prosperity, and culture had reached Main Street in the form of an architectural image that linked merchant and consumer in an alliance.

This observation leads us to the fourth axiom of Main Street architectural development: *Prosperity almost always results in aggressive building and remodelling, and Main Street will have a relatively uniform appearance because a popular architectural style will be applied to most or all of the façades, helping to unify them visually.*

Despite the visual unification of Main Street architecture, certain architectural elements were treated as exclamation points — punctuation to be used with some restraint and in the appropriate places — on Main Street: turrets, oriels, and protruding bay windows capped by towers are seen in the late nineteenth century (fig. 18). These flourishes lend a great deal of interest, and urban character, to the townscape; where a characteristic oriel is seen, it usually indicates that the location is a major intersection where a commercial merchant or speculator erected a structure. A tower at such an intersection often makes an important economic statement. Geographers use the term "peak land value intersection" for the parcels at an intersection that will bring the highest rents (property values) per linear or square foot, and these are usually occupied by services that bring a high return, such as jewelry stores and banks. In the Victorian period, when such intersections were often demarcated by these turrets or oriels, it was a testimony to the wealth of the owners and the prosperity of the businesses.

Who were the Victorian-era designers who transported and translated the architecture of classical Europe into the Main Street on the American frontier? In contrast to artisans and carpenters of earlier periods, many were industrious entrepreneurs like the Mesker Brothers, whose name appears on metal façades created in the late nineteenth century. The Mesker Brothers were sons of a tinsmith in Cincinnati and Evansville before the Civil War: Ben and Frank Mesker produced standardized components in factories in St. Louis, Missouri, and Evansville, Indiana.[29] They were joined by another brother, George, who continued the family business in Evansville after Ben and Frank moved to St. Louis. Whereas George Mesker's façades are common in the Middle West and rare in the

Figure 18. *Victorian bay-window flourishes and oriels made Main Street a highly detailed, elaborate scene for shoppers in the 1880s. Oriels like this one in Missoula, Montana, were common at high-land-value locations where important roads or streets intersected Main Street. This building contains some Romanesque treatments, including heavy masonry arches. 1994 photo by the author.*

West, brothers Ben and Frank were far more prolific: from their St. Louis factory, they mass-marketed standardized façade components that found their way to every corner of the country. Architectural historian and director emeritus of the Idaho Historical Society Arthur Hart notes that the Mesker Brothers sold 5,264 building fronts in twenty-three years, about half of them in the western United States.[30] Like other architectural-component manufacturers, the Mesker Brothers produced catalogs that illustrated their ornate products. The popularity of these components is still evident on Main Streets throughout the United States.

Architects also became more important in shaping Main Street toward the end of the nineteenth century. By the 1890s, architecture on Main Street became quite eclectic as new influences began to be felt and began to challenge the supremacy of the Italianate commercial style. Architects such as Henry Hobson Richardson (1838–1886) of Boston advocated, designed, and constructed buildings in the Romanesque style (or "Richardsonian Romanesque," as it was termed by contemporary critics). This continued the legacy of highly detailed, European-inspired buildings on Main Street. Richardsonian Romanesque buildings are symphonies in masonry: the style features large, solid masonry arches reminiscent of those seen on Roman buildings such as the Coliseum. Many buildings in this style made use of brick alternating with quarried stone (often buff-colored or red sandstone) trim. Architects influenced by Richardson created some of Main Street's grandest buildings at around the turn of the century; courthouses, city halls, and commercial buildings stood as testimony to a fascination with European building traditions and the American prowess in imitating them. Architectural historians have noted that these buildings could never truly be confused with their European prototypes, for the American counterparts were eclectic, borrowing and mixing elements to create a sense of grandeur.[31] And yet, such buildings were typically Victorian in their use of lavish detail, their pretense, and their basis in classical tradition.

TECHNOLOGICAL EXPRESSIONS:

THE INFRASTRUCTURE OF MAIN STREET

If nineteenth-century Main Streets began to look quite different by the century's end, technology as well as architecture was responsible. By the 1850s and 1860s, telegraph wires had found their way into town as express services thrived after a new form of energy — electricity — was harnessed. By the mid- to late 1880s, electricity made a tremendous impact in many towns; power poles could now be seen lining Main Street, although electricity was often brought to the rear of buildings via alleys or other easements. Electricity's most significant impact, however, came in the form of electric lighting. By about 1890, most Main Streets could boast at least one arc light, which often hung suspended by wires over the town's main intersection. Thus, electricity made obsolete the gas or oil lamps that had lined Main Street as early as the 1830s. Dependent on electricity, another major visual impact on Main Street was made by the telephone, whose separate lines required poles bearing numerous crossarms. Historic photographs at century's end often reveal seeming forests of telephone poles, each with as many as a dozen arms, lining Main Street.

Transportation technology had another major impact on Main Street in the late nineteenth and early twentieth centuries with the arrival of the electric interurban and streetcar after 1887. The widespread popularity of the bicycle in the 1890s led to demands for paving as bicycling casualties mounted on rutted, muddy streets. The 1890s witnessed the pioneering use of concrete, and a portion of the area near the courthouse so paved in Bellefontaine, Ohio, in 1893, was said to mark its first use. To suppress dust and avoid the problems created by mud, merchants often lobbied for downtown paving improvements, but interim measures included oiling or sprinkling streets to make their surfaces more stable and attractive. By century's end, many Main Streets were paved with a variety of materials, including wooden blocks and stone. Vitrified paving brick became a popular material for surfacing roads and streets. By 1920 most Main Streets were paved, as they were likely to be part of a developing network of county, state, or federal highways; the side streets, however, were likely to remain unpaved for another generation.

The water towers that served to pressurize a town's water supply are often visible from Main Street, and their style, too, has changed over the years. The earliest water towers were of wood; by the late nineteenth century, however, distinctive metal water towers could be seen. When they featured the name of the town, they served as a more literal symbol of the town's identity. Like other improvements on Main Street, the water tower symbolized the control of nature and the presence of comfort, convenience, and greater safety (from fire and disease) in town life (fig. 19).

Figure 19. *The water tank dominating one end of the Main Street of Mountain Iron, Minnesota, in about 1915 symbolizes the infrastructural improvements that accompanied progress and prosperity on Main Street. Courtesy Iron Range Research Center, Chisholm, Minnesota.*

Water towers meant that the community had installed the underground infrastructure — often wooden stave sections of water pipe wrapped in metal bands — to convey water to essential fire-fighting fixtures: fireplugs, which sprouted along Main Street by the late nineteenth century.

Whereas improvements of individual buildings brought the promise of increasing trade to an individual entrepreneur, merchants recognized the need to unify so that large-scale downtown improvements could materialize. Merchants' associations that sought to improve the entire Main Street for both the betterment of the town and for the betterment of trade downtown were common by the turn of the century. Collective improvements resulted from these unified efforts. Trees were often planted as a way of providing shade and making Main Street more attractive. Awnings were used widely to keep sun and rain off store façades and could be ordered in standard sizes by catalog; enterprising contractors, however, often erected covered wooden porches along full blocks of Main Street. These porches helped unite the façades visually and introduced a strong, horizontal element into the townscape. Improvements of any kind were amenities in that they made life more comfortable. They also helped provide the impression that Main Street was progressive, or "modern," because it now possessed the latest improvements that were seen in the larger, more prosperous cities.

EARLY-TWENTIETH-CENTURY DEVELOPMENTS ON MAIN STREET

Although popular mythology emphasizes the innovative spirit of people in small towns, accounts of entrepreneurs who adopt architectural and design innovations often reveal urban sources of inspiration for these improvements. In fact, a substantial number of urban architects designed buildings in small towns. New York was an early source area (ca. 1860) for architects, but other urban centers such as St. Louis, Chicago, and San Francisco became important in the later nineteenth century. A prosperous merchant in a small town looked to urban architects to help boost his prestige. It should be remembered that most small towns had one major goal — to become larger — and the association with a city was seen as desirable; small wonder that a number of small towns were named after cities, such as London or Rome, or incorporated the word *city* in their names (e.g., Spring City, Archer City).

Of all the cities that influenced the Main Streets of small towns, especially in the nation's midsection, it would be impossible to overestimate the significance of Chicago, which affected or even dictated architectural styles from about 1890 well into the twentieth century.[32] Chicago was in fact both a conservative force and a progressive force in shaping architecture, and it has been said that the Columbian exposition of 1893 did much to ensure that the traditional architecture of neo-classicism would dominate the American streetscape for a full generation, as it was adopted as the official style of the Exposition under the leadership of conservative architect Daniel Burnham.[33]

By about 1900, small-town Main Streets were swept by the trend that architectural historians now call "Academic Eclecticism." Using a medical-geographical metaphor, architect Louis Sullivan (1856–1924) noted that this "virus of the World's Fair" began with a "violent outbreak of the classic and the Renaissance in the east which slowly spread westward, contaminating all that it touched."[34] Having their roots in French Beaux Arts

Figure 20. *Beaux Arts and its classical emphasis created monuments on Main Street in the early twentieth century: here, the First National Bank built in 1912 appears as a sepulchral monument, its subdued trim and solid columns supporting a narrow classical façade in Newcastle, Texas. 1994 photo by the author.*

Classicism, formal styles first seen at the Columbian Exposition found their way into the small town as banks or other important commercial buildings used the style. Beaux Arts style buildings featured substantial arches and made extensive use of elaborate trim. By 1905 formal building styles rendered even small Main Street buildings into monumental shapes. When shoehorned into narrow commercial lots, banks appeared to be Greek or Roman tombs; large columns supported heavy pediments, many inscribed with Roman dates (fig. 20). Their classical building elevations with heavy, almost ponderous, corbels and bracketing provided a formal, somber tone on Main Street. Other elements of the Beaux Arts Style, including rusticated stone work, became common in commercial buildings, courthouses, and banks on Main Street.

If Chicago was in part responsible for the persistence of traditional Academic styling, however, it also claimed many innovations. Chicago pioneered what architectural historians now call the Chicago Commercial Style, which took advantage of the use of structural steel for load-bearing components. This innovative use of steel enabled buildings to be built taller than masonry construction permitted. Because it also permitted window openings to be much larger throughout the upper stories than had ever been possible before, the Chicago style involved a "quest for light," as well as strength, in buildings.[35] This style spread very quickly from Chicago to towns that were prosperous (that is, could afford new construction), and one often sees its characteristic design — windows that expand entire bays with relatively thin beams replacing large areas of load-bearing brick — on small-town Main Streets.

Chicago's legacy was a modernization of Main Street; very delicate spandrels of steel running from the first floor almost all the way to the roof tie the building together. In contrast to Victorian or later Beaux Arts styling, relatively simple architectural detailing caps the cornice of the Chicago Commercial Style. Steel also helped create somewhat more fire-resistant (but not fireproof) structures and so was touted for its both practical and aesthetic merits. Its acceptance confirms the fifth axiom of Main Street development: *The prevalent building material also helps to dictate the actual form that buildings on Main Street will take.* Architects often utilize the most accepted, least expensive, strongest, and otherwise "best" materials, especially when these materials can be made to look like other materials or encourage new styles.

The Chicago Commercial Style transformed the appearance of many Main Streets in the early twentieth century. No longer were the windows on the second, third, and perhaps fourth floors of buildings relatively tall and narrow; now they could be opened up to span almost the entire width of the building. In the Chicago Commercial Style, a very few structural members formed, in effect, braces that could support much of the weight of the *entire* building façade. This development helped blur the difference between the first story and the upper stories, for large horizontal expanses of glass became common across the face of the entire building.

Terra cotta became a common architectural material in the early twentieth century, and it too helped free architects to create new designs as well as to closely copy, even duplicate, classical motifs. Although terra cotta can be traced back to the Romans, its use in Main Street commercial buildings is especially prevalent after about 1912. Terra cotta of different colors provided tremendous variation and beauty to the townscape (fig. 21). One could see, for example, cream-colored façades with dark green, blue, or even orange, trim. When rendered into the numerous re-

Figure 21. *Terra cotta could be shaped into exotic and classical forms and brought color and detail to Main Streets in the early twentieth century. It is seen from coast to coast in towns that flourished in the 1920s. Note that this building and that at the right feature large Chicago-style window openings on the upper floors. (The lower, or storefront, portions of these façades were modernized in the 1960s.) Childress, Texas; 1991 photo by the author.*

vival styles, such as Mission Revival (fig. 22) that began in California in the 1890s[36] and diffused to smaller communities nationwide by about 1915–20, terra cotta could further show its versatility and beauty by being shaped into sculptural form. Because the use of terra cotta coincided with a neoclassical revival that became common after about 1905 from New York to Oregon, one might see Roman urns and other classical detailing recreated in the building façades along Main Street in the 1920s.

As might be predicted given Louis Sullivan's disdain for the lavish classic and Renaissance styles, however, there developed — in Chicago especially — a strong resistance to the neoclassical. This resistance had been spearheaded by Louis Sullivan himself, but many agreed that a radical change was needed. He and his followers developed a distinctive style, often called the "Sullivanesque," which found its way into Main Street when merchants and entrepreneurs could afford new construction. Sullivan's radically styled bank buildings appeared in prosperous communities such as Owatonna, Minnesota; Cedar Rapids, Iowa; and Newark and Sid-

Figure 22. *Mission Revival became popular in California by the 1890s and spread nationwide by about 1915. The style was applied to this handsome electric interurban railway station in Woodland, California. Buildings of this style attempted to recreate the lost heritage of California's golden past on Main Street. 1994 photo by the author.*

ney, Ohio. These reflected Sullivan's fascination with rarely used architectural materials (including tile and stained glass) and powerful architectural compositions, such as huge arches and bold, solid wall surfaces (fig. 23). An architectural historian has noted that "what Sullivan was being asked to do, in effect, was to create a whole new image for one of the basic institutions of life: the small-town bank."[37] In doing so, Sullivan used diverse sources: he looked to the Middle East for inspiration, and its influence is seen in his striking façades, which featured large arches and elaborate mosaic details. Sullivan used both traditional and new materials, such as terra cotta, in the architectural treatment of his buildings, and a contemporary (1912) review of his Peoples Savings Bank in Cedar Rapids, Iowa, stated that "his every design is his personal work and embodies his personality in each of the many materials used."[38] Sullivan's bank buildings, especially in the Middle West, are classic examples of this peculiar style, which was influenced by, and in part influenced, the "prairie school" architecture of Frank Lloyd Wright (1867–1959). Importantly, Sullivan introduced new *abstract* forms and shapes into Main Street architecture that represented a break with the traditions of the nine-

Figure 23. *Designed by Chicago architect Louis Sullivan and completed in 1908, the National Farmer's Bank building introduced a bold, arched façade in the Main Street composition of Owatonna, Minnesota. As a symbolic statement, this building rejects the classically inspired Victorian structures on Main Street and anticipates the "modern" architecture that would follow. Ca. 1970 photo; courtesy the Minnesota Historical Society.*

teenth century that had lingered since the Chicago Columbian Exposition. With the acceptance of Sullivan's designs, one can anticipate the rise of "modern" architecture on Main Street. It is at this point in time — ca. 1920 — that the architectural graphic of the Historic Landmarks Foundation of Indiana (fig. 4) ends; from this point on, I will use photographs of towns exclusively to illustrate the changes that have swept Main Street in the last seventy-five years.

THE AUTOMOBILE AND ITS IMPACT ON MAIN STREET

The appearance of Main Street began to change rapidly in the 1920s. Although horse-drawn vehicles and electric streetcars ruled the street until well into the twentieth century, by the 1920s a major transportation revolution was shaping Main Street; the automobile had largely replaced horses and wagons (and posed new hazards for the pedestrian). The automobile brought a new concept — parallel parking — to Main Street. Although the tradition of diagonal parking dated from the horse-and-wagon era (it is virtually impossible to parallel-park a horse-drawn wagon) and is still practiced in many towns, parallel parking saved space as it effectively widened the travelled section of the street. It also required a new set of skills in maneuvering a motor vehicle.

Because travellers along Main Street were increasingly at the wheel of automobiles, as opposed to being confined to the slow speed of wagons (and the even slower speed of foot traffic), this gave them, quite literally, a different, more horizontal, perspective. As a consequence, Main Street architecture became more streamlined, and more emphasis was placed on horizontal signage and wider expanses of "showroom" glass along the first floors. The automobile enabled people to travel farther, and thus the streetscape became attenuated, or elongated, with the coming of the automobile. Service stations and motor courts began to spring up along Main Street. In the center of town, building heights were reduced, and windows widened where new construction occurred.

These observations lead to the sixth axiom of Main Street development: *The shape of Main Street architecture is, in part, determined by the prevalent type of transportation.* This was true in the nineteenth century, but now the speed at which one traversed the street tripled or quadrupled: whereas the Main Street of the nineteenth century was never experienced at a speed greater than, say, ten miles an hour, speeds of thirty miles an hour became common by 1920. To accompany the demands of automobile traffic, asphalt-based pavement surfaces could be applied with far greater speed, and at much lower cost, than the brick or stone pavements they replaced.

The look of Main Street was always determined in part by the kind of material available for construction, and the 1920s and 1930s witnessed a profusion of new, creative architectural materials — for example, porcelain-enameled steel, glazed tiling, and extruded aluminum — that were manufactured by American industries. Glass block also became common at about this time and helped to revolutionize the face of Main Street. Thus, Main Streets are indicators of diffusion of style and technology: by identifying certain traits, such as terra cotta trim or glass block, and determining the date on which the feature was constructed or installed on Main Street, one can determine that some towns were very quick to adopt new technology, while others lagged until the element became more accepted.

As repositories of technological traits and architectural styles, America's small-town Main Streets confirm that the spread of commercial technology is usually from larger urban centers to smaller rural or remote places.

Viewed more comprehensively, the spread of Main Street architecture indicates the dominance or supremacy of urban/industrial culture in the nineteenth and twentieth centuries. What James Vance, Jr., calls the American *ecumene* — an enterprising industrial heartland stretching from the east coast into the U.S. interior[39] — had developed by the late nineteenth century and continued as a major source of materials and products into the present century. The materials manufactured in the ecumene were easily shipped over a dense web of railroad lines and a newly developing network of paved roads.

By the late 1920s and into the Depression, a new kind of architecture — Art Deco — began to appear on Main Street, but only when an otherwise weak economy could support it. Art Deco featured smooth, curvilinear, rather sensuous designs. In streetscapes from coast to coast, Art Deco coincided with the dominance of the automobile; it also coincided with the fascination for streamlining that characterized the American transportation industry. Thus, at the very time that Main Street buildings were becoming more streamlined, so too were automobiles. Streamlining swept the country, some say to sell a disheartened public on the idea (rather than the reality) of newness and modernity in an otherwise moribund economy. Trains and buses, too, acquired streamlined shapes in the 1930s. The beautiful Greyhound bus station in Jackson, Tennessee (fig. 24), represents late Art Deco–era styling. When it was constructed in 1938, this building symbolized a belief in progress and modernization. Significantly, it was during this period that neon signs began to proliferate on Main Street. Although developed earlier in the twentieth century, neon signs seemed especially appropriate when seen from a passing automobile, for they possessed an inherently energetic, flowing quality. Neon lighting further accelerated a process begun first by oil and gas lighting and then incandescent lighting, namely, the utilization of the street at night.

The Second World War slowed change on Main Street for a while, but America's fascination with streamlining and modernization continued after the war as the "Art Moderne" style flourished. Art Moderne, which might be said to be a continuation of Art Deco in that it featured many of the smooth curvilinear surfaces that had characterized Art Deco, found its way into Main Street at about the same time automobiles began to break from their smooth, almost bulbous, profiles and began to sport fins. Art Moderne buildings make especially effective use of porcelainized and

Figure 24. *The Greyhound bus station, with its gleaming, streamlined, porcelain steel surfaces, introduced smooth, sensual Art Deco or early Moderne lines to the streetscape of Jackson, Tennessee. This style coincided with the streamlining of trains, automobiles, and buses during the 1930s and helped pave the way for more modern design on Main Street. 1978 photo by the author.*

enameled steel, chrome, and tile. The use of Art Moderne for auto dealerships and service stations on Main Street seems appropriate, since the style is so flowing, like the form of the automobiles sold and serviced there. As a complement to the style itself, the large, smooth, horizontal Art Moderne advertising signs readily caught the eye of those in automobiles. These signs and buildings could be found wherever new construction took place on Main Street. Anaconda and Missoula, Montana, and Lowell, Arizona, offer beautiful examples of Art Moderne styles that flourished during the late 1940s and early 1950s.

THE MODERNIZING OF MAIN STREET

Main Street architecture may be embellished and flashy, but it can also be rather simple and utilitarian; the relatively Spartan commercial buildings erected after the Second World War that simply serve the purpose of being storefronts, with perhaps living space above them, provide a case in point. Most are rather unadorned, leaving their signage to convey messages about the services they provided. After the war, architectural trim became rather subdued or was even eliminated as the International Style swept the country. In the urban landscape, the International Style was often expressed as "modern" architecture. Glass-and-steel skyscrapers dominated the cities, but on Main Street, the incarnation was usually far more modest: buildings often expressed a simple horizontality, as building-façade ratio of width to height continued to increase in the 1950s. "Modern" style buildings employing large expanses of glass were erected along Main Street, and also in the new shopping centers that began to proliferate at the edges of towns. Because upper stories had far less utility at this time, most new construction, like shopping centers, was of one-story design. On Main Street, the lower stories of building façades were often remodelled or modernized while the upper floors retained their earlier design and might, symbolically, have remained vacant. These developments emphasized horizontality (as opposed to the verticality so prevalent in Victorian architecture) and can be seen as resulting from fundamental changes introduced by the automobile.

At this time, aluminum siding became quite popular as siding salesmen worked their way through the small towns selling material with which one could enshroud the earlier more detailed, and now less fashionable, façades of the Victorian period. In a relatively short time a streetscape could be transformed as aluminum siding was used to cover the earlier details and open up the façades, thus giving them a streamlined appearance (fig. 25), as shown in catalogs by Alcoa and other companies. Yet, for the most part, this new beauty was skin-deep; a glance toward the upper stories revealed remnants and details of an earlier era (perhaps Victorian, perhaps even Greek Revival). Thus, although the lower floors might be swept along by architectural fad and be encased in aluminum siding, the upper stories helped one to better determine the age of earlier remodellings — and earlier aspirations — along Main Street.

Here and there across the United States, one can see the International Style in Main Street buildings of larger towns: a bank, for example, that might be enclosed completely in glass and appear to be something of a modern skyscraper structure in the heart of town. These buildings often reflect, in their glass surfaces, the buildings dating from earlier periods across the street which have, somehow, escaped remodelling or demolition. The First Interstate Bank in Missoula, Montana, provides a fine ex-

Figure 25. *Aluminum siding covered the façades of many buildings as the "tin-men" (siding salesmen) sold their wares in small towns. In later years, preservationists have removed the siding, often revealing older details underneath. This classic example is from St. Paris, Ohio. 1989 photo by the author.*

ample (fig. 26) and is a reminder that the decisions affecting the face of Main Street may be made in corporate offices hundreds, perhaps thousands, of miles distant from Main Street.

It takes a good eye, but one that can be developed, to note architectural change along Main Street. Looking, for example, at the façades of a hardware store, bank, or other retail structure along Main Street, one must look beyond just simply the lower portion of the façade — that is, look up toward the roofline. This view often reveals older architectural details that might have escaped modification or alteration, as in the case of a Victorian-era commercial façade that was transformed, at eye level, into an Art Deco, Art Moderne, or modernized façade.

HISTORIC PRESERVATION AND POST MODERNISM ON MAIN STREET

During the 1960s and especially the 1970s, two seemingly opposed trends reshaped Main Street: while progressive modernization continued, historic preservation became a potent force. The American historic preservation movement, which has deep roots that reach back into the early

Figure 26. *The bold glass façade of the First Interstate Bank in Missoula, Montana, shows that the international style of building an "envelope" in glass and steel found its way into towns by the 1950s and 1960s. Note how the reflective surface of this building mirrors, in a distorted image, an older Victorian-era building across the street. 1994 photo by the author.*

nineteenth century, rapidly gained strength in the 1960s. Preservation became a household word after Congress passed the Historic Preservation Act of 1966, which with its subsequent amendments provided both funding and expertise to owners of historic structures. Historic preservationists often encouraged owners to "restore" buildings by essentially removing older trim and, sometimes, removing modern paint (through the destructive process of sandblasting, before its evils were recognized) to reveal the original brick and stone beneath. Historic preservation brought about renewed interest in maintenance as well as the aggressive marketing of the structures for their historic character. A generous subsidy in the form of tax incentives for rehabilitation of historic buildings (the Investment Tax Credit) ensured the commercial popularity of historic preservation.

The preservation movement on Main Street sometimes led to zealous action frowned on by knowledgeable preservationists: intentionally making new construction appear old. The Courtyard Cafe in Lampasas, Texas, provides an example. Using the masonry and trim of a narrow Victorian-era building as a guide, owners expanded the façade by build-

Figure 27. *The Courtyard Cafe in Lampasas, Texas, seems historic, but only the right portion of the building is; the left portion was constructed to look just like the old — a testimony to the power of popular history in shaping Main Street in the 1980s and 1990s. 1994 photo by the author.*

ing a new section that, even to the trained eye, is essentially indistinguishable from the old (fig. 27). This action resulted in the building's losing its designation as a Recorded Texas Historical Landmark and a removal of its State Historical Commission marker. In some cases, such *faux* historical construction has resulted in a building's removal from the National Register of Historic Places.

By the 1990s, historic preservationists faced a dilemma when they considered what was happening on Main Street. On the one hand, many well-meaning architects were fascinated by, and actively involved in emulating, historical building styles. On the other hand, however, those same architects often did not respect the existing historic fabric of the buildings that lined the street. They designed and built some uniquely hybrid pseudo-historic buildings in their quest to make Main Street look historic. Nevertheless, the architects' fascination with historic building styles and details over the last fifteen years expresses an acute interest in "history," however enthusiastic or misguided. Historic preservation made strongest headway on Main Street when communities adopted local preservation ordinances based on the United States Department of the Interior's Secre-

Figure 28. *In Valentine, Nebraska, the First National Bank has become an instant land-mark since its completion in 1993. The spectacular façade features a detailed Western-themed mural, with appropriate iconography for its location in the Sandhills of the west-ern Great Plains. 1994 photo by Heather Rayne Yehnert.*

tary's Standards, and when communities become Certified Local Governments (or CLGs), ensuring that they would work closely with the State Historic Preservation Offices. As will be seen later in this book, some communities elected to work with the National Trusts' National Main Street Program to balance historic preservation with continued growth and development. A highway planner for the Michigan Department of Transportation stated succinctly that "the National Trust's 'Main Street' program has renewed interest in the façades of small town commercial streets — literally the face of hometown America." [40]

That the subtle but pervasive power of the past can even shape new construction is seen in the façade of the First National Bank at 253 N. Main Street in Valentine, Nebraska. Employing an innovative, bold design reminiscent of Louis Sullivan's bank buildings, artist Jack Curran of Lincoln incorporated a magnificent brick mural into the façade facing Main Street in 1993 (fig. 28). The mural features historic rural imagery, and appropriately so, for Valentine is located in the Sandhills of Nebraska: in a sweeping composition, a herd of longhorn cattle are being driven across the upper portion of the façade, while at storefront level another brick mural features other frontier images, such as covered "prairie schooner" wagons, a windmill, a steam train, and early Native American imagery, including tipis, and bison or buffalo. Since its completion in 1993, the building has become a town landmark, made all the more poignant by the fact that the bank's president died in a tragic plane crash (which also claimed the lives of another bank executive and the Governor of South Dakota) the day after he dedicated the work to the people of Valentine on October 15, 1993. Buildings of this type become instant landmarks, but the fact that this building contains such vivid historical iconography says much about the current appreciation for American history by the public.

The historic-preservation movement has left its mark on Main Streets across the country. It was followed closely by (and actually almost coincided with) the development of Post-Modern architecture in which new construction emulates the historic features, such as ornate detailing or towers, of earlier buildings. Post-modernist and neo-traditionalist architects may also feature or recapture regional historic architectural elements, as in the case of the Poletti Building on San Benito Street in Hollister, California (fig. 29), which abstractly reproduces the historic regional bay window flavor of nineteenth- and early-twentieth-century commercial architecture in a strikingly new (1993) glass-dominated façade.

Despite a fascination with history and historic preservation, architects on Main Street endeavored to use the most modern examples of architectural designs, which is to say, they tried to have their work reflect modern or progressive rather than reactionary trends or fads. But in the case of Post-Modern architecture, architects clearly looked backward to models from the American past for inspiration, and in so doing continued a trend that began earlier in the twentieth century, when American Colonial Revivals — perhaps stimulated by the development of Colonial Williamsburg as an education-and-tourism destination — helped Americans rediscover their past. This may account for the many post offices and other retro-styled buildings that were of "colonial" style during the 1930s and 1940s. Making new buildings on Main Street look old reached something of a craze in the 1980s, however, and in some cases, buildings that would be almost undetectable as new — were it not for our knowledge that they were constructed in the recent past — appeared on Main Street. Most, of

Figure 29. *The Poletti Building in Hollister, California, features historic, regionally themed bay windows in a striking design. It was constructed in 1993 on the site of an earlier building that was destroyed in the 1989 earthquake. 1994 photo by the author.*

course, have a look that reveals their modern construction; imbricated brick with abstracted corbels; simple but powerful towers. This vaguely historic look has swept American commercial environments, from modern shopping centers to remodelled Main Streets, from coast to coast. Pediments rise here, towers reappear there; all mirror a desire to recapture features from the past.

On Main Street today, one may find historical excess; not only do some enthusiastic architects build in historic styles, they build in historic styles that are almost burlesque versions of the historic styles they are trying to emulate. For example, a second empire mansard roof may have more than one row of windows, or be much larger in scale, than an authentic mansard roof, becoming in effect a caricature of the architecture rather than a historically accurate copy of it. In the 1970s and early 1980s, and continuing into the mid-1990s, huge *faux* mansard roofs became increasingly common on new, or remodelled, Main Street buildings (fig. 30). In extreme cases, such mansard roofing might sweep down and cover the upper floors of the entire façade of the building, implying that if a mansard roof is good, more of it is even better. This, one wag noted, might be called "the revenge of the mansard."

Figure 30. *The Hollister Coffee Toasting Company in Hollister, California, features a mansard roof that, in effect, has become a false front. Treatment of this kind reveals a fascination with the past that characterizes Post-Modern or neo-traditional architectural trends on Main Street. 1994 photo by the author.*

BUILDINGS AS LOGOS: CORPORATE CHAINS
AND FRANCHISES ON MAIN STREET

Although this fascination with the past has shaped Main Street in recent decades, modern or "progressive" trends have also continued their sweep; these have often obliterated historic structures as new construction remained an attractive option. This expansion of corporate chains, and the spreading of national enterprises through franchises, has had a tremendous impact on Main Street in the last forty-five years. It began as early as the 1920s, when oil companies built pattern-book service stations that packaged the corporation's identity using a wide range of architectural styles from Art Deco to Colonial Revival.[41] By the 1960s and 1970s, nationally franchised enterprises had accompanied the automobile into the very heart of downtown. Because the corporation's product and image were inseparable, large chains refused to compromise on design. Things began to change after the mid-1970s: after more than thirty years of insisting that their standardized corporate designs be accepted on Main Street

Figure 31. *Two generations of McDonald's architectural designs on Main Street are seen in this view at St. George, Utah. At left is the older, late-1970s McDonald's with its mansard roof typical of that period, which now stands behind the newly expanded "play-place" — a large, glassed-in enclosure built at the front (right) of the older building. 1995 photo by the author.*

(in which the building became something of a "sign" in itself, as logos dominated), chains like McDonald's, Burger Chef, and Burger King began to build in more "sensitive" architectural designs by the late 1970s and early 1980s. Thus, McDonald's, which began by erecting standard white porcelain steel buildings and huge golden arches on Main Street, shifted to brick, mansard-roofed buildings with smaller Golden Arches signs that seem to "fit" somewhat better with historic structures. By the mid-1990s, McDonald's restaurants were being retrofitted with large glassed-in "play-place" enclosures facing Main Street, seemingly as a way of reaffirming the corporation's emphasis on community and family (fig. 31).

It appears to be a truism on modern Main Streets that the building of an entrepreneur will conform more to other more accepted or traditional buildings as the enterprise becomes more successful. Thus, signage may actually *shrink* in size as it becomes more recognizable and accepted. This helps to explain why McDonald's now "blends in" better on Main Street than it did at first, that is, when it was a novelty seeking attention through the use of a building as sign. In some cases, strong sign ordinances implemented in the 1970s and 1980s mandated such conformity — the goal being a return to the more "tasteful" or less "obtrusive" signage of the days when, paradoxically, there were no sign ordinances whatsoever and the streetscape was, in reality, often marked by rather garish signs that vied for people's attention.

THE STAGES OF MAIN STREET DEVELOPMENT

Time is a major factor in the look of Main Street, but that change has not occurred at an even pace everywhere. Thus, many Main Streets have experienced phenomenal change over the years while many have remained remarkably stable. And yet, even Main Streets that seem "timeless" reveal change if one knows what to look for: When studying a Main Street of the late 1990s, for example, the perceptive student often sees a subtle mixture of architectural styles that may be traceable to the nineteenth century, early twentieth century, or more recent times. Whereas this accretionary quality might offend purists, it is indeed an honest expression of the fact that Main Street is constantly evolving. A photograph or sketch may freeze Main Street in a particular moment, but time always changes the streetscape from one moment, or one vignette, to the next.

Just as architectural style and technological innovation have changed the face of Main Street, and can be discerned in broad patterns in time, so too does Main Street appear to evolve through several stages. In a pioneering study of Main Streets in Northeastern Oregon, geographer Barbara Bailey identified four stages of development.[42] As can be seen in figure 32, the first stage finds a series of individual buildings, including houses, standing along the street; the second stage witnesses the construction of new buildings and the expansion of others; the third stage sees the spread of fairly permanent buildings such as brick commercial structures; and the fourth stage witnesses these buildings increasing in height, as little open space for new construction remains along the street. Such change is also correlated with increases in population. Bailey's model appears to be applicable to a number of locations but is also dependent on regional economic factors.

MAIN STREET: DISASTER AS AN AGENT OF CHANGE

Models such as Bailey's stages of development assume that change will occur in any particular community much as it does in other, similar com-

FOUR STAGES OF MAIN STREET DEVELOPMENT

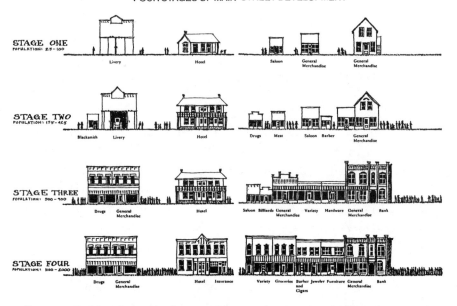

Figure 32. *In* Main Street Northeastern Oregon: The Founding and Development of Small Towns, *geographer Barbara Bailey discovered that Main Streets developed in four stages. Although some of the stages may be generalizable to other locations — with styles changing and lots in-filling through time — the character of a Main Street is also related to its regional geography and economy. Reprinted with permission of the Oregon Historical Society.*

munities. But one other factor, that of rapid local change brought on by catastrophes, must be considered.

Of the three elements that characterize the design of Main Streets — architecture, street pattern, and open space — the buildings themselves are actually the most ephemeral. Through regular processes of development and change, many buildings are altered, even demolished, when they no longer meet current demands. Some towns, however, seem to possess disproportionately large numbers of buildings of certain styles as compared to other towns with similar economies. The first question we should ask about such towns is: Has anything out of the ordinary happened here? An economic boom may explain the look of Main Street, but so, too, might a disaster.

Consider, for example, the case of Coalinga, California. The traveller visiting this small (population 9,500) town at the west edge of the San

Joaquin Valley finds downtown to be developed around a commercial intersection where attractive one-story commercial buildings, with broad porches adapted to a hot, semi-arid climate, stand near a small park (Frame Park) at the intersection of 5th and Elm Streets. Coalinga appears to be a new or modern town, for virtually all of its commercial buildings are obviously recent, and yet the town's literature states that Coalinga was founded in the early twentieth century. Why does everything look so new in a relatively old town? Virtually all of downtown Coalinga looks modern, but looking more closely on Elm Street one can see two commercial buildings that appear older, perhaps dating from the turn of the century or the early twentieth century. What, one should ask, has happened to Main Street here? A visit to the local newspaper office and City Hall provides the answer. In October 1983, Coalinga suffered a devastating earthquake — 7.0 on the Richter scale — that left much of the town in ruins, and provided an opportunity for active rebuilding using a combination of federal and local funding.

A visit to the Coalinga Historical Society's museum reveals that Coalinga in the 1920s looked like a rather typical Anglo-American town that had developed in the early twentieth century. In a letter written in 1932, entrepreneur-merchant A. P. May recollected his early building developments, noting that "several of our customers thought I was crazy to put up the row of brick stores in 1902, thinking there would never be enough business in Coalinga to fill them."[43] Concerned about fire, May noted that he built five additional galvanized-iron buildings in 1903. A closer look at earlier photographs shows that Coalinga had suffered considerable damage in the 1906 (San Francisco) earthquake and, before that, in a series of fires that prompted May to build fireproof buildings. Thus, although A. P. May was most concerned about fire, and tried to build structures that could resist it, it was earthquake damage that ultimately leveled his structures! Realizing that Coalinga was astride an active fault, the city in the 1980s changed character as merchants took advantage of a loss that they turned into an opportunity. Using more earthquake-resistant techniques and materials, they built modern-style buildings that incorporated traces of Southwestern style architecture, and thus created an attractive yet modern downtown.

Disaster can arrive in many forms. Fires, as implied in the description of Coalinga's early development, were the scourge of many Main Streets.

As two Illinois architectural historians have stated, "Unraveling the threads of a downtown tapestry, one finds that an often neglected element — fire — has contributed to the shape of the landscape."[44] A look through historical records for communities reveals the effectiveness of fires that could, within a matter of minutes, reduce a commercial district to ashes. Historians in Plano, Texas, matter-of-factly recall that "on the morning of August 27, 1881, the entire business district of Plano was burned to the ground even though the McKinney firemen made the run into Plano in just eighteen minutes."[45] A poem published in October 1895, after yet another of the "innumerable fires" to hit Plano, immortalizes the conflagration with the following lines: "Our stores are rapidly burning down, nothing left but ashes, out on the ground," but concludes, with characteristic Victorian optimism, "So rebuild boys, build up your stores, fill up your shelves and open your doors. . . ."[46] Similarly, in Willcox, Arizona, when "on May 3, 1910, a whole row of frame buildings on Railroad Avenue between the Willcox Hotel and the Maley Street intersection burned," a mass meeting was held and the town rallied, recognizing the need for better fire-fighting equipment.[47] That adobe and brick buildings were far better at retarding the spread of fire did not go unnoticed by the town's merchants; this helps explain the more "permanent" look of the town by the 1920s.

Although fires have probably had the greatest impact or effect on downtowns, tornadoes and other high, shearing winds have been among the major factors influencing the appearance of Main Street, especially in the "tornado alley" section of the Central United States from North Texas into Oklahoma, Kansas, Nebraska, and Iowa, the Dakotas, Wisconsin, Minnesota, Illinois, Missouri, Arkansas, Indiana, and well east into Ohio. Southern communities, too, are susceptible to particularly vicious night or early-morning tornadoes in late winter and early spring, and such twisters have devastated commercial districts from Louisiana through Mississippi and Alabama into Georgia, and, occasionally, the Carolinas.

The historic center of Xenia, Ohio, which features nineteenth- and early-twentieth-century examples of commercial architecture, was heavily damaged on April 3, 1974, when a twister ripped through the town leaving thirty-four dead and a hundred million dollars' damage in its wake. As preservation sentiments were not as strong as a desire for "progress" in the form of modern buildings, Xenia elected, after a painful process that included a building moratorium, to rebuild a portion of downtown using structures seen in modern strip shopping centers.[48] The result was the transformation of West Main Street from a late-Victorian streetscape (which had been witnessing the intrusion of fast food and other services on the eve of the tornado) to a shopping-strip-style commercial area that features many of the services that might normally develop at a town's edge. In the case of Xenia, historic buildings were not rebuilt, and the town's architectural character was transformed rapidly. It is important to realize, however, that Xenia was being affected by such forces *before* the tornado, and the tornado simply helped accelerate the change. Xenia is a classic example of the truism that pre-disaster conditions are intensified by disaster; time is compressed as the pattern that prevailed *before* the disaster is accelerated *after* it. Thus, the few years immediately following the Xenia tornado witnessed changes that might otherwise have taken decades to occur.

A deadly tornado that roared through the historic downtown square of historic Lancaster, Texas, on April 28, 1994, was eerily reminiscent of that in Xenia. Many historic buildings surrounding Lancaster's square were devastated. However, Lancaster vowed to rebuild its historic downtown by reconstructing all of the historic buildings as a way of ensuring that the pre-tornado character of the town would be maintained, and many were rebuilt within a year. Because the Lancaster tornado occurred at a time (the mid-1990s) and in a place (a historic community in Texas with a Main Street program), rebuilding is being orchestrated to preserve the town's historic character. Texas-born country singer-songwriter Willie Nelson, a historic-preservation advocate, appeared at concerts targeted to rebuild the town's historic center much as it was before the tornado. Xenia, Ohio, and Lancaster, Texas, would seem to have two different fates, but they both reaffirm the seventh axiom of Main Street development: *Developmental and economic forces in effect on Main Street before a disaster will be continued, and intensified, as a consequence of that disaster.*[49]

Thus it is that many Main Streets in tornado alley bear evidence to the swath of damage left by past storms. Until very recently, when historic preservation became a major force on Main Street, tornadoes and other natural disasters simply provided opportunities for merchants and owners to rebuild and get back into business using the most desirable (read "the latest") building and architectural styles. That explains why a row of buildings destroyed by fire or storm would be built using then-new styles that today have become historic in their own right. Main Streets often contain impressive visible evidence of disasters that, with the development of newer styles, "heal" by becoming historical styles with the passage of time. Whether through disasters or economic development, change is everywhere evident on Main Street.

Time, then, is a major factor in Main Street development, for it determines the way in which architectural fads and technology develop and serves as a framework for determining when peoples of various cultures migrated to different locations. But so, too, is space, for Main Street is a result of geography as well as history. That subject — the ways in which Main Streets vary across the country as a result of spatial patterns of cultural development and environmental characteristics from place to place — is treated in the next section.

2 : SPACE AND MAIN STREET

Toward a Spatial and Regional Identity

WHEN CAROL HAD WALKED FOR THIRTY-TWO MINUTES SHE HAD
COMPLETELY COVERED THE TOWN, EAST AND WEST, NORTH AND SOUTH; AND
SHE STOOD AT THE CORNER OF MAIN STREET AND WASHINGTON AVENUE AND
DESPAIRED. MAIN STREET WITH ITS TWO-STORY BRICK SHOPS, ITS STORY-
AND-A-HALF WOODEN RESIDENCES, ITS MUDDY EXPANSE FROM CONCRETE
WALK TO WALK, ITS HUDDLE OF FORDS AND LUMBER-WAGONS, WAS TOO SMALL
TO ABSORB HER. THE BROAD, STRAIGHT, UNENTICING GASHES OF THE STREETS
LET IN THE GRASPING PRAIRIE ON EVERY SIDE. SHE REALIZED THE VASTNESS
AND THE EMPTINESS OF THE LAND. — SINCLAIR LEWIS, *MAIN STREET*

Because "property developers are dedicated followers of fashion,"[1] the changing architectural styles or fads along Main Streets of American towns help to define the character of individual buildings and link them to particular periods, episodes, or events in history. But the architecture of individual buildings tells only one part of the complicated story of what is called "townscape" — all the physical features and amenities that contribute to the way a town looks and "feels." If architecture comprises the building blocks of townscape, then the way in which these buildings are formally arranged with regard to one another and to open space largely determines the "feeling," or *ambience*, of towns. Buildings are not placed randomly but are a result of many decisions. The way they are placed in any setting is dictated by the dimensions and pattern of streets, the size and shape of lots, and the configuration and design of open spaces. These spatial parameters not only shape individual towns but, as will be seen, may also contribute to the personalities of larger American regions.

This section demonstrates that the historic layout and design helps to determine the overall character of towns in general and the image of

Main Street in particular; furthermore, it demonstrates that these broader design patterns are also linked to trends or fashions through time and in space. These design-related aspects give a community both its "depth" in time and its character in geographic space.

As the epigraph at the beginning of this section reminds the reader, Main Street is often depicted as a backdrop for voyages of discovery and encounter in the American heartland. That discovery may be one of an unsettling, almost grim, realism, such as that which awaits Carol Kennicott in Gopher Prairie, Minnesota, where "dullness is made God" and her vision of transforming Gopher Prairie into a beautiful village is stifled at every turn. It might, however, also be used to symbolize a return to the familiar — literally and figuratively — as when Forrest Gump repeatedly refers to experiences in his hometown of Greenbow, Alabama, and when Faulkner refers to Jefferson (perhaps actually Oxford, Mississippi) in his novels set in Yoknapatawpha County. Thus, the words of Sammy John's popular song from the early 1970s link a personal experience — a young man's pleasurable encounter with a young woman from a small town — with a blending of longing, indifference, and nostalgia that characterized the era. After travelling together in his Chevy van, he drives her home, where

> I put her out, in a town that was so small,
> You could throw a rock from end to end,
> A dirt road Main Street, she walked off in bare feet,
> It's a shame I won't be passin' through again.[2]

The small-town Main Street that has become an evocative image in verse, song, and cinema is deeply connected to American attitudes toward both time and space: collectively, they define the small town as place in the American mind.

In a perceptual/geographical sense, Main Street is both mundane (topographic) and paradoxically "utopian" in the two seemingly contradictory meanings of utopian: it is both an *imaginary* place (literally *no* place), and also an *ideal* (or perfect) place. As a place, Main Street has spatial and geographical properties: kinetically, one must traverse Main Street while travelling into, or through, a town; by definition, Main Street occupies a central location in the community. That helps position Main Street locally, but does not address an important question. How does any particular Main Street fit, geographically, into the mosaic of larger regional or national landscapes? Is Main Street really the same from coast to coast, or are there different types, or varieties, of Main Streets? In order to answer these questions, one needs to define Main Street as a type of urban form, and then determine if that form varies from place to place, as its architecture certainly does through time.

Main Street develops in relationship to the overall urban form of a community. In terms of spatial design, Main Street has roots in a number of places. Northwestern Europe is one such source area. Just as architectural styles and building types reveal these source areas, so too does the morphology or spatial design of a community. Brian Roberts's important book *The Making of the English Village* provides a hint to the development of Main Street in this succinct observation: "All villages contain streets, but a surprisingly large number look towards a single main axis running through the settlement's centre: this is at once a highway and a front yard, a public space, the king's highway, usable by all travellers, and a focal area which helps to bind the settlement together."[3]

One can observe this tendency for a town to orient itself to a single axis by observing it as a traveller: Main Street is where buildings are joined together and define the public space and the commercial activity. From the air, Main Street is obvious as the density of the buildings is high, and their clustering or lining the street is quite apparent.

MAPPING MAIN STREET

Maps are the next best thing to flying over a community, as they too can help us place architecture in space and shed light on the design of Main Street. Students of American townscapes are fortunate in that small towns have been mapped in considerable detail from coast to coast. The topographic maps prepared by the United States Geological Survey at scales of 1:62,500 or 1:24,000 frequently contain sufficient information to permit a general understanding of downtown. On the maps of smaller communities especially, commercial buildings are often shown as black rectangles, and open spaces can be easily deduced from the maps. City halls, courthouses, churches, schools, and other important and prominent institutional structures are also shown. On these topographic maps, Main Street is easily recognized as a denser pattern of larger buildings oriented toward the main road or roads (fig. 33).

Other types of commonly available maps that contain even better detail can help us better read and interpret streetscapes. Without a doubt, the Sanborn Insurance Maps (fig. 34) are the most effective tools used by

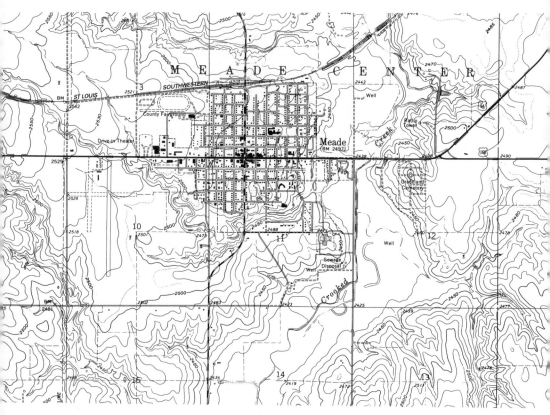

Figure 33. A USGS *topographic map of Meade, Kansas (pop. ca. 1,750), reveals at a glance the location of the town's "Main Street" commercial section. It appears as a series of black rectangles oriented toward the main road (U.S. Highways 160 and 84 at the junction of State Highway 23). United States Geological Survey, Meade, Kansas, 7.5 minute series, 1:24,000 scale, 1963; photo revised 1983.*

historical geographers. Prepared to assist insurance companies in deter-mining the risk of fire to any particular enterprise, Sanborn maps show, in detail, building location, shape or "footprint," and construction material; they also indicate where buildings may share common walls. Quite im-portantly, Sanborn maps show all buildings and structures, streets, alleys, walkways, fire plugs, and other features, such as streetcar tracks, that might affect firefighters' access to a particular building. They also depict open or vacant spaces, as these may help firefighters gain access to buildings. Since 1877, Sanborn maps have provided very accurate mapping of the elements that comprise American streetscapes. Completed for thousands of communities, including most small towns of greater than 500 popula-

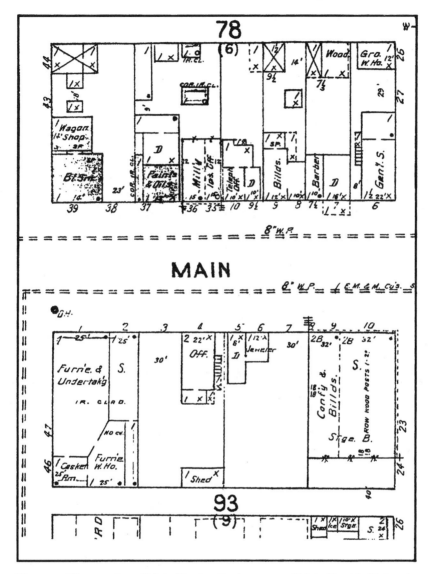

Figure 34. *The mapping of Main Street: a Sanborn map of Main Street in Enterprise, Oregon, in 1910 shows that commercial buildings occupy most of the lots as the downtown continues to urbanize during the early twentieth century. Reprinted with permission of the Oregon Historical Society.*

tion, Sanborn maps are available in the original color format at a number of historical archives, and are available in microfilm at most central repositories such as state or university archives.

In addition to the Sanborn maps, property and deed maps available in city and county records are also quite helpful. These often show the building outline, and may be used to reconstruct historic patterns of property ownership along Main Street. Another important cartographic source — historical maps in county atlases — may show individual building outlines as well as property boundaries. These often prove very helpful to the student of historic townscapes, especially when consulted with city or town directories that list businesses and their owners.

A METHODOLOGY FOR READING MAIN STREETS

As noted in the introduction, students of townscapes use three simple ingredients — building form, street pattern, and open spaces — to read and interpret the general design of towns and cities. Collectively, these spatial elements determine the visual personalities of communities. Although we intuitively know that something "different" happens to us when we experience different communities, architecture is only one of the factors. For example, a New England village with its green faced by churches reinforces a sense of pastoral or agrarian community life (and ultimately connotes a spiritual sense of community), while a Southern town in which a large courthouse sits on a square and is surrounded by commercial buildings will, naturally, convey quite a different sense (namely, reaffirm the county government's importance in the life of the town and its residents). The term "green" and "square" are quite important, for they give a spatial context to downtown in the community.

As a way of simplifying these spatial issues, urban designers and landscape architects have developed methods that permit one to read and interpret a community's visual geography. The methodology pioneered by Kevin Lynch more than thirty years ago in *Image of the City* still serves as a helpful tool for reading both the downtowns of our smaller communities and our largest cities. Lynch used five indices, or elements, that help orient the observer and enable him or her to make sense out of the townscape. They are:

1. Paths. The channels, such as streets or sidewalks, along which people move.

2. Edges. The boundaries that separate two different environments, for example, walls, creeks, and escarpments.

3. Districts. Medium to large sections of a community, such as the central business district, that have some common identifying character.

4. Nodes. Strategic points into which the viewer can enter, such as a major street intersection.

5. Landmarks. Visually prominent forms in the landscape, such as monuments and objects, that invariably draw, or command, the viewer's attention.

Using these five elements, it is possible to construct (and then deconstruct) images of the town. For example, architecture and the density of buildings enable the viewer to sense that he or she is in the downtown district; one may have traversed a *path* (road) to arrive there and have crossed an *edge* (for example, the railroad) in the process. Depending on its design, a Main Street commercial *district* may feature a *node* in that an open space is available from which the downtown can be experienced. Individual, highly recognizable buildings, such as a city hall or courthouse, may be *landmarks*; statues, fountains, and other important features may also serve as landmarks. Together, these five elements help one to define the character of a community and to better interpret how its downtown commercial area (Main Street) is experienced by both the traveller and the resident alike.

That these elements were as relevant a century ago as they are today is seen in the delightful sketches and chronicles of Lewis Miller, a nineteenth-century Pennsylvania German folk artist who drew the downtown of York (fig. 35). Miller's depiction indicates the streets, the buildings lining the street which help frame one's view, and the market-court(house)-office that stood as landmarks in the central square of York. The downtown section can be thought of as a district having a distinctive character seen in the drawing. In York, and virtually all American towns, the edge of downtown is usually demarcated by the trees of a residential district, the railroad tracks, and/or other features.

THE PLACEMENT OF BUILDINGS ON MAIN STREET

A visual synergy exists on Main Street. This central artery is comprised mostly of commercial buildings, but even civic or institutional buildings

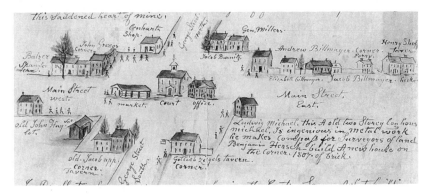

Figure 35. *Whether an image of a community is from the past or the present, Kevin Lynch's methodology for "reading" a townscape can help identify significant paths of mobility (such as Main Street itself), nodes in the form of public squares and other park-like spaces, and landmarks like the court and market buildings shown on the square in York, Pennsylvania, in a historical (ca. 1870) sketch that indicates how the town developed during its early years beginning in the late 1700s.* Lewis Miller: Sketches and Chronicles — The Reflections of a Nineteenth Century Pennsylvania German Folk Artist; *courtesy of the Historical Society of York County, York, Pennsylvania.*

(such as a city hall, courthouse, or church) become part of our image of the downtown area of a community when they are present. Whereas individual buildings themselves make individual architectural statements, their actual impact on the observer, however, also depends on their context, that is, *their relationship to other buildings and open spaces.* Just as individual bricks may create quite different patterns when arranged in different ways, a row of essentially identical commercial buildings may look quite different if they are placed in different settings, or viewed from different vistas.

Consider, for example, the Main Streets of two towns in the Red River Valley along the Texas-Oklahoma border. In the case of the buildings in Waurika, Oklahoma (fig. 36), the fact that the commercial buildings line both sides of a densely built-up Main Street restricts the distance, and limits the angles, from which they can be viewed; Waurika's Main Street possesses the feeling of a corridor or canyon, a situation that is reinforced by the fact that there are few empty lots between the commercial buildings that line and define the street. However, a similar row of buildings facing the public square in Henrietta, Texas, where the open space on the square enables the viewer to see the entire assemblage "head on" from the courthouse steps, creates a very different effect (fig. 37): rather than channeling one's view, the buildings define a node. Whereas Main Street buildings in Henrietta form a backdrop to, and actually define, a well-tended public space, in Waurika they define the singular path itself — called, appropriately enough, Main Street. Locals are aware of this difference: Oklahomans refer to the type of town plan in Henrietta as a "Texas square." Such squares are rare in Oklahoma, which, as Indian Territory, was settled much later than Texas just across the Red River.

Main Street as a term implies important action in that the adjective "main" signifies prominence and the noun "street" signifies a path that carries traffic. The two Red River Valley towns referred to above exemplify two basic models of Main Street design. In the first, Main Street is a *linear* strip or corridor lined by buildings much as a river's banks actually define its course. In the second, a *nodal* open space is surrounded (or embraced) by commercial buildings, much as the shore of a harbor defines a port. The river/harbor analogy is not as remote as it may at first seem, because both features — be they water or pavement — provide for mobility and refuge. This contrast between the *security* of a node and the *uncertainty* of following the linear Main Street outward into the distance was implicit when novelist Madison Cooper described the layout of a fictional Texas town: "Main Street ran from Sironia's Court House Square due west more than a mile before it became lost in cedared, limestone confusion."[4]

Of all the basic classification systems used to interpret towns, few have as much validity as the simple division of Main Streets into linear or nodal or a combination of the two. These spatial designs can be determined by watching vehicular and pedestrian traffic move: does the movement take place in a line or is there some central point of focus, such as a park or prominent building, around which traffic flows? This circulation-related factor (linearity or nodality) greatly affects the character of a town, for — as novelists and town designers know — our perceptions of it are influenced by how we move in relation to objects and other people.

STREET WIDTH AND LAYOUT

From a design point of view, other related factors contribute to the character of Main Street. The *width* of the street, in particular, itself affects the feel in that it affects the flow of traffic and the proportion or ratio of built-up to open space. Main Streets in the United States vary in width, but are

Figure 36. *Despite being a county seat, Waurika, Oklahoma (population 2,088), presents the simplest of Main Streets, a linear assemblage of buildings flanking a straight street. This linear Main Street is typical of towns built to serve a market center along dominant lines of transportation. 1994 photo by the author.*

commonly within the range of fifty to eighty feet; the standard dimension of 66 feet — a surveyor's chain — is common. Consider the range: The Chinese American rural town of Locke, California,[5] has what appears to be the narrowest of America's Main Streets. Its twenty-two-foot width reinforces the feeling that one is entering the confines of a canyon (fig. 38). Locke's straight Main Street is lined by two-story buildings, many of which feature porches and balconies, further enhancing its canyon-like ambience. Designed and platted in the early twentieth century, the town was designed to fit tightly against a levee in the Sacramento River delta. Locke persists as a quaint reminder of an essentially vanished way of life, and its Main Street has come to be an icon for the town itself. Locke's narrow Main Street contrasts vividly with the wide Main Streets of many Mormon towns in the intermountain west that were platted in accordance with the directive of Latter-Day Saints prophet Joseph Smith, who called for streets 132 feet (two chains) wide in the Mormon *Doctrine and Covenants*. These wide Mormon main streets, however, cannot compare to the 300-foot-wide main street of Ennis, Texas, proclaimed in a tourist brochure to be the widest Main Street in the entire United States.[6] Nu-

Figure 37. *Henrietta, Texas (population 3,213), county seat of Clay County, presents a different appearance: built around (that is, facing) a square, the town's commercial buildings can be viewed directly head-on. This type of nodally developed downtown is typical where roads converged on the community and the town platters recognized the importance of central authority, such as the county, in the affairs of the community. 1994 photo by the author.*

merous communities, including Keene, New Hampshire, vie for the distinction of widest Main Street in America.

Typically, very wide Main Streets provide opportunities for embellishment; their centers often become places in which vehicles are parked or trees planted. Thus, wide Main Streets may become more like nodes than the paths they were originally envisioned to be. Designers have long appreciated the power of trees to transform urban spaces. The trend of planting trees along streets, said to have originated with Thomas Jefferson in Washington, D.C., in 1803, spread rapidly to other eastern cities and became commonplace in American communities by the mid–nineteenth century. The regular spacing of a line of trees down the center of Main Street, such as that seen in Franklin, Tennessee, or Coloma, Michigan, effectively both architecturalizes and naturalizes the space (fig. 39). Strategically planted shade trees serve to soften the streetscape and provide shade when planted in front of commercial buildings. They were commonly employed by merchants on Main Street as a way of making shop-

Figure 38. *Street width helps to determine the character of Main Street, as this scene of the very narrow Main Street of Locke, California, shows. On Main Street, the observer is in a canyon, as buildings tightly define one's view. Ca. 1980 photo; courtesy California Office of Historic Preservation.*

ping more pleasant and the streetscape more beautiful. Deciduous trees are especially functional in the middle latitudes of America, for they provide shade in summer yet permit the sun to reach the façades of buildings during the winter months. As Sinclair Lewis would have appreciated, trees help soften the straight "gashes" created by streets.

STREET PATTERN AND THE CHARACTER OF MAIN STREET

If a town's character is influenced by such amenities, it is largely determined by the town's layout, for the way in which streets and property parcels intersect affects — perhaps even controls — the views or vistas that are experienced. Students of landscape design have noted that the surveying and layout of rural property parcels is one of the differentiating elements between the East (much of which was settled *before* rectangular planning became widespread in the late eighteenth century) and the West (much of which was pragmatically laid out in squares or rectangles after the dominant township and range system was adopted). In reality, the rectangular-grid pattern can be found in the areas of western New York

Figure 39. *Shade trees transform the streetscape. As seen in this historic (ca. 1908) post-card of Coloma, Michigan, the trees define the street right of way while softening the scene by providing shade. Photograph by C. R. Childs, Photograph Postcards, Chicago; author's collection.*

that were still the frontier in the late 1700s, but for our purposes we might say that the West begins as far east as Ohio, for the rectangular surveying of western lands began with the original surveying of the Seven Ranges of Eastern Ohio in the late 1780s.

Although American towns — especially in the Middle West and West — are often laid out in the familiar checkerboard patterns of the Township and Range System that resulted from the Land Ordinance surveys of 1785,[7] there is much variety across the country. Some eastern communities are laid out in rectangular squares, while the historic Main Streets of western mining towns may follow the winding courses of streambeds in canyons, where, in the case of Bisbee, Arizona, or Central City, Colorado, they form memorable streetscapes that fit into the stereotype or archetype of mining towns.[8] Although many Midwestern towns are laid out in a rectangular fashion, some river towns in the region, such as La Crosse, Wisconsin, or Galena, Illinois, often curve with the bends in the river. This variety in American townscapes is in part dependent on history, the topography of the site (or lay of the land), and the cultural background and vision of the people who laid out the communities in the first place. The sensitive traveller always asks design-related questions about townscape: why does Main Street curve or run straight; why does Main Street intersect with other streets at a particular angle; why are buildings built where (and how) they are; and why are certain land parcels maintained as open space while others are built up?

Main Street at its simplest is found where a straight road is lined on both sides by commercial buildings constructed solely to serve the needs of travellers and local shoppers (see fig. 34). In this pattern, Main Street represents an axial channel, or path, along which people and vehicles move. Aside from the street and sidewalks, there is no open space set aside for the public, the only center or focus of attention being the largest, or most ornate, building along the street. As geographer John Jakle has noted, this type of linear Main Street is tightly bounded by the architecture of the buildings lining it.[9] This is Main Street at its most functional, and the street reaches out to infinity in both directions.

The architecture of Main Street serves to delineate a powerful, almost urbanistically regimented corridor. Because building massing and positioning helps define townscape, Main Street has a different quality when building height varies, or when empty lots are encountered between buildings. Although these vacant lots provide a wonderful opportunity for advertising signage, they may be viewed as negative or unproductive space by speculators who would hope to see the entire streetscape built up.

TOWN SURVEYORS AND THE SHAPING OF MAIN STREET

Of course, these assemblages of buildings that comprise Main Street did not simply spring up like so many weeds. By what mechanism is a town laid out or surveyed and platted and how does its Main Street take form from seemingly innumerable locational options? In other words, who (or what) controls or determines the basic design of the plat and the selection of Main Street? Most often, this process is a partnership or arrangement between a landowner who desires to subdivide a parcel for a town, and the person who has the experience of town creation, the town platter.

Survey record books and local histories usually confirm that an individual essentially "draws up" the plat map of a community. In his classic studies of American town development, John Reps identifies many such individuals.[10] Commonly, they worked for landowners who sensed an opportunity; thus, their charge or task was to give form to a vague vision. In

Figure 40. *Town developer A. A. White of Moorhead, Minnesota, helped merchants and others visualize what Main Street would look like as he used this advertisement to promote the towns that he designed and platted. Great Northern Railway Company records, St. Paul, Minnesota; courtesy Thomas Harvey.*

virtually all the communities they platted, these town platters envisioned Main Street; usually they created narrow lots with sufficient street frontage to encourage commercial enterprises to locate on the street. Oftentimes they named it Main Street, but Market Street, First Street, or Commerce Street were also common names for what town platters felt would be the most important thoroughfare in town.

Main Street formation occurred in several stages in the nineteenth century. Individual landowners were often the catalyst for town platting in the early nineteenth century, but by the middle to later part of it, town platters worked closely with large landholders such as the railroad corporations. Of these, the enterprising A. A. White of Moorhead, Minnesota, was perhaps typical. White and his partners were active in town development in the Red River Valley of Minnesota and North Dakota.[11] That the commercial Main Street was an essential ingredient of each of White's towns is seen in the attractive promotional logo that advertised his services (fig. 40).

What configuration did these town speculators choose for Main Street? Would it follow an early road or would it blaze a new path? Would it parallel or run perpendicular to a major path of transportation such as a river or the railroad? Since the shape or form of a street itself is a major factor in determining the character of Main Street, students need to ask several basic questions: Can one traverse Main Street without turning corners or changing direction? Is the view down, or along, Main Street open, or is it blocked? Typically, town speculators and platters use straight lines to minimize problems and ensure accuracy. And thus, in most cases, the street is straight, and building walls are parallel to each other — as in the case of Bellefonte, Pennsylvania; Winchester, Kentucky; or Newbury, South Carolina. This rectangular geometry creates a feeling of order and regularity, and was a favorite plan of town promoters and platters.

There are thousands of straight Main Streets in many parts of the country, including the midwest, and they have served as the backdrop for great American fiction, including Sinclair Lewis's *Main Street*. The Main Street of Clyde, Ohio, which served as the setting for Sherwood Anderson's *Winesburg Ohio*, provides an elementary prototype: here, as in most main streets, the street runs arrow-straight and is lined on both sides, for several blocks, by commercial buildings.

To the traveller arriving in a particular community, Main Street usually is an architectural climax of two- and three-story buildings set close together. Main Street, in fact, features the highest density of buildings in the town, and the value of land is highest in this commercial district. Because most of the buildings are of standard styles (often of the late nineteenth and early twentieth century), any deviation is noticeable: the tower on a fire station or town hall may serve as a landmark to locals. As architectural critics have often derided it, Main Street is often uninspired. Its rectilinear layout may be unimaginative, but its straight lines and its predictability reflected the street's straightforward function — *Commerce*. Main Street is, above all, a manifestation of the relationship between merchant and vehicle-bound customer. Town platters attempted to ensure that commercial intercourse would occur at logical, even predictable, locations.

As noted earlier, a curving Main Street, such as that seen in Galena, Illinois, or the Gold Rush town of Jackson, California, transforms the character of the streetscape. Instead of running straight out to infinity, the curving street directs one's view to the buildings on the inside of the curve, much as the bend in a river gives one a better view of its banks. Rather than being deliberately designed for aesthetic impact, however, curving Main Streets were usually the very practical solutions of pragmatic town developers who faced the task of developing unique sites. The curving — even twisting — Main Streets in western mining towns often follow the course of the creek along which the first or earliest roads developed; a twisting Main Street usually indicates that a community developed *before* much planning could occur. Or if the design was planned, such as at the junctions or intersections of roads or where several rectangular plats were engineered to fit into each other at angles, it usually indicates that incremental growth occurred.

In some towns, such as Aurora, Indiana, or Decorah, Iowa, Main Streets may intersect with other blocks in the plat — in effect terminating one's view down the street by commercial buildings as the traveller will have to "jog" left or right to continue onward. The natural topography itself may help to determine the character of an otherwise straight Main Street. Thus, the Main Street of Telluride, Colorado, is provided an incredible backdrop — the sheer wall of a canyon looming several thousand feet above the town — as the street was designed to run parallel to the stream valley in which the town was located. This mountainous wall terminates one's view, and shapes one's impression of downtown Telluride. Such seemingly picturesque vistas often originated as functional solutions to design problems, and only later, as we seek "unique" places, do they become aesthetically pleasing or charming.

In any type of town plot, wherever *two* commercially important roads converge, the intersection will likely become the nucleus of the downtown. Its importance will often be anticipated by town platters who will create commercial lots at this location. At this important node, traffic from four directions comes into contact, and the "peak land value intersection" referred to in Section 1 is created. If no provision has been made for public space, then the intersection will be framed on all four sides by commercial buildings, and a very "urban" streetscape will be created. One's view at such intersections is controlled by commercial and civic buildings, which are usually large and ornate.

The rural farming community of Cedarville, Ohio, provides a case in point. Because the town's main streets intersect at an angle determined by early roads leading to the site along Cedar Creek, the town hall is visually dominant, terminating and controlling the view as one approaches the town from the southwest. Where there is no open space to draw one's attention to buildings across vistas, and where a street curves slightly to provide a direct view to buildings placed at the end of the street, the effect

Figure 41. *In Jim Thorpe (Mauch Chunk), Pennsylvania, the view down a slightly curving Main Street terminates at the Romanesque style town hall, which becomes an exclamation point in the landscape as one's view is channeled toward it by the slight curve of the street. 1991 photo by the author.*

can be spectacular. The Main Street of Jim Thorpe (formerly Mauch Chunk), Pennsylvania (fig. 41) features the Romanesque style town hall that arrests one's view down Main Street. So, too, does the white wooden Methodist Church in Nevada City, California, which stands like a sentinel at the northwest end of Main Street. As town planners have known for centuries, the street pattern can be designed to dictate one's line of sight toward landmarks.

Towns that have little or no open space downtown are likely to have a decidedly more "urban" or densely settled character than those with large open spaces. In America, as in the urban places of medieval Europe, townscapes that are almost completely architecturalized, especially those

with fairly narrow streets, feel remarkably closed, or close. The dense concentration of Italianate commercial buildings, located in a veritable maze
of angled intersections where two street plats obliquely meet, creates a remarkably urban feeling in the small town of Bellevue, Ohio. The feeling
is not solely created by the actual structures themselves, for similar structures exist in other towns that possess a more open feeling, but rather by
their placement in a complex configuration of angled, built-up lots; the
feeling thus is determined, in part, by the pattern of streets.

That such spatial design relationships continue to be significant is seen
in Nelsonville, Ohio. In the early 1980s, McDonald's selected a location at
a bend in the town's main thoroughfare, with the result that the tall golden
arches sign is now the most visible feature in town. Day or night, it can be
seen for almost a mile in each direction. Whether one likes McDonald's
or not is irrelevant; the placement of their sign indicates that someone
seized an opportunity to draw considerable attention to what would otherwise be just another sign in the landscape. Good siting, like good tim-
ing, is essential for effective business enterprises. This point leads to the
eighth axiom of Main Street development: *The more visible or accessible a
property or building on Main Street, the more valuable it will be as commercial property.*

Deviations from the rectangular grid provide relief from otherwise re-
lentless checkerboard patterns and capture attention. Annapolis, Maryland; Sandusky, Ohio; and Esperanza, New York, all possess remarkable
street plans. In these communities, a series of major streets radiate out
at 45-degree angles into the otherwise rectangular town plan. Wherever
these angled streets cross the regular streets, one finds unique triangular
lots. On a larger scale, Indianapolis, Indiana, has a similar plan; on a
much smaller scale, and for a more practical reason, the original plan of
Coalinga, California, found streets paralleling the Southern Pacific Railroad at a 45-degree angle from the cardinal points. Where the later, com-
pass-oriented grid intersects, one finds a proliferation of acute- and
oblique-angled intersections that disorient the visitor but have become
part of the character of "home" to residents and merchants. Rather than
being planned this way, Coalinga's street layout is simply a result of two
grids meeting at different angles.

Among the most unique town plans in the country was that of Circleville, Ohio, so named because the entire street pattern radiated, in a series
of concentric circles, outward from an Indian mound at the center of

town. This represented one of the truly creative adaptations of a town plan to an aboriginal site. But alas, practicality overcame the vision; in what has been called "the squaring of Circleville," the town was systematically squared off in the nineteenth century, leaving Circleville with a mysterious name (and a common town plan). Today one can glimpse vestiges of Circleville's circular plan in the form of commercial buildings on Main Street that have peculiar pie-shaped floor plans and oddly angled building walls.

THE GEOMETRY OF OPEN SPACE

Streets provide the basic framework for town design, but the look of the community is also dependent on the form of buildings and the spaces between them. If even a simple intersection of two streets, which may seem like a void, is really part of the townscape where people enter and interact with each other and their surroundings, then larger spaces may have symbolic importance as nodes. Whereas nodes may be rather small, such as a street corner, some may be as large as an open village green or square. When they occur at or near the center of town, these open spaces help to define the character of Main Street, for they are points in which people interact as they intersect one another's paths of travel.

The Village Green

The open space in a town may take many forms. It may result from an intentional setting aside of space for civic activities, or be more or less accidental (or temporary), as in an empty space or lot that, someday, may become the site of a commercial building as the town develops. In the smaller communities of New England, the village green is prominent. It may be square or rectangular, but is often irregular in shape. In either case, the village green is public open space that forms the nucleus or visual center of the town. Fronting on the open space are churches, town halls, and commercial buildings. Each structure is prominent, and yet can be seen as part of an assemblage of structures which, collectively, tell the story of the intimate relationship between commerce, religion, and civic affairs that characterizes small-town life in early New England. The area encompassing the village green is a district in the true sense of the word, for it is spatially contiguous and of consistent design. The visitor or resident is well aware that he or she has entered the district, for it possesses a distinctive visual character or "signature."

Figure 42. *A New England village green at Guilford, Connecticut, provides a nearly stereotypical example of Main Street at its most bucolic. 1971 photo by the author.*

The village green has become synonymous with New England (fig. 42), and in a few cases appears to have spread with migrating New Englanders who moved westward into the Middle West. Thus, at the center of the aptly named New Haven, Ohio, one finds a small village green. In a scene reminiscent of New England, the town hall and church face this irregularly shaped verdant spot at the center of town. When such towns become just a little larger, or more prosperous, the green is likely to be nearly surrounded by the downtown commercial buildings, as is the case of the nearby towns of Plymouth and Lodi, Ohio.

Through time, the village green usually changes in use. Whereas it may have started out in the earlier nineteenth century as a functional space where animals might graze, by the late nineteenth century most village greens were public meeting places that reflected the development of Victorian values: the importance of *time* (as seen in the clock), *order* (as seen in the regularized paths cut into the public space), *democratic values* (as seen in the access to the public meetings at the village hall), and the increasing importance of *leisure* (as seen in the familiar gazebo, whose delicate Victorian structure harmonized with the surrounding buildings) in the late nineteenth century. So popular has this nostalgic image of the gazebo become that today one finds such trim bandstands on greens that were empty open spaces thirty years ago, when it seemed that the small town, and its architecturalized visual heart, were headed for extinction.

Among the most interesting open spaces at town centers are the triangular greens found where Main Street branches. Where there is sufficient trade, commercial buildings will line both streets and face a green which gradually increases in width with distance from the main intersection. As revealed in a bird's-eye-view illustration (that is, in fact, a unique type of a map of a community's downtown),[12] the green at Chagrin Falls, Ohio, is among the most beautiful of Ohio's small triangular downtown open spaces (fig. 43). Here in Chagrin Falls the works of man and nature are brought together and the oblique view — a common cartographic technique in the nineteenth century — helps give the scene an aura of harmony, tranquility, and order. When experienced from the perspective of a pedestrian, the green is a verdant space delineated by solid rows of Victorian commercial buildings. This triangular open space incorporates two basic design elements: the reassurance and predictability of straight lines (in the form of building fronts and streets) and the visual tension of an acute angle that directs one's view toward the building façades. Intuitively, perhaps, the nineteenth-century designers of Chagrin Falls learned the power of acute angles in channeling or focussing vistas.

The Public Square

The geometry of much of the Midwestern and western landscape, is, of course, usually less dramatic than the irregular street patterns that converge on the stereotypically irregular village green. In much of America, town plans that are rather predictably rectilinear (or, to use a Mormon expression heard farther west, "right with the compass and right with God") are common. Public space at the center of town is likely to occupy one rectangular (or square) block. In reality, rectangular planning can be traced to the seventeenth century on the eastern seaboard, where communities like New Haven, Connecticut, and Philadelphia, Pennsylvania, were platted by the late seventeenth century. Some of Anglo America's most interesting rectangular-shaped towns are found in New England and the Middle Atlantic culture areas. These types of town plans found their way west with the frontier. The public square was one of the important in-

Figure 43. *The Chagrin Falls, Ohio, green, a triangular piece of land at town center, is beautifully depicted in this detailed view from the lithographed panoramic bird's-eye map by J. J. Stranahan, publisher, in 1883. Note the bandstand on the tree-lined green. Author's collection.*

gredients of town design in the late 1700s and early 1800s. Upon this square may be found public buildings, or, as is often the case, the square may remain unbuilt upon and will then be faced by the public buildings. Thus two basic types of squares (open and closed or built upon) can be identified.

Medina, Ohio (fig. 44), provides a perfect example of the open square plan. As laid out by town platter Elija Boardman, a Connecticut Yankee, in 1821, Medina possessed a large rectangular open space around which commercial lots were developed. This public square has remained open — that is, has not been built up with structures — to the present.

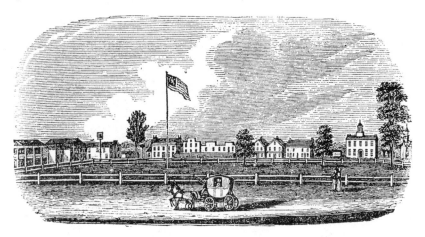

Figure 44. *Medina's open square is a large node at town center. Its openness provides ex-cellent views or vistas of the commercial and civic architecture that surround the square. 1846 lithograph by Henry Howe, in Howe's* Historical Collections of Ohio, *1847.*

One of the lots across from the square was set aside for the Medina County Courthouse, and thus it faces, or fronts on, the open space, much as churches front upon the village green in various parts of New England. A similar situation can be seen in Canfield, which originally served as the seat of Mahoning County. Here, the former courthouse stands promi-nently at the south end of a long rectangular green, a vestige of the town's halcyon days before the county government moved to Youngstown. A careful observer of the American landscape could trace these open squares into the upper Middle West (e.g., Owatonna, Minnesota), the great plains (Broken Bow and Table Rock, Nebraska), and the upper South (Hermitage, Missouri, and Ozona, Texas). In these communities, the square with its beautiful shade trees presents the appearance of a spa-cious oasis, especially on hot summer days. It also provides an excellent lo-cation from which to view the prominent architectural façades of com-mercial, civic, and institutional buildings that face the square.

A second type of square — that which is closed (or built upon) — is also rather common, especially in places that were intended to serve as seats of government. When the county courthouse is built on the square, it be-comes a distinctive, typically American space — the "courthouse square." Of America's 3,066 county seats (including 64 parishes in Louisiana) in the lower forty-eight states, approximately a third feature a courthouse prominently situated on the square. Lagrange, Indiana, provides a perfect

Figure 45. *This view of the county courthouse at Shelbyville, Tennessee, epitomizes the centrality of the square in town and its importance to the county's residents. Commercial buildings downtown face the square. 1973 photo by the author.*

example of the type; when seen today surrounded by the buggies of Amish folk and the automobiles of other residents who come to town, it is a striking sight. More typical is the large county courthouse in Shelbyville, Tennessee, which sits on a square that seems to shrink periodically as automobiles park closer and closer to the courthouse on what was once a large, lawn-covered square (fig. 45).

The Public Square as Central Place

Because commercial lots are often planned and sold by town platters, Main Street is usually an integral part of the downtown image in such county-seat towns. There are several options for designing a county seat, and town platters have left us with an interesting variety. The centrality of the county seat, when coupled with rectangular or square county boundaries — as is often the case in the Middle West and the upland South — provides some of the finest examples of spatial order and uniformity on the face of the earth. Even though a roughly circular — or hexagonal — political unit would provide better potential for equal access to the courthouse, the Middle West still retains a tremendous degree of rectangular centrality, for which it owes the rectangular land surveys of the U.S. government no small debt.[13] In *Corn Country*, Homer Croy related one of the great anecdotes concerning Midwestern centrality:

> Two towns in Nebraska were fighting for the county seat. The matter was determined by an election at which every person in the county could vote. The people of Osceola did some thinking; then had stiff cardboard maps printed in the shape of the county. The voters were asked to balance these cutout maps on a pin, or a pencil, then look to see which town was nearest the balancing point. That settled it. Osceola won.[14]

Many communities adopted the argument that a centrally located county seat provided the most equitable way to serve the county's population — a good example of the close relationship between civic and commercial motivation in town development. As a result, the centrally located county seat might be a relatively insignificant place whose centrality was its greatest virtue. There are numerous examples of the logical result of arbitrarily dictated centrality in the hierarchy of urban places: namely, a centrally located county seat that is not the most populous town in the county (e.g., Hartville and Bloomfield, Missouri). Whatever the case, one of the truly impressive vestiges of nineteenth-century political geography is the small county seat (such as those in Arkansas and Missouri), often numbering no more than a few hundred people. In these towns, a small, partially developed central business district faces a courthouse square with a modest but nevertheless disproportionately impressive courthouse building located in the middle of it. So strong was the interest in centrality that a number of towns permanently forged their names with geometry — at the expense of older, more familiar, or even classical names. Central City, Centerville, Le Center, and the fanciful Centralia are all statements to the importance placed on central location.

How is Main Street development related to these seemingly abstract spatial decisions? There is some evidence that town morphology itself was affected by decisions of centrality. In central county seats, roads often converged from at least four directions on the county courthouse. Very often a town speculator would donate a central block of property for the courthouse, and, in many centrally located towns, the business district grew around the courthouse.[15] Historian Lewis Atherton noted that the morphology of two Minnesota towns was probably significantly affected by the results of a county-seat decision. In this case, "loss of the county seat perhaps accounted for Chatfield's business district developing along one main street instead of centering around a square occupied by a courthouse or municipal building."[16] Its competitor, Preston, developed around just such a square; and the town is in fact just about central to the Fillmore County boundaries.

A town's design results from many factors, including the location and persistence of trade routes and more abstract concepts of symmetry and centrality. Just as zoning today can affect town morphology, so too could speculation. In many county seats, commercial properties were deliberately located facing the courthouse square, a recognition that the courthouse could serve as a magnet to commercial enterprises. Thus, although many towns were laid out around a public square; whether that square was to become a dominant focus often depended on the location of a county courthouse or the crossing of two major thoroughfares to create and sustain business.

Whereas traditional linear "main street" towns develop along only one axis, a town based around a square is really a special example of a node located at the junction of two arteries. This is especially true of parts of the South and the Middle West, where the public square in the county seat is often a gathering spot or focal point. As the expression goes, "All roads lead to the public square." The later trolley or interurban lines in the Middle West, which usually duplicated the pattern of major roads, often circled the public square.[17] Helen Santmyer, in her classic work *Ohio Town*, characterized Xenia but might have been talking about a thousand county-seat towns when she succinctly stated that "the courthouse square is the heart of town."[18]

Considered geographically, counties in which the county seat is located central to the county borders are common only in the South, Upland South, and lower Midwest.[19] E. T. Price's map showing central courthouse squares bears a striking relationship to the distribution of central county seats (fig. 46).[20] The only major exceptions appear to be the county seats of Virginia, many of which were too early to be built around a square, but many of which are nevertheless located at or near town center. Price's map shows a strong distribution throughout the upland South and the lower Midwest. The central courthouse square is rare in the Northeast and uncommon in the western U.S. This helps explain why

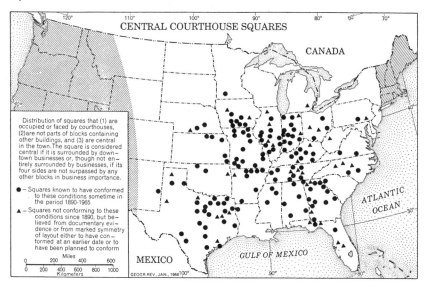

Figure 46. E. T. Price's map of the eastern U.S. showing the distribution of courthouse squares. Copyright by the American Geographical Society and reproduced with permission from the Geographical Review, 1968.

certain Western towns like Missoula, Montana, or Prescott, Arizona, have a decidedly Midwestern or lower Midwestern quality: their squares make them appear quite different from other county seats in the region.

A further example of this centrality can be found, in the negative sense, in the peripheral "river town" county seat. There is a distinctive river town morphology.[21] In a river town, Main Street usually parallels — but is one block away from — the river; thus the backs of the stores, rather than their façades, face the river. Oftentimes the railroad will lie between the waterfront and the first block of businesses. Rather than relating to a public square or park, Main Street and the commercial district stretch along the river in a decidedly linear arrangement. If a river town were also a county seat, the courthouse would likely be peripheral to Main Street for two reasons. First, many river towns gained county-seat status after they were well established, so that the courthouse, even if given its own generous block of land, would be in an "afterthought" location with reference to the main commercial street. Second, it is highly unlikely that a river town would morphologically develop around any square, since the focus of the town is a linear interface with the river.

Even those towns originally intended to be county-seat river towns could do relatively little to change this commercially-oriented state of affairs. Hastings, Minnesota, is an example. Platted with a generous public square, the town's business district nevertheless grew two blocks away from the square along the river. This left the Dakota County courthouse relatively isolated, despite the fact that a major road (Vermillion Street) intersected the waterfront one block away from the courthouse square. In another example of a transportation-related feature influencing Main Street, the town of Newcastle, Wyoming, developed on a railroad line and served the nearby coal fields, and is located nowhere near the center of Weston County. Not surprisingly, Main Street developed toward the railroad, leaving the courthouse somewhat peripheral: it stands at one end of the Main Street commercial business district.

To return to those rectilinear and geometric "square" places that so characterize the Middle West and portions of the upland South, one needs to understand the alternatives available to town platters in the late eighteenth and early to mid-nineteenth centuries on what was then the American frontier. In his seminal article on American town planning, E. T. Price identified and described four major types of rectangular central courthouse square plans: the Block/Shelbyville, the Philadelphia/Lancaster, the Harrisonburg Square, and the Four block square (fig. 47). The most common of county-seat plans in the region is what Price called the Shelbyville plan. So named for its prototype in Tennessee, the Shelbyville plan features the county courthouse on a square that is simply one of the blocks of the town plan reserved as public space. Travelling down Main Street, one is aware of the courthouse square as a verdant node, above which looms the dome or cupola of the county courthouse, forming as it were an exclamation point to the horizontal flow of traffic on Main Street. This Shelbyville plan permits the business district to develop around the square, and I have described elsewhere the likelihood that such towns will be located in the center of a particular county.[22] Texas has dozens of courthouse squares of the Shelbyville type: Waxahachie, Granbury, Georgetown, Hillsboro, and Blanco are among the better-known examples. Where the county seat is located at the center of the county, and the roads meet at the center of town, the courthouse square is liable to be faced or surrounded by rows of substantial commercial buildings. This reaffirms a connection between the seemingly abstract or ideal geometric concepts of space (centrality) and the more mundane actualities (building location) of what is constructed in the landscape.

In addition to siting, the actual design and architecture of the centrally

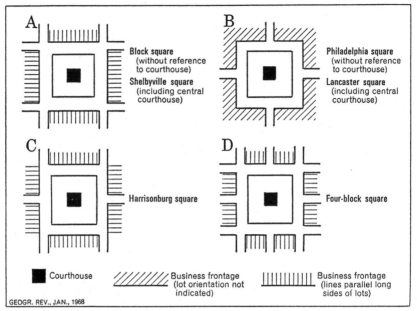

Figure 47. *Delineated by E. T. Price, four major types of courthouse square plans are found in the eastern United States. Copyright by the American Geographical Society and reproduced with permission from the* Geographical Review, *1968.*

located county courthouse is affected by centrality, which is in turn a reflection of anticipated commercial activity. As architectural historian Willard Robinson noted of nineteenth-century Texas courthouses:

> Because of tensions created by the demand to orient each block around the square to the front of the courthouse, similar portals were generally required on all four façades. At mid-century, specifications for new courthouses typically called for four façades alike — even in the occasional instance when there was not actually an entry in each of the sides. . . . The identical façades . . . were appropriate for the geometry and circulation of the plan, and gave equal attention to the commercial property on all sides of the public square.[23]

Robinson further speculated that "the same relationships between the square and its surroundings that produced the need for four similar or identical façades also dictated that the tower should normally rise from the center of the building rather than from a corner or side — it was essential that the county landmark be equally prominent from all sides."[24] Thus, the form of public buildings, like that of commercial buildings, is

Figure 48. *The Shelbyville style courthouse square in Decatur, Texas, demonstrates the power of centrality in landscape planning on the nineteenth century frontier. Like its prototype in Shelbyville, Tennessee (fig. 45), the building marks both the center of town and the center of the county. 1994 photo by the author.*

in part influenced by the dynamic urbanistic forces that link mobility and trade. The centrally located county courthouse is among the better expressions of such powerful centripetal forces that create nodes.

Even from a considerable distance, Decatur, Texas, demonstrates the importance of the county's magnificent red-granite-and-sandstone courthouse, for it can be seen for miles. When one arrives downtown, the courthouse positively looms over all the other buildings around the public square (fig. 48). The traveller to Decatur may feel that he or she has seen this courthouse before, and indeed, the courthouse in Waxahachie, Texas, is a virtual carbon copy of the Wise County courthouse in Decatur, both having been designed by the same architect at about the same time (1895). An illustration of Waxahachie's square during the times when a booming economy filled the square with wagons loaded with cotton bales (fig. 49) reveals how significant the central courthouse square was (and is) in the life of the town. As illustrated in engravings and photographs, it confirms the town's image of itself as a center of production.

Townscape not only has an indelible impact on residents; it also can

FARMERS SELLING COTTON ON THE SQUARE.

VIEWS IN WAXAHACHIE. TEXAS.

Figure 49. *Leslie's engraving of "farmers selling cotton on the square" at Waxahachie, Texas, depicts intense commercial activity: on what is presumably market day, wagonloads of cotton bales crowd the courthouse square in this 1890 scene.* Frank Leslie's Illustrated Newspaper, *Texas edition, 1890; courtesy Special Collections, the University of Texas at Arlington Libraries.*

make a vivid impression on the visitor. One of my associates, William Dunaway, who was born and raised in Decatur, Texas, recently had the opportunity to trace his family's roots back to Shelbyville, Tennessee. On a research trip to Shelbyville, Dunaway was amazed by Shelbyville's similarity to his hometown in Texas: Shelbyville and Decatur both center on a courthouse square whose townscape is dominated by the late Victorian-era courthouse; both courthouse squares are on a high point of land from which one can view the surrounding landscape; both squares feature all major businesses facing the courthouse; and both courthouses can be seen for miles in every direction. Shelbyville and Decatur are classic examples of nodally developed central places laid out in rectangular fashion. Dunaway wondered: Could there be a connection here? The answer came as he researched the founders of Decatur and realized that they brought those Tennessee traditions of town building with them to the Texas frontier in the 1840s–1860s. The Shelbyville plan served as a model that spread throughout the south and lower Midwest by the mid-nineteenth century. The invention of the Shelbyville square and its rapid diffusion confirms the ninth axiom of Main Street development: *Although the most significant innovations in Main Street design occurred in urban areas and spread to the frontier, local decisions that developed on the frontier also affected the design of Main Street.*

Variations of the Square

According to urban historians, the grid plan that spread rapidly westward with town and agricultural settlement is easily reproduced and permits equitable, accurate division of land and property. Texans and Tennesseans could trace their towns' squares to a source area in England. The central square as a unifying element in British town planning seems to date from its use for the new town of Londonderry (Ireland), which the British created in 1611 as part of their colonial expansion. The British soon used the square in the New World, for it helped add a dimension of order to the uncertainty of founding and sustaining towns in the wilderness. By the time the British adopted the square for purposes of colonizing, it had been known widely in the European planning and design professions, whose practitioners experimented with numerous variations, such as offsetting squares or linking them to angled streets.

In the hands of talented town designers, the grid can be used to create memorable townscapes. One of the most effective variations on the grid finds a corner subtracted from each block at the center of town, creating in effect a square within squares (fig. 50). In this plan, an open space is created where streets must intersect: traffic usually flows around the park or building placed in a circle or square at the intersection. Because the corners of the surrounding blocks are notched, the commercial buildings matching the 90-degree "nooks" are designed into the corners. This plan provides interesting visual variety that is lacking in plans where all buildings are simple rectangles. Originating at least as early as William Penn's design for Philadelphia in 1683, this "Philadelphia Plan" became common in western Pennsylvania, central Ohio, and Indiana in the early nineteenth century. Several varieties of the Philadelphia plan can be found in the East, Middle West, and South. Geographer Hugh Wilhelm has called them "diamond squares,"[25] a term that ostensibly refers to the "diagonal" placement of the square by shape, but interestingly implies something of the radiance of this type of plan as streets run directly out from (or into) the square at its center.

That the central space in a Philadelphia style square provides a superb

Figure 50. *Philadelphia-inspired "circle in square" plan towns, such as Gettysburg, New Oxford, and Shippensburg, Pennsylvania, reveal that all elements in the landscape are defined by a simple yet powerful geometry. The plan diffused westward in the early 1800s and is seen here in the town of Angola, Indiana, where all through traffic must circle around a monument at the town center. 1976 photo by the author.*

place to erect a monument is apparent in a magnificent historic view of the square at Mt. Vernon (Knox County, Ohio; fig. 51). The monument is visible from all roads, forming a landmark at the end of the vista down the town's two main streets. In many northern towns, a monument to the Union's most famous Civil War generals may face southward as if to perpetually protect the town. In the South, e.g., West Point, Mississippi (fig. 52), a Confederate monument faces north for much the same reason. Most monuments of this type were erected in the generation following the Civil War, and they brought our small towns an element of the formal architectural beauty of Europe's Renaissance, which also commemorated deeds of the past. When graced by monuments of this type, an otherwise common townscape takes on additional significance, becoming a symbolic place that embodies collective memory of shared sacrifice and loss.

According to historian Gerald Danzer, public monuments of this type are significant because they connect an individual with his or her group and "they have both a horizontal and a vertical dimension — that is, they serve as rallying points for group solidarity at one point in time, binding a

View of Main Street and Public Square Mt. Vernon O.

Figure 51. *A historic view of Mt. Vernon, Ohio, shows the sense of order created in a classic Victorian-era downtown, where a Civil War monument has been placed in a Philadelphia style square created by the subtraction of a corner from each adjoining block.* Graphic News 8, July 2, 1887; courtesy Cincinnati Historical Society.

community together horizontally, but also vertically connecting the present generation with a heroic past and a fulfilling destiny."[26] They also subconsciously reaffirm the inseparability of time and space.

Because the main roads intersect at the center of a Philadelphia style square, all traffic must flow around anything erected on it. When the square contains a building, it is called a Lancaster type in recognition of the prototype in Lancaster, Pennsylvania. Any building constructed on such a square will become the most visually dominant structure in town. All roads seem to lead to it, and the building appears even larger than if it were positioned off to the side of the main flow of traffic. Thus, when a large courthouse or city hall is erected on such a square, the effect is overpowering. The Parker County courthouse at Weatherford, Texas, seems almost surreal, for it can be seen for miles in all four directions. When

Figure 52. *In West Point, Mississippi, a Civil War monument stands at one end of Main Street, serving as a reminder of past sacrifices and the town's white citizens' allegiance to the Confederacy during the Civil War. Typically, such monuments rise about a generation after the events they commemorate. 1978 photo by the author.*

erected in 1886, it was not only the largest building in town; it was the largest building in the entire county.

One can trace this plan as far west as Arizona, where it appears at Florence in Pinal County. In west Texas, the Presidio County courthouse at Marfa provides a superb example of the important relationship between building form and town layout in a community with a Lancaster type plan (fig. 53). The courthouse can be seen from virtually any place in town. It is the first building one would see gazing up Main Street from the depot. It commands one's view of the commercial streetscape, for the vista along the street literally terminates at the courthouse: thus the commercial buildings help direct or channel one's view toward the courthouse. This relationship confirms the inseparability of government and commerce, and is a reminder of the historical fact that government control provided order to a potentially chaotic and dangerous settling of the western frontier in the nineteenth century.

Whether open or closed (built upon), the square is a powerful element in the design of American towns. It has served as a significant literary de-

Figure 53. *The Presidio County courthouse at Marfa, Texas, is built on the Lancaster style plan, with the view up Main Street from the railroad tracks terminating at this impressive public building. 1993 photo by the author.*

vice that anchors the community in time and place. As William Humphrey related in the saga *The Ordways*, the square in Clarksville, Texas, could serve as a regional metaphor:

> The shady streets of Clarksville radiate from a spacious square, from the plaza in the center of which, bedded in wild roses, rises a tall marble shaft surmounted by a Confederate foot soldier carrying a bedroll on his back and a canteen at his side, resting his musket, and shading his eyes to gaze over the rooftops towards the Southwest, in which direction the view is almost limitless.[27]

This description sets the scene for a quest that will contrast Clarksville with the towns of southwest Texas that are the creations of another culture — the Hispanic peoples of the great Southwest.

The Plaza
In contrast to Anglo American communities of the eastern seaboard, the Middle West, and the South, the towns founded by the Spanish were, with the exception of a few Florida communities, usually located in

arid or semi-arid areas. The irrigated fields and habitation presented a contrast to the desolation of the surrounding countryside. In describing his arrival at the then small community of San Antonio in the Republic of Texas in September 1839, medical doctor-geologist-botanist John Leonard Riddel wrote:

> a broad verdant valley opened to sight in the midst of which appeared, as if created by enchantment, the city of San Antonio de Bexar. It stands alone, surrounded by a country really held by the savages, unmarked by cultivation or improved, and at present almost sterile desert from the effects of fire & drought. It reminded me of Tadmor in the desert mentioned in the Scriptures. . . .[28]

Most Anglo travellers to Spanish (and, after 1821, Mexican) towns of what is now the Southwest commented first on their adobe and stone architecture (as described in Section 1) and then upon the spatial layout, which, like most Anglo American towns, was often rigidly rectangular. Indeed, the Southwest is a rich repository of urbanistic designs inherited from the "three peoples," as geographer D. W. Meinig called them, who now inhabit the region: Native American, Hispanic, and Anglo American.[29] That Native American communities in the region possessed a time-proven ability to protect themselves is seen in an analogy drawn by Father Dominguez in 1776: "Its plan resembles that of those walled cities with bastions and towers that are described to us in the Bible."[30] It should be recalled that the pueblos were so defensible that the Puebloan Indians revolted in 1680, driving the Spanish out of an area that had seemed to be conquerable. The Spanish, however, would return to continue establishing communities in the 1700s.

As Anglo American town speculators and developers moved south and west creating Main Streets and squares, they encountered sophisticated Hispanic town plans that, in some cases, could be traced back several centuries. For example, when Anglo traders and merchants reached Santa Fe in the 1830s and 1840s, they experienced a town plan that had evolved into a rectangular form, with a central plaza, since its founding by governor Juan de Oñate in 1608. These Hispanic towns often evoked an old-world or middle-eastern quality, being constructed of "natural" materials. The Spanish introduced rectangular town planning — and open public spaces — into their developing network of towns in this part of the New

World by the late 1500s, but it should be remembered that Native Americans in Meso America — notably the Aztecs — were familiar with the grid and had used it for their communities in the Valley of Mexico long before the Spanish arrived.

That largely French communities also may be developed in reference to squares is seen in the prototypical Jackson Square in New Orleans, which is shown as the *Place d'armes* on early maps of the city (ca. 1718). A review of early French town plans in North America reveals that the earliest communities were often fortified and irregular in shape, but were often designed around the central *Place d'armes*. In Europe, the French had designed such towns as early as the thirteenth century for their *bastide* towns, and so it is not surprising that they were prone to use it in their fledgling communities in the New World.

In the earliest years of Spanish community development in the New World, fortified, irregularly shaped plans were common. These gave way to orderly communities after the Spanish realized that their first century of settlement had been chaotic and relatively ineffective. Several scholars have identified the Spanish *Law of the Indies* (1573) as an important document that dictated how communities would be platted. The Spanish adopted a strict code of rectangular town platting, and often laid out their towns around a rectangular *plaza de Armas*, or military parade ground, that also served as the town center. This plaza was surrounded by civic and commercial buildings, and was recognized as the center or heart of the community. In the American Southwest and adjacent northern Mexico, the plaza was usually a large, dusty open space in the early years of a town's development, but was considerably softened by improvements, such as bandstands, trees, and flower plantings in the late nineteenth century.

Spanish-Mexican townscapes reflected a sense of order, as the plaza and environs were *planned* and *regulated* to reduce confusion and express or illustrate the power of the crown in controlling commercial, social, and religious activity (fig. 54). In his classic study of Tejano (Mexican Texas) communities in the period 1821–36, Andrés Tijerina noted that settlements were required by law to be orderly in design:

> The town plat was actually a square. The principal town square or
> plaza was in the center with perpendicular streets oriented to the four
> ordinal directions. Each city street as well as the plaza itself was set to

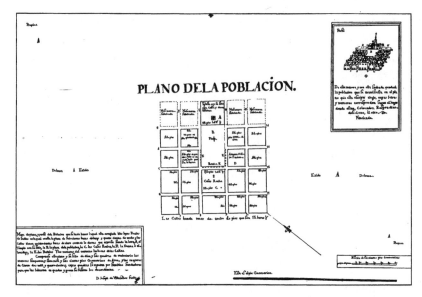

Figure 54. *The Plano de la Población of San Antonio, Texas, 1730, reveals a strong sense of rectangular geometry and the centrality of an open plaza around which were located important civic and religious buildings.* Herbert Eugene Bolton, Texas in the Middle Eighteenth Century, 1915.

standard measurements, so many *varas* or yards (approximately) in length and width. The east side of the plaza was designated for ecclesiastical structures such as the cathedral, chapel, or chancery. On the west side were the government and public buildings such as the *casa capitular* or state house, the customs house, and the governor's palace.[31]

In reality, of course, most Spanish-Mexican communities deviated somewhat from the ideal. Nevertheless, this striving for order in the landscape affected many communities, and their resulting townscapes serve to identify them as Hispanic in origin. That these communities are somewhat similar in basic geometry and the positioning of important buildings reveals the power of centralized, repetitive decision making in widely separated frontier communities; it is also possible that town platters in two separate cultures (e.g., New England villages and Hispanic Southwestern villages) followed the general guidance of Renaissance (1400s–1600s) and even earlier Roman and other classical engineers and architects, such as

Marcus Vitruvius Pollio, who encouraged geometry, order, and symmetry in town design as early as the first century B.C.

It is tempting to consider the plaza a purely Hispanic or ultimately Mediterranean element in town design, but its acceptance in parts of Latin America and the Southwest may also relate to its intrinsic compatibility with Native American culture. Anthropologist Frank Waters noted, "Life on this continent from earliest times has revolved about the central plaza," and that the plaza "was the center of the people's outward communal life and the focus of their religious thought and ceremonies."[32] Because these plazas incorporated a circle into the square, Waters further asserts that they were, in essence, great mandalas.

> A mandala, the Sanskrit word for circle, is a geometrical design expressive of the unity and wholeness of all Creation, a design which produces an effect upon its maker. Its basic form is that of a four-petalled lotus with infinite variations in the shape of a cross, a square, or a circle divided by four, but always with four as the basis of the structure. Mandalas have been found everywhere, in all ages.[33]

A structural anthropologist would interpret the persistence of the circle-and-square motif in design as answering basic needs, such as ascribing order, or recognizing the totality of the universe, in geometric form.

As Hans-Peter Schwöbel noted, "Geometry has proven to be one of the mainstays of all civilizations," and the persistence of mandalas may be related to the fact that "geometric shapes display certain aesthetic characteristics," and "are simple, clear, exact, regular, abstract, adaptable, repeatable, and transposable."[34] In this regard, a geometric (square) node at the center of a community — whether it be a Native American pueblo village, the Spanish plaza, or a public square in an Anglo American town center — may be evidence that our towns are more "universal" in their design and meaning. To the economic or pragmatic explanations of town design, then, we might add the spiritual or metaphysical: the way a town is designed fits a sense of cosmological order; the way a streetscape looks is determined by many factors, but "landscape tastes" are definitely among them.[35] This leads to the tenth axiom of Main Street development: *Although the layout of Main Street may seem largely functional, its design is also related to deeply held aesthetic values about the way space should be arranged.* The methods by which this collective aesthetic is perpetuated can be either positive or punitive (that is, carrots or sticks), but serve a similar purpose. In New Spain, incentives came in the form of grants; under Mexican rule an *empresario* system often encouraged trade and commerce. Failure to conform to mandates in either system could result in accidents such as fires or even deliberate confiscation of property and enterprises. As merchants have long known, social pressures, too, tend to enforce a conformity. In that their design is so persistent, Main Streets may reflect the prevailing ethos and values of North American society.

On yet another level, of course, the Spanish plaza — like other centrally positioned open spaces in a community — symbolizes the power of authority and the need to control life on the frontier. It also provides unique perspectives from which to view the townscape. From the plaza, one could view the adobe or masonry buildings surrounding, or enclosing, the open space. This reinforced the sense of colonial protection, and the centralization of activities, that the Spanish brought to the region. In Spanish-Mexican towns, all community life focussed on the plaza; many homes fronted on it, as did civic buildings and churches. Typically, commercial buildings faced the plaza or lined the narrow streets that led to it.

San Juan Bautista, California, was developed around such a plaza. Named after St. John the Baptist, the town developed adjacent to one of California's twenty-one missions; the beautiful and historic mission San Juan Bautista faces the rectangular plaza. Whereas many wealthy or prosperous colonial Spanish towns, such as Alamos Sonora, featured plazas surrounded by colonnaded buildings, the two-story adobe Castro House and Mission San Juan Bautista on the plaza are rather modest. Nevertheless, these features serve to identify San Juan Bautista as a center of importance on the California frontier of the early nineteenth century. Despite the fact that considerable stylized commercial preservation and rebuilding has taken place in the town, the buildings in San Juan Bautista are among the better surviving examples of the interplay between architecture and environment (that is, buildings in relationship to their surroundings) that is a hallmark of Spanish and Mexican design. The regularity and rectangularity of the open plaza at San Juan Bautista reveal the intentions of the ideal model, as do the plazas at Santa Fe and Mesilla, New Mexico (fig. 55), and Roma, Texas. The Hispanic townscape is characterized by built-up streetscapes of adobe or masonry buildings flanking

Figure 55. *The plaza at Mesilla, New Mexico, is typical of the restored streetscapes based on Hispanic heritage in the Southwest. The prominent church stands facing one side of the plaza; commercial buildings (left) face the remaining three sides. 1979 photo by the author.*

relatively narrow streets that "funnel" the traveller or resident into the plaza. Thus, in both the Anglo American realm and Hispanic culture area, Main Street can serve much the same purpose — to orient the traveller and affect human behavior through design.

Remembering that streetscapes are assemblages of buildings in relationship to the street and open spaces, a look at a Hispanic Main Street, such as Tucson or Santa Fe in the 1870s and 1880s, is instructive (fig. 56). Whereas individual buildings in an Anglo town have "footprints" that reflect deep property parcels (that is, narrow lots running toward the center of blocks), Hispanic towns often featured buildings that fronted on the street but had spaces (for courtyards and gardens) behind the buildings. Note, too, that the original placement of buildings in a Hispanic townscape differs from the Anglo practice in that they usually had no setback (that is, they are built up to the sidewalk), and could be expanded more or less organically as they were called upon to serve new uses.[36] They exemplified Hispanic concepts of community and family that were transformed upon the arrival of Anglo Americans after the U.S.-Mexican War

Figure 56. *A Tucson streetscape of circa 1884–1885 shows that the adobe buildings of Hispanic culture were an important design element that could be modified by Anglo American façades and signage. Courtesy Arizona Historical Society, Tucson.*

(1846–48) was concluded by the Treaty of Guadalupe Hidalgo (1848) and the subsequent Gadsden Treaty/Purchase (1853).

Architectural historians have noted that the buildings of Anglo merchants tended to be more detailed — that is, architecturalized with "high style" trim (for example, Greek Revival or Italianate) and elaborate porches, but that Hispanic architecture had a more cubic and solid massing with fewer and smaller window openings. This, of course, tended to affect the character of the streetscape in that fewer openings (doors or windows) made the Hispanic streetscape seem more tectonic or solid. Streets tended to be narrower, and thus the Southwestern Main Street retained some of the qualities seen in its Spanish, North African, and even Native American antecedent communities, such as, respectively, Almaden, Spain; Marakesh, Morocco; and Taos, New Mexico.[37]

MAIN STREET AND THE RAILROAD

The coming of the railroad in the nineteenth century often had profound effects on Main Street as commercial centers proliferated. In towns that had been platted or developed before the arrival of the iron horse, the railroad may have pulled commercial development away from the early center of town, in effect stretching or attenuating the central business districts. In others, the railroad may have actually run its tracks on major streets as a concession for developing to, and hence through, town. In the late 1830s, Xenia, Ohio, encouraged the little Miami Railroad to run through the town center using Detroit Street as a right of way; until 1968, residents and travellers often commented on the railroad's presence as trains rumbled right next to the courthouse square. On occasion, trains stopped and their crews searched for automobile owners who had absent-mindedly parked on, or too near, the tracks, thus blocking the train's progress. La Grange, Kentucky; Thurmond, West Virginia; and many Middle Western and Southern towns (such as Saluda, North Carolina) witnessed the penetration of the railroad into the town center.

The position of the tracks with regard to Main Street greatly affects the character of downtown, and the alternatives are almost infinite: sometimes the tracks and streets are at oblique or acute angles, as in the case of Wasco, Oregon, where the railroad slices the south end of Main Street at a diagonal. In others, the railroad and the major street intersect at right angles. Usually the railroad depot is at the edge of the business district, but in some rather unusual but memorable cases, the railroad tracks may actually be at the heart of town square — as in the most interesting Galva, Illinois, where the main line of the Burlington Railroad cuts through the center of the square, a quite literal version of Leo Marx's "machine in the garden," as trains rumble through what would otherwise be a more peaceful small-town center. In cases where the railroad ran close to the Main Street, it became an essential element in how the town would be perceived and remembered. Novelist Rose Wilder's nostalgic *Old Home Town* provides the reader vivid descriptions of the town's commercial center and railroad; unlike most novels, however, *Old Home Town* includes a stylized map that shows the prominent location of the railroad. The railroad and the depot occupy one-quarter of the square's frontage.[38]

In the American West and Southwest, the railroad had a profound effect on Main Street. As interpreted by D. W. Meinig,[39] the railroad symbolized the coming of Anglo American cultures. Las Vegas, New Mexico, provides a case in point. Located near the historic plaza, the Hispanic section of town remains quite distinct from the Anglo American Main Street which developed about a mile away in the vicinity of the AT&SF railroad depot. As Ellen Threinen noted, until 1879 and the coming of the Santa Fe railroad, "Las Vegas looked like a typical Mexican town."[40] Architecturally, the Anglo building styles and techniques would come to dominate the region, but Hispanic traditions would continue to help define the character of Southwestern townscapes, including Main Street. Spatially the railroad both reaffirmed the separation of Hispanic and Anglo peoples in many Southwestern towns, much as it created a dividing line in American towns generally.[41]

Whatever their relative positions, railroad and Main Street development (except in the smallest communities that never had a railroad) are inseparable; some of our finest travel accounts note the character of towns from train windows. As Robert Sayre noted of small Iowa towns, the railroad passenger experiences places from a higher viewpoint, in effect getting a more comprehensive "side" view from the window of the train rather than looking ahead, as do those in control of a moving vehicle such as a horse and wagon, or, later, an automobile.[42] Symbolically, one commands the townscape from a train, as this is the vehicle that has precedence over vehicular and pedestrian traffic as it encounters the street at grade.

MAIN STREET AND REGIONAL IDENTITY

From this discussion it is apparent that the appearance of townscapes is largely a result of the time in which they were settled and of the re-alignments that took place through changes in technology, especially transportation. However, it is also apparent that the cultural hearth (cultural source area) from which communities developed was important in shaping their Main Streets. This is especially true during the early development phases of Main Street, when regional vernacular architecture constitutes a high percentage of the community's buildings. Diffusion (the spread of a trait from its source to a particular location) is a key factor as regional styles are quite identifiable: New Englanders, Southerners, and the Spanish all brought ideas about architecture and town design with them, and America's historic townscapes are a result of this "cultural baggage" as well as other factors such as environment and technology.

Novelists have been most adept at capturing the regional diversity in American townscapes. William Humphrey was particularly perceptive when he wrote, ". . . in the towns of northeast Texas, such as Clarksville, the South draws to a stop," and, about another geographic region, "The Texas of cattleherds and cowboys, of flat little sun-swept towns with low sheet iron buildings strung out along a single Main Street, the Texas of the West, lies farther on in time as well as space."[43]

A vivid description of Main Street in Guthrie, Oklahoma, is found in a collection of stories entitled *Firesticks* by Diane Glancy. In relating that Guthrie is constructed of the regional, red-colored soil that "was like the Indian skin that came up from below the surface of my dreams, and reached into my thoughts," Glancy describes Main Street as

> Rows of red brick buildings hunched around an early sun. The buildings of Guthrie were turn of the century, some restored, some boarded and vacant. The brick and red-stone buildings the same as the red soil that stained the snow and had stained my shoes and clothes. How many years had I seen that red soil splattered on cars that came from country roads to Guthrie?[44]

The issue of color is important in describing townscapes. The color of brick, for example, is determined in part by the chemistry of the clay as well as the temperature at which bricks are fired. Brick color may therefore vary locally, but some colors — such as the reds described by Diane Glancy — are quite diagnostic and memorable aspects of place. Although Munsell soil charts will permit one scientifically to identify the peculiar red color of Oklahoma and North Texas landscapes and townscapes (and can in fact be used to accurately classify the color of *any* clay, brick, or stone objectively), Glancy's words beautifully link the characteristics of place to the human condition in the region. Geographers have long tried to characterize the essence of place, but usually fail unless they take such subjective perceptions of it into account.

In fact, geographers have made but modest headway in characterizing towns. Whereas most historical and cultural geographers have described rural (agrarian) patterns of American landscapes, none has yet described, to my knowledge, how American towns developed regional identities or personalities. This section encourages future scholarship by identifying several major regional patterns of townscapes. Like all townscapes, the images they represent are combinations of buildings (building material, style, color), town plans, and street patterns. Painted in very broad strokes, the following patterns, based on my thirty years of field experiences and the inspiration of the works of historical geographers (from the seminal works of Fred Kniffen beginning in the 1930s to the recent, comprehensive interpretations of D. W. Meinig),[45] emerge:

The New England Village. Although the ideal New England Village is largely a stereotype created in the nineteenth century,[46] it is one of the important settlement types. Age, or time of initial settlement, is an important factor, for the area developed relatively early (in the 1600s) and had both a religious and a corporate identity. As noted by landscape historian John Stilgoe, some New England townscapes very nearly attained the ideal set out in an anonymous 1638 essay entitled "The Ordering of Towns," which called for the meetinghouse (religious building) to be "the Center of a whole circumference," surrounded by a circle of houses.[47] In reality, of course, many New England villages were small hamlets based in part on a marginal agrarian economy. In terms of actual design, they varied considerably. The juxtaposition of wooden buildings lining relatively narrow streets is often seen in early lithographs. In some locations, the streets converged on a village green that is often, but not always, irregular in shape. Guilford, Connecticut, provides a good example (fig. 42), but New England possessed many such communities, and they could be found as far south as Long Island, New York, by the early 1700s.

In the early New England village, church architecture is dominant, and rural buildings may be seen close to town center, as farms often clustered at or near these intersections. Main Street commercial architecture varies; those villages that developed in the late eighteenth century and early- to mid-nineteenth century buildings often possess clapboard sheathed vernacular frame buildings, but stone is also used in construction. The "New England large" house is common, and it served as both residential and commercial buildings in many New England villages.

In reality, of course, many New England villages became industrial communities by the mid- to late nineteenth century, much like the fictional mill town of Bedford Falls in Frank Capra's classic film *It's a Wonderful Life* (1946), but the general public still thinks of the region as rural. Although village greens are popularized in the literature, in reality there is a good deal of linearity to the New England village. Nevertheless, visual focal points and nodes do dominate, especially in the late nineteenth century and early twentieth century, when, consciously or unconsciously, townspeople reinforced or even created village identities centered on the village green. Geographically, the New England village pattern extended from New England (by way of upstate New York) to — in modified form — northern Ohio and Michigan by the early to mid–nineteenth century, despite the fact that it was essentially obsolete by the mid 1700s in its source area.

The Midlands (Middle Atlantic) Hearth. Eastern Maryland and southeastern Pennsylvania are the source area from which townscape designs spread westward into central Ohio and Illinois, thence to Iowa, Missouri, and Nebraska. This is the region immortalized in Lewis Atherton's *Main Street on the Middle Border* (1954), where "villages a few miles apart speckle the midwestern countryside."[48] The morphology of towns in its Pennsylvania source area was studied in a pioneering work by Richard Pillsbury,[49] and Alfred Wright described the form of communities in Ohio.[50] Rectilinear (grid) planning is very common, though early road patterns strongly influence town designs here. Linearity and centrality are seen in the townscape, though, in the earliest settled areas, irregular road patterns may form the nucleus of downtown. The Philadelphia (circle in square) pattern is common in Pennsylvania; unpainted red brick and native stone are the dominant construction materials for commercial buildings, with extensive use of wood, cast iron (Ohio), and cut stone (Indiana) for trim and detailing. As these towns prospered in the nineteenth century, Main Street developed extensive Victorian Italianate detailing. In the western part of the area, Chicago and St. Louis are visibly important centers of influence on the commercial architecture. These "Midwestern" towns have served as locales in American fiction, including Sherwood Anderson's *Winesburg, Ohio*, the numerous works of Theodore Dreiser (including *A Hoosier Holiday*), and the more recent science-fiction stories of Ray Bradbury (for example, Green Town, Illinois, in *Dandelion Wine*). The Main Street of Hartford, Michigan, seen in the postcard view in fig. 3, is typical of the Middle West.

Lower Tidewater/Deep South Commercial/Marketing Centers. After initial settlement in the 1600s to early 1700s, these communities spread from Virginia and the coastal Carolinas westward by the early nineteenth century. This townscape pattern extends as far west as southeastern and eastern Texas, an area that was settled by Anglo Americans during the period 1835 to 1860. Town plats vary considerably; classic market towns in which

Figure 57. *Newberry, South Carolina, features a classic Greek Revival courthouse (left) and classically styled and inspired commercial (bank) buildings facing the public square in this 1973 photograph. Together these buildings conspire to imitate the aura of the Acropolis in a small Southern town. Photo by the author.*

Main Street surrounds the square can be found (fig. 57), but they are considerably more rare than linear towns. Commercial buildings are often of red brick with detailed corbelled parapets; extensive awnings (often metal) and porches cover the sidewalk; commercial buildings on lots that sit several steps higher than the street are quite common here, as, for example, at Inman, South Carolina; Crawfordville, Georgia (fig. 58); and Demopolis, Alabama. Buildings are commonly painted white, though unpainted red brick is also common. Many of these towns had substantial African American populations (as high as 60%) and heavily racially segregated businesses in the period before about 1955. Confederate war monuments (again, many facing north) are seen. Although the "antebellum" character of the region is often promoted in many towns in the deep South, Main Street in this area reveals the Civil War to have been an important watershed; much of the character of Main Street in the region dates from reconstruction times, when the capital of northern entrepreneurs resulted in a booming textile (cotton) industry and aggressive construction of late-nineteenth and early-twentieth-century buildings (fig. 59).

Figure 58. *The buildings on Main Street in Crawfordville, Georgia, are set several steps higher than the street, a typical configuration in towns of the Upland South — a pattern that reaches westward into Missouri and north and central Texas. 1973 photo by the author.*

Upland South. A legacy of several eastern coastal hearths, especially midlands and tidewater, towns developed here in the later eighteenth and early to mid-nineteenth centuries. Nucleation and centrality are very strong traits; many town centers focus on public squares reached by a network of irregular roads converging from the countryside. The county courthouse is often central to the town in centrally located county seats. Red brick is a dominant building material, often superseding clapboard by the early to mid-nineteenth century. Commercial buildings on Main Street may have distinctive flourishes, such as round ("eye") attic windows

Figure 59. *Crawford, Mississippi, presents a classic Southern small-town appearance, with simple red-brick buildings, large awnings, and a huge Coca-Cola sign on the side of a building facing Main Street. 1978 photo by the author.*

above the upper floors. The "southern" tendency for the building lots to be several steps (often more than two feet) above the street, with the curbing configured into steps, is seen in many of the region's towns, such as Winchester, Kentucky. This pattern of townscapes extends into north and central Texas and into Missouri. Towns in the region have served as the locales for much Southern fiction, including Faulkner's novel *The Town* and William Humphrey's *The Ordways*.

Western Transport- and Marketing-Oriented Towns. These are based on prototype designs that originated farther east, but are especially well developed from Kansas and the Dakotas west to Montana. Main Street is usually linear; though some of these communities feature public squares, the dominant orientation of the town is to a linear Main Street which inevitably interacts with a railroad. The railroad itself may either parallel or run perpendicular to the Main Street. In these western agricultural towns, Main Street and the railroad have decidedly separate but interrelated functions: to move goods and people to market. The railroad depot may form a major visual element in the townscape; grain elevators are often a dominant feature, as is the grange hall on Main Street. These rural service

Figure 60. *Main Street in many towns in Minnesota, the Dakotas, and the Far West is oriented toward the railroad. Hastings, Minnesota, is typical of the genre: being both a river town and a railroad town, its Main Street parallels the main lines of transportation and its grain elevator, center right, is an important landmark. 1971 photo by the author.*

centers feature very utilitarian Main Streets, with some Victorian embellishment where the economy or cultural traditions permitted (fig. 60).

Villages of the Mormon Culture Region. These are characterized by rectangular town planning in which the business district lines a very wide Main Street and church buildings are located on the prominent public square at the center of town. Street width was determined in part by Mormon prophet Joseph Smith's City of Zion Plan that called for all streets to be 132 feet wide. In one sense, the Mormon Villages are mid-nineteenth-century adaptations of the New England Village in the semi-arid West, and their appearance is a result of church ideology and values as well as the prevalent economy in this region. Mormon Main Streets are devoid of bars and the buildings of fraternal orders; the ward chapel is the most significant building in town. Architecture is of the standard commercial styles; adobe business buildings were once more common, but due to attrition, they are rare today (fig. 61).

Southwestern Townscapes. The downtown may either develop around a plaza or square (in which case a good deal of centrality is evident) or,

Figure 61. *Main Street in Mormon towns is usually wide and is devoid of bars and the buildings of fraternal organizations. In this view of downtown Monticello, Utah, the Mormon Chapel is seen at right, and businesses line the opposite side of the wide Main Street. Compare this wide Main Street with its narrow counterpart in Locke, California (fig. 38). 1969 photo by the author.*

more commonly, develop parallel to the main route of travel (in which case Main Street will be linear). Main Street usually parallels the railroad. Buildings may be adobe, fired brick, stone, or wood; they will often be painted light (beige, white, buff) colors and have awnings covering sidewalks; trees are sometimes planted for shade. Awnings are a rather distinctive feature in the streetscape and can be classified into several types: curved convex corrugated metal, as seen in North-Central Texas, and straight sheet or corrugated metal in West Texas, New Mexico, and Arizona. Gallup, New Mexico, and Winslow, Arizona, are archetypes located on the Santa Fe railroad and the historic Route 66, and in the hands of director Oliver Stone became anonymous "Southwestern" locales for a rampage of mayhem in the 1994 film *Natural Born Killers*.

Figure 62. *In the Anglo American Southwest, arcaded and colonnaded storefronts convey a Mediterranean or Latin American quality; the arcades also provide an important amenity — shade — in a hot, dry region. Most of these features date not from the earliest years of Anglo settlement in the 1880s but rather from the early twentieth century, which witnessed a search for regional identity. 1989 photo of Gila Bend, Arizona, by the author.*

Main Streets in the Southwest often feature elaborate arcading or colonnading. In towns in the lower elevations of the Southwest (e.g., Gila Bend, Arizona, and Westmoreland and Calipatria in California's Imperial Valley), these colonnades help provide a Spanish or Mediterranean quality, but rather than being authentically Spanish or Mexican, are likely an early-twentieth-century fad associated, in part, with the popular mission style (fig. 62). The ultimate stereotypical Southwestern townscape, perhaps, is found in the Phelps Dodge (New Cornelia) Copper Company town of Ajo in southwestern Arizona's Sonoran Desert. Ajo has a spacious palm-lined "plaza" surrounded by arcaded buildings and seems quite historic despite the fact that it actually dates from circa 1920. The Southwestern Style continues to be popular, as seen in the design of the new county courthouse in America's most-recently created county — La Paz County, Arizona — a rambling single story adobe-style building, complete with Spanish Colonial trim, that was completed in 1994. As this regional idiom has been so clearly defined by developments in Santa Fe, the style seems quite natural — even in areas never actually settled by the Spanish and

Generalized Regional Patterns of American Townscapes

ca. 1770-1900

LEGEND

Hearth Area

Route of Diffusion

Edge of Zone of Influence

RVF '94

0   Miles   500

Figure 63. *This U.S. map of regional townscape types reveals the spread of major cultural groups and the diffusion of townscapes from hearths. Map by the author, based on field work and numerous sources listed in the bibliography, including Conzen, 1990.*

not having a Pueblo Indian tradition. The spread of the Santa Fe Style into this part of Arizona seems quite natural in a culture that now expects all Southwestern towns to have this adobe, pueblo appearance.

When these general patterns are depicted on a map (fig. 63), they reveal broad paths of migration and provide an overall picture of diversity by region, but do not explain the intriguing variety or spatial variation of townscapes *within* larger regions. For example, a typical western mining town Main Street found in Eureka, Utah, which is proximate to Mormon townscapes, may, in turn, be proximate to railroad-oriented Main Street towns such as Wells, Nevada. Also, there is an underlying pattern of smaller ethnic communities that would otherwise be lost if we were to focus only on the broader regional patterns: in northeastern Nevada, one can also find the small community of Paradise Valley, home of late-nineteenth-century Italian settlers who, along with other ethnic Americans, left their mark on the town. Thus, although there is some validity to the general regional patterns, they explain some, but not all, of the variation from place to place. A closer look at the patterns of Main Street development (which requires extensive travel and the consultation of historical photographs of Main Streets), reveals that subtypes of general townscapes exist at the sub-regional and local levels. Two examples are noted below:

Industrial Subtypes. Example: Mining Towns. Economy is extremely important in shaping a Main Street's identity. A distinctive subtype of towns based on mineral exploitation is widespread, and especially common in the Western United States.[51] Main Street may be rectilinear or follow curving creekbed/topographic patterns, but often shows a very rapid sequential architectural development. Originally tents, then wooden false front (Greek Revival or Italianate), then brick or stone buildings are erected, as the town becomes more established. Extensive use of detail is found on balconies; signs calling attention to competing services proliferate, giving Main Street a decidedly urban look. There is little centrality: public buildings such as courthouses are not conspicuously positioned, rather being placed much as other commercial buildings.

Local/Sub-regional Design Flourishes. Example: Central and Northern California (Coastal and intermediate valley towns). Main Streets in many central and northern California communities feature the extensive use of wood during the Victorian period; rectangular, detailed bay windows and oriels are common. Wood rather than masonry is prevalent in many areas due to, in part, the potential for earthquake damage. The plaza (or, more correctly, the public square) is seen, but linearity is dominant. Commercial activity in the town often focusses on the railroad. Extensive use of porches roofed in shakes or shingles covering sidewalks serves the purpose of protecting people from the sun in summer and the rain in winter.

Climate may be said to have an effect on the look of Main Street in that materials weather differently under different climates. For example, brick and mortar effloresce distinctively in arid climates, the white or "sun-bleached" look attributable to a build-up of calcium salts that would wash away in a more humid climate. Similarly, the higher acidity in rainfall in areas of greater industry, such as the industrial Middle West or East, may stain brick or stone. Paint, wood, and metals likewise weather differently, and at different rates, under different climatic conditions.

The broad patterns portrayed on the map account for the interaction of two cultures — British (Anglo) and Mexican (Hispanic) American. Beneath its generalizations one can find small areas where other ethnic cultures have made an impact on the design of the small town, as, for example, the German influence in Hermann, Missouri, and New Braunfels, Texas. Significantly, however, most ethnic influence in the nineteenth century seems to have been confined to the vernacular architecture of houses and institutional buildings, such as churches and, occasionally, town halls and other civic buildings — not commercial buildings. Only rarely does ethnicity express itself in the commercial buildings along Main Street in the middle to late nineteenth century. More typically, even ethnic craftsmen on Main Street of the period followed mainstream designs that were illustrated in catalogs and building plans; the Main Streets of the period are a testimony to the power of standardized designs in effecting assimilation. Thus, when the late Victorian Italianate–styled Medegovich building was constructed in Bisbee, Arizona, in 1902, only the surname of this entrepreneur appearing on the pedimented gable — and not the architecture or design of the building itself — hinted at the owner's Serbian ethnicity.

The major factor influencing the look of American townscapes is, of course, popular culture. My extensive travels, photograph collections, and notes reveal that American townscape design appears to be influenced largely by national popular trends, and secondly by regional conditions, including economy and perceptions of the physical environment, and lastly by local factors such as craftspeople. Therefore, it is often possible to identify a Main Street's regional location using a series of clues, such as materials and building siting and detailing (including porches, window and door styles, etc.), but these take a trained eye. A perceptive traveller can identify subtle visual clues to detect regional traits that appear commonly in some places (like multistepped curbing/sidewalks in upland Southern towns) and rarely or never in others (centrally located county courthouses are virtually absent from New England).

A closer look at townscapes in any region usually reveals delightful and unique flourishes that set some Main Streets apart from others, such as the distinctive second-story porches on Main Street commercial buildings in towns in Ohio's Hocking Valley coalfields; these "overhanging porches" or "balconied porches" appear to be unique in the entire country in that

Figure 64. *"Overhanging porches" on Main Street commercial buildings are unique to the coal-mining towns of Ohio's Hocking Valley. Shawnee, Ohio, represents a localized center of otherwise rare architectural details. 1988 photo by the author.*

there is such a high percentage of buildings with this distinctive trait concentrated in about a dozen towns (fig. 64).[52] Because architects often use local materials to reduce cost, many of our townscapes are indeed wonderfully localized despite their use of standardized styles. The buff-colored limestone commercial buildings of the Texas Hill Country, the yellowish sandstone buildings in diverse locations such as Hot Springs (South Dakota) and western Kansas, and the red sandstone buildings in parts of the Southwest, including Gallup, New Mexico, are reminders that Main Street involves both mainstream influences and local interpretations (fig. 65). Commercial buildings in Tishomingo, Oklahoma, offer stunning examples of the use of pink Oklahoma granite in concert with the distinctive red brick seen in that part of the country. These architectural treatments help anchor the town to a particular area despite the fact that much of its basic architecture can be seen elsewhere.

Ultimately, the regional look of our Main Streets relates, in part, to the dominance of various nearby urban centers in their design and economy; thus, Minneapolis–St. Paul platters, architects, and foundries have affected Main Street in the northern plains; Seattle and Portland affected

Figure 65. *Local craft and a national pattern: the stonemason's art is seen in the construction and detailing of this beautiful buff-colored limestone Central Block building, which was constructed in 1905 in Hot Springs, South Dakota. 1993 photo by the author.*

Oregon and Washington townscapes; Austin, Texas, had an affect on much of central and west Texas, and so forth. Certain major urban centers such as New York, Chicago, and San Francisco affect Main Street over huge areas. This confirms that Main Street is designed on a widely shared, frequently reproduced prototype that is easily, almost intuitively, adopted by developers. The eleventh axiom of Main Street development, then, is: *Main Street develops as designers conceive, and then share, an image of how a town should look; this information normally diffuses from larger to smaller places, that is, from cities to towns, and is translated by locals into material form on Main Street.*

More research needs to be conducted into how innovations spread into the entrepreneurial sector of communities, that is, how building designers and merchants adopt new or exotic traits — and how they invent their own. I believe that the Caribbean region's impact on porch details on Main Streets in the Southern and Southwestern United States would be one very fruitful area of concentration. So, too, would the importation of environmentally sound urban-design solutions, such as shutters and vents, that spread from one similar climatic region to another: the extensive use of corrugated metal awnings on Main Street in the American South and Southwest and in the Australian frontier in the nineteenth century offers another provocative direction of study.

America's Main Streets are indeed tied to geography at various levels — national, regional, local — but most of this design was originally unconscious, or rather unselfconscious (that is, towns did not attempt to appear, say, "Southwestern" in the nineteenth century when Anglo Americans were moving west and attempting to dominate Hispanic culture). Only after successfully establishing positions of control and power (as Anglos did, for example, in the Southwest after the turn of the century) do town developers and merchants seek colorful ethnic or regional charm. It is apparent that *national* trends, above all, shaped Main Streets and that their shaping was related to a powerful need to assimilate first, and diversify later.

There are signs that Main Street design reflects a need to recognize diversity in the face of overwhelming assimilation. This has become apparent in the late twentieth century, when regional or ethnic identity is marketed by communities. On Main Street, the search for regional identity has taken on a touch of the fanciful or bizarre as certain towns have

Figure 66. *Biwabik, Minnesota, promotes its ethnic traditions by creating stylized folk architecture on Main Street (note the building at far left and the banners hung from simulated gas lamps lining the street) and has many counterparts, especially in the Midwest. 1990 photo by the author.*

deliberately attempted to create townscapes that recapture the original ethnic heritage of their residents, whether it be Swiss (as in southern Indiana, which calls itself "America's Switzerland") or Bavarian (as in Gaylord, Michigan, where even the Bob's Big Boy statue sports Bavarian dress!). Merchants in Sugar Creek, Ohio, added Alpine motifs, including detailed porches, balconies, and gables to their Main Street to achieve a Swiss theme; some communities in Minnesota perpetuate their Finnish and German ethnic heritage through themed architecture on Main Street (fig. 66). This type of themed remodelling has been taking place since the 1950s and 1960s.

According to geographers Steven Hoelscher and Robert Ostergren, the ethnicity that is rediscovered in these communities is often selfconscious and has become inextricably tied to tourism, especially in the "Old European Homelands" in the American Middle West.[53] Landscape architect Michael Hough decries the fact that "every town that has seen better days and can boast of a past has an eye to capitalizing on its own historic specialty for tourist entertainment and dollars."[54] Mira Engler notes that such "themed" towns in Iowa are based on four "experiences": the Ethnic Heritage Experience, the Frontier-Pioneer Experience, the Good-Old-Town Experience, and the County Charm Experience.[55] Whereas historic preservationists oppose veneering a town's real heritage under exotic, often incongruous, elements such as half timbering and European gingerbread, few will deny that such alterations bring in tourists. The questions that merchants and others on Main Street need to ask, however, are: How long will such themed popularity last? How reversible will these architectural embellishments be if people tire of them? Preservationists often argue that towns seeking to capture an exotic or folksy heritage may overlook the power and significance of their own real local history in image building and marketing.

Ultimately, of course, each town must be considered a unique entity with its own personality. Like human personalities, Main Street may portray a number of characteristics, such as innovativeness, ingenuity, conformity, imitation, predictability, and even bizarreness or outrageousness. Being a manifestation of the dreams and actions of individuals — individual architects, individual town platters, individual merchants, individual consumers — Main Street's character is at once personal and universal. Overall, however, one must be impressed with how effectively standardized architecture and design (e.g., building form, street pattern) created a readily identifiable "American town" appearance from coast to coast in the nineteenth century. Although our Main Streets may have individual personalities and regional characteristics, they are instantly recognizable as American.

If Main Street as an image is dependent on a combination of several factors — including architecture or building form, property-parcel size and shape, street pattern, and the configuration of open spaces — then these in turn contribute to the character of regions, or at any rate contribute to a sense of regional identity, which, paradoxically, appears to be growing at a time when many pundits and scholars have predicted that a national identity would engulf the entire country. Historic regional elements in townscape design are often quite subtle: the colors of buildings, their details, the types of awnings and porches. These, nevertheless, are part of their character.

Strong regional identities persist, if not as an authentic part of their character as towns then as almost theatrical sets. In places like Santa Fe

Figure 67. *Taos, New Mexico, an example of the chic Southwestern style, features romanticized Pueblo style architecture mixed with Spanish Colonial details that has become a stylized cliché of the region. 1982 photo by the author.*

and Mesilla, New Mexico, standardized Anglo architecture overwhelmed Hispanic architecture by the turn of the century. In fact, Santa Fe appeared rather more like a prosperous Indiana town in the late nineteenth century than a Hispanic town. Only with the rise of tourism in the 1920s did Santa Fe become aware of its Hispanic-Indian roots. Anglo entrepreneurs who developed the La Fonda Hotel selected a romanticized style incorporating Indian and Hispanic themes, including simulated adobe walls and viga beams in 1922, and the rest is history. Since the 1940s, Santa Fe has themed its architecture and design through a series of increasingly restrictive design requirements. Whereas today's visitor may think Santa Fe to be authentically regional, it is in fact a mostly contrived landscape much like a theme park.

Thus, through a panoply of stylized stereotyped Southwestern designs, Santa Fe (and, for that matter, Taos) have developed a stylized regional character that is as much a result of popular culture as it is actual location[56] (fig. 67). Southwestern historian David Weber recently noted that "entire towns — such as Madrid, Cerrillos, Sedona, Tombstone, and Jerome — seem to have more in common with theme parks or resorts than they do with the living communities, yet these places have come to represent the 'authentic' Southwest."[57] Both visitors and residents should be aware that these recent trends, like the search for ethnic roots or the quaint regionalism described above, have created fictional townscapes that are eagerly consumed by those in search of history. That subject — the shaping of images of Main Street by popular culture — is the subject of the next section.

3 : IMAGE BUILDING AND MAIN STREET

The Shaping of a Popular American Icon

THE SMALL TOWN IMAGE CONSISTS OF SOUNDS, SMELLS,

CONVERSATIONS, PATTERNS, VISTAS, AND EMOTIONS. IT IS A PARADOXICAL

TRUTH THAT WE SLOWLY CREATE OUR SMALL TOWNS IN OUR IMAGE, AND THEN

THEY SLOWLY REBUILD US IN THEIRS. IMAGE IS SUBTLE, YET IN DETERMINING

WHAT WE VALUE ABOUT SMALL TOWNS, IT POSSESSES GREAT POWER.

— JAMES BARKER, "THE SMALL TOWN: ORDER AND IMAGE"

As it evolved in time and space, Main Street became the commercial and social heart of the American small town; as it developed in our collective thought, Main Street became an integral part of American culture. Because many people left small towns in the early to mid-twentieth century, these places became repositories of memories. Main Street was always associated with place; now it also became an intrinsic part of our view of history. It may surprise some to learn that, in the early part of the twentieth century, the small town as exemplified by Main Street was not held in especially high regard. Architect-educator James Barker noted that "a number of us possess a subtle schizophrenia concerning the small town image. We love it for its picturesque qualities and its sense of community, but we hate it for its narrowness of thought and its slowness to respond to change."[1] We have always been, and perhaps ought to be, ambivalent about small towns, for they provide security at a price: conformity.

Despite our ambivalence toward them, small towns offer a seeming virtue in their constancy. In the popular mind, small towns seem to change less than their surroundings, and this helps explain why they seem to be havens *from* change. Despite America's involvement in two major wars, and its experiencing rapid technological and social change in the twentieth century, the nation's small towns seemed to change less than the world around them. In the small town, it seemed, the pace of life was slower, offering the type of security and nostalgic longing portrayed in episodes of the *Twilight Zone*, whose creator, Rod Serling, grew up experiencing the small towns of western New York before he attended Antioch College in the idyllic small town of Yellow Springs, Ohio. Like many shapers of popular culture, Serling helped to create a mind-set about the small town and its Main Street. In describing a harried executive's return to a small town where all cares could be forgotten, Serling penned the following unforgettable prose image:

> Beyond the station was a small village square with a bandstand. A bed of flowers went halfway around the square and added reds and whites and blues to the deep green of the town. A summer afternoon and a small town with a village square and a bandstand and people in old fashioned dress. In his whole life . . . he had never felt such a stirring deep inside, such a hunger to see a place again. . . .[2]

The image is all the more poignant when we realize that the man only found this idyllic community after calling out its name (Willoughby) and stepping off a moving train to his death; thus, the small town becomes heaven to those stuck in the modern hell of the present.

In their Cold War–era films and television shows, science-fiction writers creatively used the small-town square to contrast the predictability and reassurance of small-town life with the terrors of the unknown. One particularly chilling scene in the original 1956 *Invasion of the Body Snatchers* depicts the residents of the fictional small California town of Santa Mira, California, grouping in the public square as they methodically load alien pods onto trucks. The townsfolk are viewed from the second-story window of a commercial building by stars Kevin McCarthy and Dana Winters, and the audience shares the witnesses' horror, for the heart of a once-idyllic small town has now become the marshalling point of nightmarish activity destined to dehumanize every town in America. The elevated perspective of this scene is significant, for it normally conveys a sense of serenity and control in small towns (as was noted earlier in the popular bird's-eye views of the nineteenth century) but now only serves to compound the sense of terror. It is significant that the heart of the small town is the setting for this disturbing film, which has been interpreted as a metaphor for the concern about world Communism taking over the minds of Americans during the 1950s — a reminder that the perceptions of the small town are always tied to the era or time period in which they are conceived. And yet, a rather enduring design image of the small town has emerged in American popular culture during the mid- to late twentieth century. When portrayed in film and on television, places like Willoughby and Santa Mira rely, respectively, on beautifully constructed sets of the type seen in the earlier Andy Hardy films of the 1930s and 1940s, or actual locations in towns such as Sierra Madre, California. Rod Serling and many other television and film writers scripted the classic or "typical" Main Street into their plots, and it appeared as a row of trim brick commercial buildings that used the street, sidewalk, and public square as center stage. This popular imagery generates the impression that all Main Streets are much alike, when, in fact, real small-town centers are rather diverse. Most towns featured on television and in films simplify complexities. An essential role of Hollywood (and of most novelists, for that matter) is the actual creation of stereotypes that can be easily recognized and readily incorporated into the story, and the idealized small-town streetscape has served fiction well.

RE-CREATING OUR VANISHED TOWNSCAPES

In reality, the varied Main Streets of small-town America are in various states of preservation or decay — that is, their health continues to reflect the power of time and space in affecting the local setting. As depicted in Larry McMurtry's *The Last Picture Show*, Archer City, Texas, is an example of the downside of Main Street in the 1950s. Most often, however, portrayals of small-town Main Streets, such as those in food and automobile commercials, depict relatively prosperous communities. And yet, as if our actual and celluloid towns are not enough to satisfy our collective fascination with the past, historically recreated villages have sprung up to emulate them. The typical tourist today — both American and foreign visitor alike — has developed a strong appreciation for American history, and seeks out communities that convey it. Promotional wording for the popular book *America's Living Past* informs interested readers that "it is theoretically possible to travel across the length and breadth of America and visit sites that bring to life the entire scope of U.S. history."[3] Bowen was referring to largely fictional, but educational, historic communities such as Old Sturbridge Village in Massachusetts, Old World Wisconsin, and the Stuhr Museum of the Prairie Pioneers in Grand Island, Nebraska, where the visitor steps back in time to experience America's small-town past.

What, we might ask, are these historic towns and villages *really* like? How would they compare with their real counterparts during the historic periods they depict? Such questions will lead the traveller to places like Ohio Village, which is more or less typical of the genre of re-created nineteenth-century communities. Ohio Village is located at the northern outskirts of downtown Columbus on the property of the Ohio Historical Society. Beckoned by signs off the Interstate 71 freeway urging the visitor to visit Ohio Village, the visitor steps back in time to the year of about 1853 or 1854. This, it will be recalled, was the time period in which Henry Howe first recorded the idyllic, prosperous communities of the Midwest. Ohio Village, however, is not truly historic: it was created in 1971, when the state legislature released supplemental educational funding to the Ohio Historical Society's budget. Ohio Village was conceived as a modest educational project, several buildings depicting town life in the mid-nineteenth century. Originally intended to be an adjunct to the interpretive efforts of the Ohio Historical Society, Ohio Village has become an important tourist site in its own right.

Ohio Village is remarkable for its late-frontier appearance. Most of the buildings are simulated wood frame, but the school and certain commercial buildings are of red brick. To enter Ohio Village, one passes the doctor's office, and houses; walking along a rather wide boardwalk lining a variously muddy or dusty Main Street, the visitor soon arrives at the public square. Ohio Village is carefully designed to center on this node — the public square. Around the square are various commercial buildings such as the hotel, the tin shop, the bank, and the apothecary or drug store. Classic in their Federal Style Greek Revival lines and their simplicity, these buildings appear to be original from the period of the 1830s or 1840s. The brick general-merchandise building shows a hint of early-Victorian architecture, but most of the buildings are older and might have appeared in Howe's early illustrations. The architecture was selected to reflect the

Figure 68. *This war monument in Ohio Village occupies a portion of the square. Such monuments serve as landmarks that link events and dates and thus provide history lessons to a community. The square serves as a nodal center of community life. 1977 photo by the author.*

transition from the earlier nineteenth century to the later nineteenth century and thus places Ohio Village squarely in time as pre-industrial.

As the heart of Ohio Village, the public square is ingeniously designed to convey information about the past. As squares go, it is rather small (approximately 100 feet on a side). Part of the square is devoted to a small, rectangular piece of land on which stands a Mexican-American War monument (fig. 68). Shaped like an obelisk and surrounded by iron posts that are ringed by chains, it stands about 8 feet in height and forms the centerpiece of the square. Trees have been planted on this sacred ground in the square, presenting a picture of beauty and serenity. Like most true nodes, the square in effect focusses the observer's attention inward, that is, it helps create a mood of introspection.

Like its counterparts everywhere, Ohio Village makes modern concessions to accommodate visitors. Lining the storefronts are small signs indicating that tintypes and photographic portrait views can be taken of the family. One can watch leather goods and items of tin being made and purchase these items. If one were to go behind these buildings, however, one would see barrels, crates, and other seemingly historic features that convey the impression of an older era, but are strategically placed to hide appurtenances such as the air-conditioning and heating systems of these buildings. These buildings are climate controlled, enabling visitors to learn and to shop in comfort — something that never characterized the good old days. Many visitors think Ohio Village is "real" — despite the Historical Society's pointing out that it is not.

Ohio Village represents a small commercial center at the time when Henry Howe might have visited. Howe would have sketched its prototype at the dawn of the era of photography, when the daguerreotype was just coming into vogue. Within a short time, photography would revolutionize the way Americans perceived their surroundings and the way memories of Main Street would be shaped. Howe's early scenes of many other communities throughout Ohio, as well as Virginia and as far west as California, are captivating, for they capture considerable architectural detail; they also often depict intense activity along the streets by showing people and livestock.[4]

Lest the reader might be led into thinking that Ohio Village is an idealized abstraction — an edited version of history — and that historic scenes such as those drawn or commissioned by Henry Howe are reality, it must be noted that even creditable photographers and illustrators were often quite selective. Consider, for example, a New Philadelphia, Ohio, scene by Henry Howe. In a beautiful lithograph (fig. 69), the town's courthouse and a row of commercial brick Victorian buildings convey the impression of a well-ordered Main Street scene. However, by comparing Howe's *original* photograph (fig. 70) with the illustrations that appeared in Howe's books, one can see that Howe himself edited the illustrations for the public. Whereas the original photograph of New Philadelphia features the courthouse and the commercial brick Victorian buildings prominently, it also contains (on the left side of the photo) a false-front wooden building that was to be removed; in fact, Howe's photograph reveals the words "cut off here." One must ask how many undesirable buildings were omitted as victims of selective editing, lost to posterity, or, as film makers might later say, wound up on the cutting-room floor. It is easy to understand that older or shabbily maintained wooden buildings were expendable in Henry Howe's day, for his was a time when masonry implied stability, wealth, and permanence.

Figure 69. *This lithograph of New Philadelphia, Ohio, appeared in Henry Howe's His-*
torical Collections of Ohio (1907) *and shows the downtown as consisting of substantial*
masonry buildings. Like many other illustrations in this period, this was based on a pho-
tograph. Courtesy Ohio Historical Society.

While this may seem a disingenuous way for a chronicler to treat a
place, it should be realized that people have edited Main Street for more
than a hundred, perhaps a hundred and fifty, years. This selective editing
process on Main Street ensures that we see it as it *should* have looked
rather than as it *actually* appeared. Henry Howe and other travellers marvelled at what they saw in the American countryside in the nineteenth
century, but they often made it appear even grander, neater, or more prosperous than it actually was.

Victorians like Howe (and his New England mentor John Warner Barber), who recorded townscapes while living in an era that sought permanence, recognized that architecture reflected the collective commercial, social, and even spiritual accomplishment of Americans. The towns
they experienced varied in their design: many were based around public squares; many others were simply developed along their Main Streets.
Ideally, however, all featured the latest in highly detailed Victorian archi-

Figure 70. *A photo of New Philadelphia, Ohio, taken by Philip Strickmaker for Henry Howe in 1887 shows the dilapidated wooden false-front building (left) that was omitted in the final illustration. The words "cut off" indicate where the photo would be cropped before being reproduced in Henry Howe's* Historical Collections of Ohio. *Courtesy Ohio Historical Society.*

tecture by the late 1880s, indicating they were prosperous places. The Victorians were not alone in showing only the best side of Main Street, for the process continues to this day; chambers of commerce, development groups, and individuals have a tendency to show the image of Main Street they want us to see. The twelfth axiom of Main Street development, then, is: *The image of Main Street that reaches the public is often a selected or edited version depicting what the street should look like rather than an objective or random view of it.*

As noted in Section 2, monuments in public squares often served as important statements of community events and sacrifices. Naturally, chroniclers such as Henry Howe and the makers of historical atlases recorded these. Memorial monuments like the one at Chatham Centre, in Medina County, Ohio, were erected in the memory of the soldiers of Chatham township who gave their lives to the service of their country during the rebellion. Such monuments served as inspiration to contemporary historians. The historians who designed Ohio Village thought it natural that a monument of this type be erected on the square. They had ample source material. An illustration from one of the beautiful historical atlases of Medina County, Ohio, features several properly attired Victorians observing the monument, which is crowned by an eagle and features the shield with crossed flags (fig. 71). This memorial rises on a small knoll at the intersection of two major roads. Historical investigation revealed that the monument was depicted rather accurately in the atlas, but that the scene was rendered more attractive by the placement of people and the omission of litter.

Here and there throughout the United States, travellers even today can find actual streetscapes that, somehow, managed to escape either demolition or well-meaning preservation efforts. They reveal that there was a good deal of truth in the Victorian lithographs and engravings of the last century. New Vienna, Ohio, presented such a townscape in the late 1970s. Main Street consisted of a row of virtually intact commercial Victorian buildings whose façades had remained unchanged; their original Corinthian columns, corbels, and other Victorian trim remained unmolested. The signage along this street was phenomenal, too, for its uniformity. It appears that one sign painter had gone through the entire Main Street and painted most of the signs, giving this town a visual uniformity that many communities lacked.

Of course, time has not treated most towns as well as it has New Vienna and its fortunate counterparts in different parts of the United States. In many cases, one often finds towns with boarded-up façades — streetscapes that have, in effect, closed down — where commercial trade has shifted, either to other parts of town or farther away, perhaps to shopping centers. The Dakotas and Texas have innumerable small towns with boarded-up façades; towns where Main Street appears as if the merchants "just up and walked away," as one old-timer put it, in a relatively short time (perhaps in the 1950s or 1960s). Some of these townscapes have hardly changed at all.

Figure 71. *The Civil War monument in Chatham Centre, Ohio, was depicted in a contemporary Victorian atlas in 1886. Such scenes were rather accurate but somewhat stylized, in that people in fancy Victorian dress were added and litter removed.* Historical Atlas of Medina County, Ohio, 1886; *courtesy Ohio Historical Society.*

They remain as forlorn reminders that time has passed many Main Streets by, leaving them isolated in time and space.

Other Main Streets, however, present quite a different appearance, and it is obvious that there has been considerable restoration and renovation. These towns often seem too good to be true — that is, too authentic — and many are. If American small towns have been idealized, in literature and popular culture, this has found an expression in the landscape; many have been preserved into something more attractive than ever existed in the past. This leads to the thirteenth axiom of Main Street development: *Interpretations of a community's past affect how its historic structures and other features will be treated: a contempt for the past will hasten the destruction of the reminders of the past, while a romanticizing of it will help preserve its historic fabric.*

Re-Creating the New England Village

Historical geographers and other students of landscape history delight in comparing real places with idealized descriptions of them, and, as the evidence accumulates, it appears that the New England Village became the first of America's small-town landscapes to be idealized. According to geographer Joseph Wood, many New England villages we experience today have been stereotyped. In an insightful article, Wood recently noted that many real New England villages were not as charming and picturesque as the model villages that have become created through a slow, subtle, and nearly subconscious process of image building.[5] Interestingly, the process was begun by intellectuals in the nineteenth century, who sought — and found — in the New England villages a refuge from the quickening pace of urbanization and industrialization that was changing the character, and the racial makeup, of America. This New England image was actively marketed by merchants. Presently, New England village landscapes sanctify an idealized past as part of their tourist economies.

Woodstock, Vermont, is typical. In his critical interpretation of the village today, social historian James Howard Kunstler wrote this description, which would serve as an archetype for all "historicized" New England village centers:

> Here is the quintessential New England town of America's fevered imagination in all its fine-honed details: the village green bordered by streets of white clapboard houses, stolid churches and a handsome red-brick inn; the charming little commercial district with well-kept shops and cozy restaurants; the dignified old civic buildings unsullied by the affronts of Modernism; the brook that burbles through the heart of the village crossed by several quaint, iron-railed bridges; the

whole community of buildings wedged into a narrow valley between abrupt wooded hills so as to afford a pleasing sense of compactness and enclosure.[6]

Kunstler goes on to state, however, that the town of Woodstock never looked quite this way, or quite this good, in the past.

The New England Village became a stereotyped, romanticized community as early as the nineteenth century, and this perceptual iconization was facilitated by a growing middle class with income that permitted recreational travel on a rapidly developing railroad network. By the time Patti Page sang about the "quaint little villages here and there" that seem to beckon the traveller, in her 1952 song "You're Sure to Fall in Love with Old Cape Cod," the process was essentially complete.

Re-Creating Main Street on the Middle Border

This romanticizing of place helps us better understand the popularity of New England as a tourist destination, but how and why did our more typical Main Street marketing towns of the Midwest also become idealized, albeit at a somewhat later time, more specifically in the latter half of the twentieth century? Whereas religion and colonial values are associated with New England (that is, they are "covenanted" towns, according to Page Smith),[7] why would a mundane commercial center in the middle section of the country be romanticized? In this regard, two towns of the same name, Georgetown, Ohio, and Georgetown, Texas, might be compared side by side (figs. 72 and 73). Both developed as county-seat towns in the nineteenth century, and both are places where twentieth-century commercial developers along Main Street have sensed that history sells. Since the mid-1970s, entrepreneurs have carefully restored many of the façades. The trim is painted very creatively, often in contrasting colors that accentuate its detail. Strong sign-control measures have resulted in a visual uniformity along Main Street: signs are often mounted flush to the buildings, and are not highly illuminated, for they would then appear garish (that is, un-historic). These signs often feature lettering that appears to be old or old-fashioned, and from these clues it is obvious that preservation has been an active force on Main Street. A sense of late-nineteenth-century history permeates both places.

These two towns epitomize an entire class of historic communities,

Figure 72. *Georgetown, Ohio, possesses a revitalized downtown centering on a square that is in turn faced by restored Victorian-era buildings. By the late 1970s, many towns had begun to manifest a renewed sense of their history; repainted buildings featuring historical color combinations and historically themed signage helped create the image of Victorian-era prosperity in modern times. 1979 photo by the author.*

which are known as "Main Street communities" in the parlance of developers. Nationwide, in recent years, Main Street has become quite important as a visual icon. One sees — throughout the entire country — rehabilitated Main Streets that bear the look of preservation. The trees are trimmed very neatly, the colors are very carefully selected, and there is an overall look of visual uniformity that had been lacking some years before. It would be impossible to overestimate the power of the popular history that has swept America in the last twenty-five years. It has transformed many small-town Main Streets that had become rather forlorn by the 1960s and early 1970s into showcases by the 1980s and 1990s.

The late 1960s to the late 1970s was a crucial period in this transformation, the ten years in which much entrepreneurial preservation took hold. As the process was unfolding, I asked a general question: How, and why, was Main Street gaining such appeal at a time when the small town had been declared dead by a number of academicians?

To answer this question, I deliberately made a pilgrimage to Marceline,

Figure 73. *Georgetown, Texas, also features a revitalized square faced by historic commercial buildings, most of which have been restored to maintain a historic appearance. Taken more than fifteen years after the previous illustration, this photo demonstrates that preservation efforts have been sustained and have had a profound effect in the retention of historic buildings. 1994 photo by the author.*

Missouri, in 1972, where I found a rather ordinary Main Street that obviously dated from the late nineteenth century and had struggled to maintain its share of the retail trade (fig. 74). Merchants and residents of the town were at once optimistic and pessimistic about Main Street's chances of survival. Although there was some talk of revitalization, Marceline showed the characteristic signs of decline: several buildings had been abandoned, and merchants eeked out a living in others. The landscape showed Main Street's long struggle to attract trade. On the sides of a few of the buildings one could see signs that dated from the early years of this century. One old sign for Nabisco featuring a "Uneeda Biscuit" slogan appeared prominently on the side of one building.

In conducting research in the files of Marceline library and of the local newspaper, I located a beautiful photograph (fig. 75) of that same Main Street, which was called Kansas Avenue when the photo was taken in 1905. That same "Uneeda Biscuit" sign was prominent in this historic photograph, and was apparently new at the time the photographer set up

Figure 74. *Main Street in Marceline, Missouri, presented this appearance in 1972 as the author travelled there in search of Walt Disney's hometown. Disney is said to have insisted on capturing the Victorian-era quality of these rather typical two-story buildings. Marceline's buildings at this time were in various states of deferred maintenance on the eve of the American discovery of the "real" Main Street America. 1972 photo by the author.*

the camera to record the scene for posterity. In reality, the streetscape of Marceline in the 1905 photograph presented a somewhat austere appearance. Gaunt power poles lined this street, and the buildings had a relatively ragged profile: although most of them achieved two stories in height (indicating that substantial commercial progress had been made), some buildings were one story and, in a number of cases, there were empty spaces between the buildings. Nevertheless, there was an overall look of modest prosperity in the town in 1905, even though the Main Street was unpaved. To the dismay of some merchants in 1905, Marceline's streets, even in the business section along Main Street (Kansas Avenue), were a quagmire of mud in wet weather, dusty in dry weather, and what one critic called an "equine latrine" throughout much of the year, as horses

Figure 75. *Marceline, Missouri, in 1905 was where Walt Disney experienced the town and began his lifelong love of Main Street. This historic photograph reveals Main Street to be unpaved and lined by telephone poles. Business signs like "Uneeda Biscuit" on the sides of buildings (center right), as well as projecting from storefronts (note "HARDWARE" sign at left), are typical of the era. Courtesy Missouri Historical Society.*

left piles of droppings in the street as they plodded along pulling wagons or hauling riders.

From these historic photos, Marceline, Missouri, appears to be much like any other "typical" town in the United States, but its streetscape has a much deeper meaning. Walt Disney (1901–1966) spent his early years in Marceline, growing up in a frame house not far from the business district. Disney would have seen the town when its Main Street looked like the 1905 scene I discovered in the historical files. Those who knew Disney say he never forgot his early years in Marceline, for they were formative in developing his early character. His years in Marceline were relatively happy, far better than the years of near poverty in Kansas City and later Chicago. Understandably, then, Walt Disney looked back on Marceline in particular, and the small town in general, with a great deal of nostalgia. It symbolized his youth and a freer — and perhaps fairer — time for him.

IMAGINEERING MAIN STREET USA

It is not surprising, therefore, that Disney selected a small-town Main Street as the main entrance point for his spectacular new theme park in

Figure 76. *As seen in Disneyland (above) and Walt Disney World, Walt Disney's Main Street is narrow by most comparisons, only thirty-five feet wide, and serves as an ingeniously designed pedestrian environment that channels the observer toward a plaza after experiencing a very memorable public square. The tower of the Disneyland & Santa Fe Railroad Station is seen in the distance. 1975 photo by the author.*

the orange groves of Orange County near Anaheim, California, when he created Disneyland in 1955 (fig. 76). Disney called this streetscape "Main Street USA." What Walt Disney created, however, was rather different from what he actually saw in his early years in Marceline. It is true that some of the buildings that Disney created possessed some of the architectural character seen in towns like Marceline, but Walt Disney and his cadre of designers, including John Hench, Marvin Davis, and Harper Goff, very carefully engineered the streetscape. There were few or no open spaces between buildings; every commercial building was more or less the same height; the buildings were approximately five-eights the size of their prototypes, and thus seemingly more approachable or less formidable; streetlamps, trees — everything was very carefully selected. A Disney biographer has noted that "the storefronts of that period were so important to Walt Disney that he worked out two hundred specific color shades with his artists. He wanted them to look the way he remembered them." [8] The effect was certainly successful, "for Walt Elias Disney relived his boyhood in a small town when he walked along Main Street."[9] As if to confirm the axiom that architects on Main Street use modern building materials, Disney and his designers employed a new material, fiberglass, in re-creating Victorian details. Fiberglass was light, durable, and cheap, three important prerequisites that helped reduce the cost, and speed construction time, in the creation of Disney's elaborate Main Street USA.

In the early 1970s, I corresponded with the Disney staff regarding Walt Disney's fascination with Main Street. Robert Jackson, publicity manager for Disneyland, responded with skill and candor: "The architecture was personally selected by Walt Disney, himself a Midwesterner by birth and during his early life. He felt that America's 'Innocent Years' at the turn of the century were best depicted by this structural style — and that this introduction into the special realm of Disneyland would be the perfect 'mindsetter.'"[10] Those close to Disney knew how powerfully his youth in Marceline had affected him. It came to symbolize innocence and purity. Therefore, in keeping with an image of unsullied youth, everything he created in Disneyland would remain spotless at all times.

Towns other than Marceline also served as sources of inspiration for Main Street USA, for Disney involved many of his designers in the project. Although Marvin Davis appears to have been most influential in the overall design of Main Street USA, the person most involved in conceptualizing its architecture was Harper Goff. Disney and Goff were both model-train buffs and had met accidentally at a model-railroad hobby store in London, England, in 1951. Goff, an artist, soon found himself working for Disney, and prepared sketches of a number of early concepts for theme parks, including one that would have been named "Disneylandia." Goff and Disney discussed, and visited, Walter Knott's "Knott's Berry Farm," a Western-themed park in Anaheim, and were impressed. However, whereas a rather rural, more or less frontier, small Western town was one of the early concepts, it was Disney who favored the more substantial, mostly brick, two-story Victorian architecture. Goff complied by drawing buildings he remembered from his youth in Fort Collins, Colorado. In response to an interviewer's questions about this Fort Collins source of Goff's inspiration, Goff replied:

Yeah, I was born in that little town . . . Fort Collins, Colorado. My
Dad owned a newspaper there, the Fort Collins Express Courier, and

Figure 77. *The City Hall in Disneyland faces the public square, and is a credible replica, albeit reduced in scale, of Second Empire architecture inspired by the Larimer County courthouse in Fort Collins, Colorado (compare this with fig. 78). 1995 photo by the author.*

> I grew up there. It was a very prosperous town. We had banks that looked like banks, you know, and there was a Victorian city hall. I was born in 1911 and these buildings were around when I was a kid. When I started working on Main Street, I had photographs of Fort Collins taken. I showed them to Walt and he liked them very much. Disneyland's City Hall was copied from Fort Collins . . . so was the Bank building and some of the others.[11]

In this regard, it is instructive to compare the beautiful, Victorian Second Empire city hall in Disneyland (fig. 77) with its prototype, the Larimer County courthouse in Fort Collins (fig. 78), which was located on a square downtown in more or less the Shelbyville pattern. Ironically, this courthouse was demolished in 1957 and replaced by a more modern building. Today some of the other buildings that may also have inspired Goff are undergoing restoration and help capture the feeling of late-Victorian-era prosperity that Harper Goff and Walt Disney fondly remembered in their small-town boyhoods.

Figure 78. *The Larimer County courthouse in Fort Collins, Colorado, served as the prototype for the City Hall in Disneyland, but is an otherwise rather representative example of high-style Second Empire Victorian architecture. It was built in 1888 and demolished in the 1950s. Courtesy Rheba Massey, Fort Collins Public Library.*

Because Main Street USA has been so influential in the creation of popular images about small-town America, it is appropriate to ask several questions about Goff's role as one of the designers who worked closely with Disney: How accurately, one might ask, did Goff reproduce the buildings he remembered in Fort Collins? And, more to the point, how representative of small-town America were the buildings that Goff reproduced? Answers to these questions can help us more fully appreciate both the actual role that Fort Collins may have played in influencing Disneyland's Main Street USA and the relationship between Disney and members of his design team. Although Fort Collins is a large community today (population 100,000), in the time of Goff's youth it had about 8,700 people — large enough to have a streetcar system, yet still small enough to possess the quality of a town. In reviewing historical photographs of Fort Collins from the 1910s and 1920s with Fort Collins local-history coordinator Rheba Massey, it became apparent that Goff synthesized elements from numerous high-style Victorian buildings rather than copying, detail for detail, any particular building. Certainly Goff's City Hall on Disneyland's public square is not an exact copy of the Larimer County Court House: it is smaller and embellished with different Victorian details than its alleged prototype in Fort Collins. In fact, Goff's City Hall possesses window details and tower proportions that are more like those of the B. F. Hottel House (a Second Empire–styled Victorian residence built in 1882) that stood in downtown Fort Collins until its demolition in 1962. Goff's City Hall in Disneyland is also reminiscent of other historic Fort Collins buildings, including the Fire Station, and the "Old Main" building at Colorado State University; these buildings probably helped inspire Goff, for they were landmarks in the earlier twentieth century. They were also rather representative of Victorian-era buildings in prosperous American towns.

In using Fort Collins for partial inspiration for Main Street USA, Harper Goff also appears to have remembered urban-design features that were absent in Disney's boyhood town of Marceline, which was smaller in size, and much simpler in design, than Fort Collins. Because the earliest town plat in Fort Collins was laid out at right angles to the Poudre River in 1867, and the town's later (1880s) addition was laid out at a 45-degree angle to that original plat, the Fort Collins Central Business District possesses a number of angled intersections that provide visual variety. As translated by Goff, these may have inspired the ingeniously angled intersections that Disney and his designers placed about halfway down Main Street USA. Fort Collins also offered other inspirations: its Union Pacific depot is located at the end of Pine Street and effectively terminates one's vista down it, as does the depot in Disney's Main Street USA; so, too, did the Colorado and Southern depot on La Porte Street, which marked one edge of the Fort Collins business district.

In reality, Fort Collins was, and is, rather more complicated and prosperous than Marceline. By the time of Goff's youth in Fort Collins, a number of the commercial streets were undergoing beautification as the trolley (streetcar) tracks were landscaped into medians, and a small landscaped traffic circle was added to the intersection of College Avenue and La Porte Avenue. With its grass and trees, this circle became an important visual node, as postcard views of Fort Collins during the heyday of its trolley service confirm. It is possible that Goff's memory of Victorian architectural details, angled intersections, the small circular green, and the prominent depots — all rather refined, urbanistic touches — helped contribute to the original Main Street USA design. In characteristic Disney fashion, Walt Disney endorsed ideas from Goff and others on his design team that would help create a composite, synthesized image of the virtually perfect American small-town Main Street. This helps explain the narrow width of Main Street USA, about 30 feet, in comparison to the typically much wider streets of most American towns, including Marceline and Fort Collins. The narrow width of Main Street USA is likely a result of its being proportioned to better match the reduced scale of the buildings proposed by the design team and accepted by Disney. Thus, Main Street USA is a composite of abstracted designs from many communities, including Fort Collins as remembered, and reinterpreted, by Harper Goff.

Despite using Fort Collins and perhaps other prototypes, however, Disney is said to have insisted on certain things he remembered about his small town, and it is instructive to compare Main Street in Disneyland with Main Street in Marceline to see which features were retained and which were omitted. Significantly, Marceline has an open public square located close to the Santa Fe Railroad Station. In reality, the square in Marceline is rather mundane — simply one of the block squares of the town's grid plan (fig. 47) that possesses a few benches and, with its trees and simple street lights, serves as a park. The square created in Disneyland, however, possesses an aura of magic: being designed more closely to a Philadelphia square model, traffic must circle around it. This public square creates an element of drama and even grandeur, for it features well-tended (even sculpted) trees and bushes, iron fencing, a cannon, globe lights, and Victorian-era styled benches (fig. 79). The public square in Disneyland is open — a classic node — and is faced by the commercial and institutional buildings that front it.

Walt Disney and his designers very carefully designed this public square in Main Street USA to be the main entry point into the entire theme park, and it is one of the most memorable nodes ever designed. The square or park at this point leads directly to Main Street. By experiencing Main Street's square first, one steps back in time and in the process is exposed to a visual mythology about the small town. All of the buildings — the emporium, the city hall, and the other commercial buildings — conspire to leave the visitor feeling immersed in the Victorian period. In one of the more insightful interpretations of Disney's design

Figure 79. *The public square in Disneyland is carefully designed and impeccably maintained. Although the visitor can see grass and vegetation, fences keep people on the paths and off the lawn. The Second Empire style Emporium buildings and others facing the square help set the historical mood. 1975 photo by the author.*

genius, Christopher Finch explains the rationale for placing Main Street between two visual focal points:

> His [Disney's] plan called for a railroad defining the perimeter of the park, with its main station situated right at the entrance. Once past the station, the visitor would have to pass down Main Street — a reproduction of the heart of a small Midwestern town such as Disney himself might have known as a boy. Entered from a small square on which a town hall and a fire station were situated, Main Street was calculated to correspond with one of the archetypes of the American imagination . . . it would establish the right ambience, so that visitors would be in a receptive state of mind . . . people on foot would be drawn down Main Street by the imposing edifice at its far end — Sleeping Beauty's Castle — the likes of which seldom has been seen in any Midwestern town.[12]

Disney chose the time period carefully. He is reported to have stated, "Here is America from 1890 to 1910, at the crossroads of an era . . . the gas lamp is giving way to the electric lamp, and a newcomer, the sputtering 'horseless carriage' has challenged Old Dobbin for the streetcar right-of-way. . . . America was in transition. . . ."[13] Historians will note that the automobile actually arrived at around 1900, not 1890, but Disney favored a broad, two-decade time period straddling the turn of the century. Despite the financial panic of 1893, America continued its period of growth, based on aggressive business consolidation, during the time period selected by Disney. The actions of business would soon lead to a groundswell of populism, even socialism, as scandals rocked the business world and government. And yet, a collective, selective memory as translated by Disney recalls these times as the good old days. It is this "innocent" time period that has been highly romanticized in American fiction and film for three generations. Time, as well as place, is required to evoke such nostalgia, and both have been reshaped in the popular culture.

At a recent conference, a number of preservationists and architectural historians were asked to name their favorite place and many named, quite significantly, places dear to their *childhoods*. Could it be that these places are our favorites because we were unaware of the *real* forces that effected them even then? Historian Richard Snow has admitted something that few historians would dare, namely that Disney's Main Street (and for that matter, Disney's depiction of history) though only partially true, is ". . . a triumph of the imagination." Snow summarized the opinions of many when he revealed the love affair he developed with Disney's Main Street when he was ten years old:

> I was enchanted by all the rides, but the thing that made the strongest impression on me was Main Street, Walt Disney's evocation of the small-town America of his youth. I remember standing there in the dusk while the lights came on. I watched them outlining the busy cornices while a horsecar clopped quietly past, and suddenly I wanted to stay in this place forever.[14]

If more scholars were this candid, we might be able to better understand Disney's effect on the public, and on the history profession itself. Like Snow's, my first experience with Disney's Main Street USA at about thirteen years of age was simply unforgettable; more to the point, it was one of the seminal experiences that started me in search of real American towns, to find what inspired Walt Disney and to determine how well he succeeded in capturing their environments and essences.

I have written elsewhere that Main Street may appeal to a sense of collective innocence in that our youths are times of relative simplicity before we experience significant personal, economic, and sexual responsibility.[15] Main Street and other idealized place images may be points of refuge for Americans who would just as soon turn back the clock if it meant recapturing lost innocence and simplifying their lives. Significantly, Disney is clearly a parental figure when he so manipulates space and time to reassure a culture. I will leave to Disney biographers the task of determining whether Disney himself was ever able to find adulthood or had regressed in his "nearly total lack of affection for his family" and his lack of sexual interest during his "formative years" as intimated by Judith Adams.[16] To some critics, Disney's remaining something of a child himself accounted for his uncanny ability to appeal to the "child" in all Americans.

Whatever his motives and reasons, Disney certainly touched a deep collective chord when he created Main Street USA. Significantly, the public square in Disneyland (which, according to some architectural critics and historic preservationists, cannot be considered a real place at all, but rather some spurious assemblage of buildings) has become one of the most sacrosanct places in America. Few sensitive visitors, or "guests" as Disney calls them, have failed to be gripped by the beauty of the public square that forms the main introduction point to Disney's theme park. It has been said that Disney's favorite place in the theme park was an apartment above the firehouse which looked right down into the public square to observe the activity. Using this commanding location, Disney could observe the public interacting with the environment that he had created, and by all accounts Disney was reassured by what he saw.

So, too, was the public. More than forty years after its creation, the public square in Main Street USA certainly remains one of the best places to sit and watch people who interact with each other, move through a quintessential pedestrian environment, and are noticeably awed by it. Compelling in its beauty and scale, Main Street is at once reassuring because its square embraces and surrounds the visitor and exciting because a view down Main Street reminds us that there is always something beyond the small town: on Disney's Main Street, the visitor's glance is drawn down Main Street to Sleeping Beauty's castle at the other end. It is symbolic and interesting that Walt Disney elected to feature *two* major architectural points to anchor Main Street: Sleeping Beauty's castle at one end and the Victorian Railroad Station at the other. These two landmarks, both symbolically Euro-American in design and form, anchor the viewer in fantasy and folklore on the one hand and history on the other. The castle and the railroad station help orient the visitor as they draw the visitor into the park. In this regard, Disney's Main Street design builds upon some of the best lessons of urban planners since ancient times, the power of landmarks to define and terminate vistas.

In creating Main Street with its emphasis on detail, form, and pedestrian scale, Disney anticipated postmodern design trends that would reshape the American landscape for two generations after his death. These designs sprang in part from Disney's genius, but they had deep historical roots. I think it worth stating that Disney grew up in the shadow and with the memory of Daniel Burnham's "White City" at the Chicago 1893 World's Fair, for Disney's father worked as a carpenter on that project. Inasmuch as Daniel Burnham went on to become a spokesman for "the city beautiful" movement, it is not too far-fetched to consider Disney's wonderful creation — Main Street USA — as a realization of the idealistic early-twentieth-century belief that cities should be carefully designed and a joy to behold. As irreverent as it may seem to some, Main Street USA must be considered in the context of other urbanistic movements that sprang from the heartland city of Chicago. Disney scholar Karal Ann Marling further notes that Main Street (and Disneyland in general) was also partly inspired by the 1939 Railroad Fair in Chicago that caught Disney's imagination, for as a model railroader he sought to create his own "layout" which ran around the perimeter of the park;[17] thus, miniaturization is also an essential aspect of Main Street USA as created by Walt Disney and his imaginative team of designers.

And Main Street USA certainly fits into the genre of intensely designed and orchestrated space/place. On every inch of Disney's Main Street USA, from the public square to the Plaza, architecture, street furniture, and all aspects of the streetscape are historically themed and carefully engineered. It is this sense of "history" that nearly overwhelms the visitor. All of the street lights are patterned after the "whiteway" lights that lined Main Streets in the early twentieth century. The park benches, wrought iron railings, plantings — everything on Main Street is carefully designed to convey a feeling of the late Victorian period. Even the trees and bushes are carefully sculpted and tended. On Main Street USA, most visitors imbibe the ambience of the past, but they are in fact participating in something far more elementary; their attitudes and perceptions are being shaped through a type of social engineering. This leads to the fourteenth axiom of Main Street development. *Main Street is essentially a stage upon which several types of human dramas are performed simultaneously, each character or actor in the drama having a designated role that is dependent on his or her relationship to the "set."* Whether one stands behind the counter or in front of a store window brings with it different expectations. Disney was the ultimate merchant on Main Street, and visitors to Main Street USA are the ultimate customers.

In Disney's Main Street USA, architecture becomes the façade that creates the impression that all was right with the world in the small town at the turn of the century; it implies that commerce (and merchants) thrive along Main Street, and that society and a community are working together in harmony. Of course, Disney's Main Street does not feature those inevitable services that indicate the other, or darker, side of life. There are no funeral parlors, pool halls, or bars. It should come as no surprise that Disney created small-town America as it *should* have been. His Main Street mirrors a pre-adolescent period free from the change and turmoil that characterizes much of life. Significantly, Disney chose both the horse-drawn streetcar and an omnibus as the main conveyances that would take visitors who preferred not to (or were unable to) walk. The horse car symbolizes the mid– to late nineteenth century — most of them had vanished by about 1900 to 1905 — while the internal combustion engine's intriguing, somewhat cantankerous popping sound became more commonplace *after* 1905, meaning that Disney took liberties with time, that is, he had it both ways: only in Disneyland could vehicles that had replaced their predecessors and those predecessors co-exist. Visitors can ride these trams and omnibuses from the public square all the way through Main Street to the Plaza, the point from which the visitors could then experience any of the other five major worlds in the theme park. The Plaza is a significant element in the design of the Main Street USA complex: if Main Street and the public square symbolize childhood or youth, then the Plaza would seem to signify late adolescence, for here we must make decisions which can take us further backward in time (Frontierland), to distant places (Adventureland), or into the future (Tomorrowland).

Historians may ask the following question: In creating Main Street USA, did Disney and his designers *really* attempt to reproduce places like Marceline and the Fort Collins of yore, or simply create a generic, stylized town? In reality, they came closer to reproducing the spatial design of some of the small towns in the American midlands source area, especially in southeastern Pennsylvania, notably those intriguing townscapes that feature the unique "circle in square" Philadelphia plan. Comparing Disney's Main Street square to these open squares reveals that they are approximately the same size (about 100 feet across), that is, relatively small. Whereas most American small towns have rather larger public squares, say, 300 feet across, the public square in Disneyland is deliberately designed to be smaller (as are the buildings themselves) than was normally experienced in most "real" Main Streets. That the "circle in square" Pennsylvania towns come very close to matching Disney's scale of Main Street would seem to indicate that they served as the prototype for Main Street USA (figs. 80 and 81), and these places were well known to some of Disney's designers. On the other hand, however, these Disney designers appeared to possess an intuitive genius or sense of design that simply may have "imagineered" that as the proper configuration and scale in which to design a small town. To them, a square of that size would have "felt" right.[18]

What concerns, even infuriates, historians and scholars most about Walt Disney is that he created an abstracted image that it is so tempting to confuse with reality. Disney masterfully abstracted his experiences in Marceline and worked with his designers to capture the essences of other towns to produce a small-town image that has nearly universal appeal. In so doing, Disney intuitively knew that *all* planned townscapes — including those Main Streets created in the eighteenth and nineteenth centuries — were in a sense engineered to create effects. Even the vistas down Main Street USA were carefully designed to have significant features (the Railroad Station and Sleeping Beauty's Castle), or, as Disney himself is reported to have said, there should be a "wienie at the end of every street."

Disney's aggressive and enthusiastic "imagineering" is often misunderstood as duplicitous. In the late twentieth century, it has become apparent that Disney either knew more about image building than given credit for, or that he was a pioneer in shaping values: Disney intuitively knew that images were as important as substance. As shaped by Disney and those who worked for him, images took on a life of their own. Sociologist Ben

Figure 80. *A circle in a square: Disneyland's public square is ingeniously designed to create a sense of intimacy yet just large enough to permit groups of people to move through it. While appearing to be a circle, the verdant island at the center of this square is actually triangular, with rounded edges that permit the pedestrian and horse-car traffic to move smoothly around it. 1975 photo by the author.*

Agger has noted that "postmodern capitalism creates capital out of images and images out of commodities, utterly blurring the boundaries between the real and imaginary."[19] Evidence suggests that this process has been in operation for some time. The nineteenth-century town platters, entrepreneurs, and designers who created "real" places and patterned their architecture and even their names after classical places were doing much of what Disney did. This study suggests that Main Street has *always* embodied the essence of image building, and research on Main Streets suggests that we as scholars and students of history, geography, sociology, and other disciplines should re-study the "real" world in order to determine how "imaginary" much of it actually is. This leads to the realization that even "real" places are shaped by concepts of how they should appear, and hence how they will affect us. If looked at iconographically, the small-town Main Street would then emerge as one of our most mundane and yet metaphorical places; whether experienced from a park bench in Disneyland or an actual town such as Marceline, Main Street serves to re-

Figure 81. *Prototype circle in square: the central squares of numerous towns in eastern Pennsylvania, such as Gettysburg and Hanover, are designed to much the same scale as Disney's Main Street square. 1978 photo by the author.*

mind us that *all* places are both real and imaginary. This was as true in the nineteenth century (when civic and commercial structures looked like the Parthenon) as it is today (when the buildings on Main Street strive to capture the air of the idealized prototypes in Disneyland).

At symbolic levels, Disney's engineering of the small-town environment in Main Street USA is revealing because he so beautifully captured the essence of the romanticism of the small town. Disney himself was moved by the originals, and shaped them into an icon that affects the way we will view its "real" counterparts. To the general public, Main Street USA in Disneyland was very credible in that it featured towers and architectural turrets where they seemed logical, and even though the trim was fairly lavish, it was subdued enough to remind one of Main Streets in the relatively prosperous period during the "McKinley Era" at about the turn of the century.

Students of urban design know that Disney possessed an element of genius in that he carefully designed this Main Street to have an intersection about halfway between the public square and the plaza. That intersection provides a node of activity where merchants have materials on display outside and where towers can form visual exclamation points for the architecture. Looking down one of these side streets, one sees trees that convey the feeling that the commercial streetscape is yielding to a residential area. But in reality, the trees seen behind that intersection on Main Street are the trees of Jungleland, so close is the juxtaposition between one "world" of Disneyland and another. The entire Disneyland theme park is magnificently engineered into only about ninety-six acres of space, which is smaller than the area encompassed within the city limits of most American towns! In world history, few places this small have had such a powerful effect on so many people.

In keeping with his ability to create magic through place, Disney used night to his advantage. Because Main Street USA is experienced at night as well as during the daytime, Disney provided marvelous rim-lighting on the buildings. Incandescent bulbs were strung along all of the cornices to convey a very stylized and ornate appearance, enabling the architecture and the streetscape to "shine" at night as well as in the daytime. The Main Street electrical parade runs through the area at night, and Main Street at night provides a kind of visual excitement that was rarely, perhaps never, actually seen in the small towns of America. Rim-lighting of this kind was, however, common in pavilions and the grand buildings of expositions. Like many of Disney's creations, rim-lighting in this context brings a touch of the exotic or even whimsical to Main Street, rather reminding one more of the festive environments of parks and fairs than the Main Street of the typical American small town. Historian and social critic Jon Weiner recently noted that "Disneyland's Main Street is a fiction; the real Main Streets of real small towns at the turn of the century were not so nice" [20] — an understatement borne out by architectural historians and historical geographers. And yet, as architect Paul Goldberger accurately noted, Disney produced "a kind of universally true Main Street — it's better than the real Main Street of the turn of the century ever could be." [21] That Disney's Main Street seems so universally beautiful comes as less of a surprise when one realizes that Walt Disney was rather sophisticated and widely travelled: in fact, Tivoli Gardens in Copenhagen, Denmark, was said to have greatly impressed Walt Disney in 1952 — a seminal year in the early designs of Disneyland. [22] Disney and his designers reportedly were impressed by an exhibit called "Yesteryear's Main Street" at the Museum of Science and Industry in Chicago, which was sponsored by General

Figure 82. *Hyperdesign: Main Street USA in Walt Disney World at Orlando, Florida, has a very ornate quality, largely because the buildings are taller and more lavishly detailed than its more restrained and more realistic counterpart in Disneyland. Both, however, use a view up Main Street toward Sleeping Beauty's Castle to the same effect that designers of Lancaster style squares used in real towns (see fig. 53). 1978 photo by the author.*

Motors.[23] Disney's Main Street, which, according to WED (which stands for Walter Elias Disney) imagineering historian David Mumford, "is actually a typical representation of a Walt Disney imagineering project, since it represents a collaborative effort by many creative people,"[24] was thus inspired by many places.

I have noted elsewhere that the Main Street that Walt Disney revealed to the world in Disneyland in 1955 was not the same as that Main Street USA that later developed in Walt Disney World in Florida in 1971.[25] A comparison of the two streetscapes (figs. 76 and 82) reveals that the architecture in the Florida park has a much more lavish, overly ornate, perhaps almost burlesque, quality. In fact, whereas the Disneyland Main Street USA is fairly credible, Main Street USA in Walt Disney World is almost bizarre in its architectural treatment. The buildings are taller, and the architectural trim appears much more lavish, and is far more accentuated or stereotyped as gingerbread architecture, than anything ever seen in small-town America. This difference should not be surprising when one realizes that Disney carefully engineered every design feature of Disneyland, but he died in 1966, a full five years before Walt Disney World opened. Whereas Walt Disney's creation in California embodies the true spirit of Walt Disney as a designer, the theme park in Florida reflects another, newer, generation of Disney imagineering.

That newer generation of Disney design reflected in the Florida theme park seems to have been carried away with architectural hyperbole: Disney World's Main Street USA is a caricature of Disneyland's Main Street USA, which in turn is a caricature of the Main Streets of places like Marceline and many other towns. Nevertheless, Main Street in both parks features a number of very familiar elements, including a movie theater where up to four to six movies play at one time. This concept was revolutionary when it was developed in the California park in 1955, but it seemed to be accepted as commonplace by the time the Florida park opened in 1971. An air photograph or guide map (fig. 83) would reveal that Main Street is in fact an isolated or sequestered environment that turns its back on the real world outside, or, as one astute observer noted, "stress . . . worries . . . frustrations . . . all seem to melt away as guests . . . enter the Main Street Town Square."[26] Leaving her car in the lot before entering Disneyland, the visitor finds herself in an area that is completely architecturally controlled; where all of the deliveries are never seen, for all the delivery vehicles enter from the back and are invisible to the visitor. Having now become a "guest," the visitor is channeled through Main Street and moves through a very carefully controlled environment that is, in a manner of speaking, also climatically controlled, because both Florida and California have such a generally benign climate. Disney's Main Streets have two main visual exclamation points — the Railroad Station and the Castle — which always anchor the visitor, so that the Main Street experience is very kinetic and yet reassuring. Both Main Streets are enjoyable as commercial and social environments. Once inside, the guest is surrounded by other people who are going to behave.[27] Main Street is a democratic if not plebeian environment, and that is part of its mass appeal: as one observer noted, Disney "chose to glorify the ordinary, small town origins of the common citizen rather than to contrive an aristocratic, elegant realm suitable for a ruling class."[28] That Disney was "one of us" is underscored by the mass appeal of his Main Street. We feel comfortable there as we fill the role of consumers of both products and place.

Figure 83. *A bird's-eye view reveals Disneyland's Main Street to be a key that extends from the park's entrance (bottom) to the park's center at the plaza. This oblique view, which clearly shows the public square (lower portion), the linear Main Street with its small intersection, and the plaza (top), helped visitors orient themselves to Disneyland during the 1970s. Author's collection.*

MAIN STREET AFTER DISNEY

If this description of the Disneyland and Disney World Main Streets sounds familiar, and it should indeed, that is because it has in fact become the model of the typical American shopping mall, where the visitor or shopper leaves the car in the parking lot and enters an environment that is climatically controlled, and where the real world is left outside. In malls, as in Disney's Main Streets, every aspect of design and circulation is carefully orchestrated (fig. 84). This should come as no surprise, for many of the designers of shopping centers and malls in the United States have visited Disney's parks in order to develop a much better understanding of how people move through, appreciate, and patronize a retail environment.[29]

It is ironic that Walt Disney, who was politically conservative and espoused rugged individualism, actually produced an environment that embodies such nearly total social engineering and control. According to architectural critic Jane Holtz Kay, Disney's Main Street and shopping malls embody both "public persona" and "private autocracy."[30] The autocratic control of theme parks, of course, is linked to safety and security, and is perhaps one reason why shopping centers are highly successful, and highly criticized by those who feel that such places are "contrived." Malls, too, are able to control behavior using their "private" status. As William Kowinski succinctly stated in his classic article entitled "The Malling of America":

> Malls are designed for Disney's children. Stores are pressed close together; they have small low façades. In fact, everything about malls is minimized . . . the mall is laid out with few corners and no unused space along store rows so that there are no decisions to make — you just flow on.[31]

Few can deny the attractiveness of mall environments to a generation of retail shoppers drawn to the relative serenity and the climate control of the shopping center. That such malls are a current incarnation of Main Street is borne out by the flourishing social life and the persistence of marketing and craft fairs within today's shopping centers. The relative visual uniformity of shopping centers from coast to coast should not be particularly surprising; they, like Disney's Main Street, are archetypal environments of popular culture (fig. 85). This has caused architectural critics to

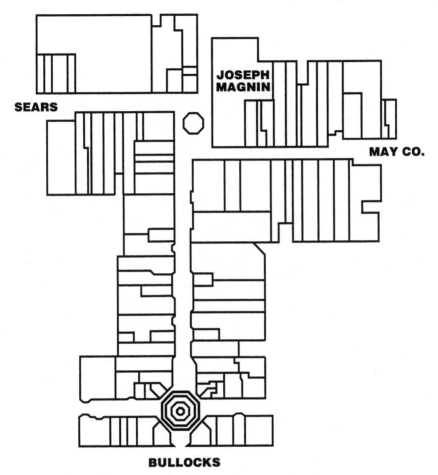

Figure 84. *The Mall as Main Street. This diagram of the South Coast Plaza Shopping Center, a mall in Costa Mesa, California, reveals many of the same design elements seen in Disneyland's Main Street USA — notably an important intersection of four radiating axes (bottom) and a linear thoroughfare running into another point of decision-making where a carousel is positioned (upper center). The similarities are more than coincidental, as many shopping center designers have studied Disney's Main Street. Computer graphic based on a 1975 map in a kiosk at the mall.*

blast the lack of "imagination" of their creators while, ironically, reflecting nostalgically on the days of the *real* American town in, perhaps, the 1880s when, critics contend, there was far greater "individuality."

In reality, of course, this was not the case; as we have seen, by the 1880s Victorian-era Main Streets had developed into highly standardized forms.

Figure 85. *Nodality, an important aspect of urban design, is designed into the Valley River Shopping Center in Eugene, Oregon. Designers placed a small seating area and a cluster of street lights where two pathways, or streets, intersect. 1978 photo by the author.*

Their major architectural components could — like McDonald's — be found from coast to coast. That scholars lament the standardization of the mall while praising the architectural integrity of historic Main Streets reveals the power of nostalgia in affecting even the most educated of our citizens. Whatever else one may say about the typical shopping center, it is an abstracted reincarnation of Main Street, where pedestrians have the right of way over vehicular traffic, where *all* store façades are attractive and where all of the merchants agree to maintain regular hours and carefully control their signage and sales pitches — techniques which avoid the appearance of haphazard or eccentric individualism.

Sociologists have long known that people visit shopping centers for far more than commercial reasons. More than twenty years ago, when Edward Tauber insightfully stated that "not all shopping motives, by any means, are even related to the product,"[32] he introduced the concept of "sociorecreational shopping." Several very revealing articles over the last dozen or more years have shown that shopping centers are important places of social interaction where people may wind up meeting future spouses and friends; where families go simply to stroll, to see people and to be seen by them; where young people go to "hang out" and socialize. Whereas academicians may condemn this type of behavior as manipulated or inauthentic, it is in fact one of the major reasons why commercial and marketing towns have existed for centuries. This may be stated as the fifteenth axiom of Main Street development: *Despite its market-driven businesses, Main Street is primarily a social environment.* Main Street is an integral element in the "collective consciousness," as geographer Alan Baker used the term, to refer to landscape creation and perception that is linked to a national identity.[33]

The Malling of Main Street

Although street pattern that directs such behavior is one of the most enduring aspects of the townscape, it can change. In the 1960s and 1970s, many Main Streets were closed to traffic in the hope that a pedestrian environment would improve retailing downtown (that is, increase the number of people), and Main Street would thus be able to directly compete with shopping centers that were drawing away its trade. Typically, the creation of a downtown mall involves closing the street and providing unlimited pedestrian access to shops. It reduces the noise, danger, and pollution of the automobile, and provides additional — often ample — space for street furniture, benches, sculptures, and lighting. In short, the Main Street Mall introduces the element of nodality lacking in most linear Main Streets.

Morristown, Tennessee, represents an extreme example of the malling of Main Street. In the early 1970s, the town began a major renovation project to bring (or keep) people downtown. In a design very reminiscent of two-story enclosed shopping centers or malls, Morristown built an elaborate reinforced-concrete set of walkways that attempted, in effect, to give pedestrians access to the upper stories as well as the lower (or street-level) shops. The result can best be described as bizarre in that pedestrians and shoppers found themselves face to face with Victorian trim that was intended, by the merchants who originally erected it, to be at the roof or parapet line of the building.

Some towns in southern California and the Midwest sought a compromise by restricting but not curtailing through traffic. In these cases, Main

Figure 86. *Mall or Main Street? Faced with the threat of shopping centers in the 1960s and 1970s, many small towns restricted traffic on Main Street and enhanced the street. Others, like Fillmore, California, beautified it using plantings. Cover sketch from the city's General Plan of 1967.*

Street is considerably narrowed, and trees and shrubs planted to create a more idyllic, verdant landscape at town center. Significantly, the towns that have tried these solutions usually do not have public squares or greens at their center, but have narrow, straight-line Main Streets that planners and developers sense needed "improvements" in order to compete with malls (fig. 86).

Since their development in the 1970s, many downtown malls on Main Street have failed, and many have witnessed the removal of barricades and obstructions that had once closed Main Street to vehicular traffic. In retrospect, these Main Street malls were well intended, but most did not reverse the loss of retail trade. In fact, some critics noted that they may have *accelerated* the decline, because shoppers normally desire to have or keep the retail enterprise or store that they wish to shop at in sight. Parking several blocks away from a store off Main Street actually made the shopping center more, rather than less, attractive. Main Street had faced tough, seemingly untouchable competition, and merchants and town planners realized that something more drastic might be needed to reverse the deterioration on Main Street.

The Disneyfication of Main Street

In the last twenty-five years, Main Street has become influential in the merchandising and marketing of services and products. In a few cases, historic towns actually have managed to overcome shopping-center competition and have been revitalized through aggressive preservation activity. Medina, Ohio, is a fine example of a town that has used its "image" in marketing; an anecdote will help to describe its power on individuals. In 1988, I was driving from Columbus to Cleveland, Ohio, and a friend was following me in another vehicle because he needed to continue on from that point. We had driven through several towns including Medina, and we paused for lunch just before reaching Cleveland. Upon stopping, the friend who had been following me in the other car walked up to me and said, "What was the name of that town that we just went through? It was fabulous . . . like stepping back in time." I said that the town was Medina, Ohio, and that he had indeed stepped back in time, in a manner of speaking, because the townscape that he saw was very carefully engineered. I had studied Medina in the early 1970s and have been recording the fascinating "historic" changes that continue to take place on Main Street there.

There is an interesting story behind the redevelopment of Medina's townscape. The town had entered a period of decline in the 1950s and early 1960s. Faced with the possibility of vacating their historic building downtown on the square, the Phoenix Bank took a radical, rather revolutionary step: its directors decided that they would rehabilitate the Phoenix

Building instead of building anew by either tearing down the building or moving to the edge of town. The Phoenix Bank spent more than a million dollars on restoring the bank to its original splendor. Upon its re-opening, the Phoenix Bank became a landmark on the square — an example of initiative applied to redeveloping and stabilizing urban decline that had been decimating many communities across the country.

Merchants, too, had been pondering the question of how to revitalize Medina, for a small shopping center on its outskirts had begun to lure trade away from the downtown. Should they consider urban renewal? Should they modernize to compete with the shopping center? Like some of the directors of the Phoenix Bank, a number of the merchants had visited Disneyland some years earlier on trips, and they agreed to revitalize Medina instead of tearing down the downtown. Some noted that they had "something as good as, and perhaps better than, Disneyland, for it was really historic, an original," as one merchant told me. Thus began the process of Medina's restoration in the early 1960s. The county courthouse, a Second Empire–style Victorian-era building, had been slated for demolition, but the merchants and many others in town objected, urging instead that the county restore the building rather than tear it down. The Medina County courthouse restoration was a classic example of revitalization, and it, too, served as a catalyst for the rest of the area around the square to develop.

Being one of the towns in Ohio's Western Reserve district, Medina has a large open square in the center (fig. 44) — a design rather reminiscent of the often-romanticized New England village green. It is this area around the square in Medina that has become a treasure. The literature about the revitalization of Main Street by Medinians is quite instructive, for it has political overtones as well as an underlying economic reality. The literature produced by the bank features color photographs and a historical account of how the community developed and was restored. One phrase is particularly revealing: "Main Street USA — guarded by towering oaks and maples, and a fiercely protective citizenry — public square Medina has become renowned as an example of one of the most effectively restored business sections in America."[34]

Those words are featured next to the American flag flying over the landscape of the public square, which is almost completely surrounded by two- and three-story Victorian commercial buildings that appear to be part of a movie set (fig. 87). These words are quite revealing because there is, technically speaking, no street actually named "Main Street" in Medina! The term "Main Street USA" is right out of Disneyland, and it serves the community well in marketing the restored downtown.

Medina has indeed become something of a stage setting in that new construction mocks the old, which is to say, a number of the buildings around the square may look old even though they were built just a few years ago. Service stations and buildings housing services that were less attractive — and less cost-effective in an area of increasing rents as restoration proceeded — have actually been torn down as property values increased for lots facing the historic square. On their sites one now finds new buildings built to look historic. These may deceive the current visitor into thinking that the entire townscape is Victorian in appearance and always has been since the 1880s. In fact, new construction in Medina has filled formerly open gaps in the townscape and also removed some less attractive or unappealing buildings that did not appear to be historic. Some critics felt that urban revitalization in Medina had turned into preservation frenzy.

Around Medina's square, the merchants were urged to paint their buildings in certain more "historic" colors, and the result of this effort is highly detailed, multicolored trim in which a particular façade may have as many as three, and sometimes five, individual colors. Regarding the subject of historic colors on Main Street, however, many architects in the 1970s and 1980s consulted contemporary guidebooks and style books from the period 1890–1910 to determine which colors were popular. They followed directions, accenting the elaborate trim with varied colors. Nevertheless, a careful look at historic photographs reveals that buildings on real Main Streets were often painted in fairly simple color schemes; white, buff, and green being common. Thus, the renovation architects may have introduced colors more typical of the elaborate bay-windowed Victorian "painted lady" townhouse of San Francisco, or Walt Disney's versions of the small town as seen in the Disney parks, than what Main Street actually looked like ca. 1900. Preservation architects also recommended that certain historic sign types be installed to replace more modern signage. Thus, one sees historic serif-styled "old-fashioned" lettering on signs for modern businesses. These and other "improvements" create the impression that everything in the downtown is truly historic; thus, by stepping

Figure 87. *Medina's public square is the site of numerous public events and serves as a powerful node. Built in the early 1980s, its Victorian gazebo or bandstand is a copy of a historic bandstand in Belleville, Ohio. 1986 photo by the author.*

into Medina's public square, one does indeed seem to be stepping back in time. Along with the restored Medina County courthouse, the Phoenix Block remains the town's major landmark; but many other significant buildings, many of which have been restored, surround Medina's square and help create the impression that time has stopped here.

One of the centerpieces creating this effect is Medina's gazebo, or bandstand, on the public square, as seen in figure 87. This seemingly historic structure serves as a place for public oratory, band concerts, and other events. It has a high Victorian gingerbread quality, and appears to the visitor as if it has been there for a century, when in fact it was constructed recently — in the early 1980s — based on the plan of a historic gazebo in the central Ohio community of Belleville. In point of fact,

Figure 88. *A newly constructed historic gazebo or bandstand in Grapevine, Texas, has become a symbol of the town's revitalization efforts. Its image is seen on the window of a drug store on Main Street. 1994 photo by the author.*

Medina never had a bandstand this ornate, nor one in this particular position, even though it is pictured on the official "Historic City of Medina" letterhead stationery. The early bandstand in Medina was a much more modest structure that served similar purposes, but never looked quite as grand as the one that stands today. One might say that Medinians decided to build a bandstand of the kind that *should* have existed rather than one that actually existed. Thus the visitor to the square in Medina today sees a townscape that is actually *more* Victorian in appearance than it was during the Victorian period! Thus are images and archetypes created and sustained.

The bandstands or gazebos seen in many public open spaces (such as squares) today are in fact somewhat more common now than they were just thirty years ago. Those that somehow managed to survive the rebuildings of the twentieth century are authentic, but many are replicas of others; some, in fact, are fanciful versions of bandstands. Nevertheless, they appear to be quite accurate to the casual observer, for they seem to fit in their public spaces. When confronted with an empty lot along Main Street in Grapevine, Texas, developers erected a bandstand — and almost instantly created a significant *node* along Main Street where none had existed. That bandstand has become a symbol of the town's revitalization efforts (fig. 88). These bandstands, of course, are quite evocative: they signify social function; they are places from which music, speeches, and political oratory emanate; they are associated with a kind of nostalgia on the one hand and patriotism on the other. They are landmarks where the public comes together to discuss politics as well as to socialize and to be entertained, to hear music and to be inspired. These, too, often owe much to Disney and others who romanticize history and urge us to recreate the past in the contemporary American town.

As one studies Main Street revitalizations, it is apparent that they may begin with the community's original design, but that they usually enhance it. Among the most common techniques for making Main Street work as a design is the enhancement of any nodal space, or even the wholesale creation of such nodes that now serve as greens, vest-pocket parks, or squares. The nodes help introduce an element of centrality and enclosure, and in so doing attempt to influence our perceptions of Main Street as a safe social environment.

Cinema and television further reinforce the image of the small town as a secure place developed around a central node: thus, the fictional but otherwise unremarkable railroad-oriented prairie town of Black Hawk, Nebraska, that was the setting of Willa Cather's *My Ántonia* (1918) was transformed, at the hands of USA television network writers, into a rather idyllic town developed around a beautiful public square faced by trim commercial buildings. Although Cather only briefly alludes to a few of the commercial buildings in town and never reveals its layout, in this 1995 made-for-television movie version of *My Ántonia*, much of the activity in town takes place near the town's prominent gazebo. The theory that historically recreated villages and towns can further influence popular images of such places is borne out by the fact that this version of *My Ántonia* was filmed at the Stuhr Museum of the Prairie Pioneers in Grand Island, Nebraska. A collection of historic structures moved to the park-like setting created the ambience of a frontier agricultural town. Other simulated historic villages and towns, including Ohio Village, have served as movie sets — yet another example of popular culture further influencing popular culture via "edu-tainment." This process has become so pervasive that it can be stated categorically that when Main Streets are revitalized, they are often redesigned through a process that de-emphasizes their linearity and emphasizes (often enhances) their nodality.

Walt Disney helped sell the combination of small public square and linear Main Street as a prevailing image of small-town USA; in the latter half of the twentieth century, that design pervades old and new retail environments alike. In that some of our real towns have copied the inspiration of Walt Disney in attempting to capture the appearance, even the essence, of small-town prosperity and values, we witness a remarkable example of life imitating art. The nostalgic small town or hometown centers in many themed places of popular culture, including the Six Flags Over Texas park (and successor Six Flags parks around the United States) and Marriott's Great America — all of which developed in the 1960s and 1970s — owe much to Disney. The hometown square at the Marriott's Great America theme park near San Jose, California, requires the visitor to walk under the railroad tracks (as at Disneyland), entering the hometown square before moving into different areas. Of course, the hometown square features a gazebo, a fire station, and a number of other familiar but romanticized buildings designed to create feelings of nostalgia. As a way of verifying the underlying educational purpose of this environment, a plaque at the entrance to Marriott's Great America states:

> Marriott's Great America is dedicated with pride to Mr. & Mrs. Jay Willard Marriott who began, as so many have begun, with only each other. Together they dreamed, and because this is America where dreams can come true, theirs became the worldwide Marriott Corporation through their persistence, labor, courage and faith. As you go through this park, may you enjoy many fun-filled hours, and in leaving, take with you a lasting sense of the true greatness of America.

These words are instructive, reminding the student of the American landscape that theme parks and reconstructed images of America at different periods constitute part of the popular-history curriculum as written by shapers of popular culture. The visitor may leave with the impression that life was more meaningful and of higher quality in the past, but the lesson is also one of hope for the future. Suspending disbelief, some visitors may believe that these theme park–style landscapes accurately reflect the character of the small town in the past. Such landscapes are at once

optimistic and didactic; they embody the belief that people can be in-
structed to develop such values through instructional (if entertaining) experiences. In this regard, such landscapes are indeed educational as well
as entertaining, and it should be remembered that Walt Disney was, above
all, a tremendously successful educator — which may help explain academicians' disdain for him.

Disney was also something of a secular humanist, and thus one looks in
vain for a church on Main Street USA. Disney's abiding faith in material
progress helps explain why Main Street is such a popular icon: it is typically American in that it features the material culture of prosperity as the
underpinnings of economic security and community strength. Whereas
the initial popularity of the New England village in the nineteenth century centers on the romanticized theme of religious and spiritual values,
Main Street USA helped romanticize the small-town entrepreneur's secular role — and helped assure its nearly sacred place in an American culture that sought to balance material attainments with social consciousness. Viewed retrospectively, Main Street USA is as much a statement of
the Cold War as it is Disney's early-twentieth-century childhood. Whatever Disney's motives, one must credit him with popularizing the words
"Main Street USA" that now appear so commonly as the names of business enterprises along Main Street (for example, Main Street Hardware in
Georgetown, Ohio [fig. 89], or Main Street Ltd. in Shelby, Ohio, or Main
Street Gifts in Grapevine, Texas). As historians, we know that this reference to Main Street is recent nomenclature: when businesses developed
on Main Street in the past, they would not normally be named "Main
Street" at all, but would instead bear the names of the entrepreneurs who
developed the business, for example, Smith's Hardware. Main Street was
a rather anonymous concept; Mr. Smith would rather have one know
the business as his enterprise. In the past, an enterprise's commercial personality was associated with an individual or family, not a generic place-
marketing concept such as Main Street. Disney, of course, changed all
that forever in 1955.

The National Main Street Program

This discussion of image building based on phrases or words (Main
Street) and images (historic commercial buildings) brings us, inevitably,
to the National Main Street Program. As originally conceived by the National Trust for Historic Preservation, the Main Street Program was in-

Figure 89. *When the word "Main Street" appears in the names of businesses, they are very likely new businesses seeking a historic identity. Main Street Hardware in George-town, Ohio, provides a case in point. 1978 photo by the author.*

tended to reverse economic decline in small towns. Developed as an inspiration on the part of historical architect Mary Means and her colleagues at the National Trust in 1977, the prototype Main Street program selected three towns (Hot Springs, South Dakota; Galesburg, Illinois; and Madison, Indiana) that were desperately in need of revitalization and rehabilitation. The Main Street Program assisted merchants by forming an alliance under the leadership of a Main Street manager. He or she would help develop a positive image for the town, and this image would help reverse deterioration of the declining downtown. Preservationist William Murtagh identified four major areas in which the Main Street program seeks to rehabilitate buildings and revitalize businesses: design, promotion, cooperation, and economics.[35] The Main Street program requires team-like cooperation; merchants must agree to maintain similar hours, to restore buildings, and to develop a positive, even aggressive, attitude toward marketing their resources in the hope of winning customers. It creates a team out of individuals, uniting them as they seek to promote the Main Street by building an identifiable, marketable image.

The developers of the National Trust's Main Street Program would no doubt be appalled to think that they owed a debt to Walt Disney, but the reader will recall that it was Walt Disney who pioneered this type of enterprise for the American shopping public in 1955. As popular culture specialist Margaret King recently noted, "it was Disney who first taught Americans how to *see*, that is, *visualize*, Main Street as they experienced it in Disneyland."[36] Twenty years before the Main Street Program, Disney helped bring Main Street into the public consciousness. As in the case of the Medinians who learned to see, that is, actually *appreciate*, their community after experiencing Disneyland, many Americans returned from Disneyland to their home towns and learned to see them anew. Disney packaged Main Street as a commercial environment that was patently "historical" and aesthetic, and helped pave the way for later efforts to revitalize Main Street. Disney, too, pioneered teamwork in building and marketing images of place to the public, much as the revitalizers of "real" Main Street communities do today.

The National Main Street Program has developed surely and steadily over the years; its namesake is still run by the National Trust for Historic Preservation in Washington D.C., whose Main Street office assists many communities throughout the country. But success is contagious, and the states themselves have also spun off incarnations of the Main Street Program using the ideology and methodology that was developed by the National Trust in the late 1970s. These may operate out of departments of economic development or tourism, though most work rather closely with State Historic Preservation Offices. Some, like the program in Texas, operate out of state historical commissions. And so, creating economic opportunity on Main Street has gone hand-in-hand with the historic preservation of Main Street. The program has a very visible manifestation; it has encouraged merchants to remove more modern trim that might have enshrouded a building to reveal older architectural features underneath. The program has also worked carefully to ensure that management is effective along Main Street, and that Main Street merchants work together in carefully promoting and orchestrating an "image" of downtown (fig. 90).

The cumulative or overall effect of the Main Street Program has been to either stop change along Main Street or to reverse it, so that the street-

Figure 90. *Lampasas, a Main Street Program town in Texas, bears the look of restoration and redevelopment based on a four-part approach to revitalization. Such communities can often be distinguished by carefully selected paint schemes and a high degree of maintenance that preserves — and sometimes backdates the appearance of — the historic commercial buildings. 1994 photo by the author.*

scapes are often backdated in appearance. Sometimes through the placing of awnings or the careful selection of signage and paint, these buildings begin to take on a visual uniformity that unites them as a retail marketing package — much in the way Walt Disney marketed his Main Street. From the prototype program in the late 1970s, Main Street spinoffs developed in Arizona, Texas, Kentucky, and twenty-five other states; by the early 1990s, over half the states in the United States had a Main Street Program (fig. 91). At first, most of these states implemented perhaps three to five test cases, towns that had considerable historic character but were economically uncompetitive and were threatened with the loss of their historic character. Many of these communities became successful, stabilizing the attrition that had earlier occurred on Main Street. Subsequently, others were spawned, and today there are several hundred communities across the U.S. that can claim to be, or have been, Main Street communities.

Main Street has become an icon that is both commercial and educational. Main Street persists because we instinctively believe that architecture and design affect behavior and can enable us to keep a sense of our

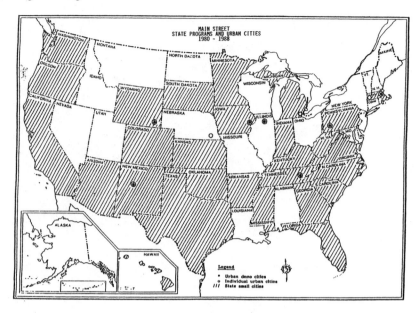

Figure 91. *This map of Main Street Program participation shows that the majority of states possessed Main Street communities by the early 1990s and that these were distributed from coast to coast. In the mid-1980s, the program was expanded to assist selected cities. Courtesy Main Street Center, National Trust for Historic Preservation.*

roots, a valuable asset in times of great social and economic change. As one observer noted, "a Main Street based on human size and human scale makes it possible to connect intuitively with our ancestors." [37] Preserving Main Streets seems natural — in retrospect, inevitable — because they are significant social and economic investments. Their preservation, then, would seem to ensure that we preserve the best of our past, and the best of our historic character as a people.

THE IMAGIC PRESERVATION OF MAIN STREET

As I have noted elsewhere, historic landscapes like Main Streets are preserved in many ways. [38] A continuum exists from actual preservation to visually preserved landscapes rendered photographically or artistically. Among the most interesting small-town landscapes are those that are "imagically preserved," such as the Main Street scenes that appear as murals on the sides of buildings. Here the viewer sees a depiction of a long-vanished scene from, say, the Victorian era superimposed on an otherwise contemporary or modern scene. When done creatively, the effect can be stunning, for the side of the building becomes a window into the

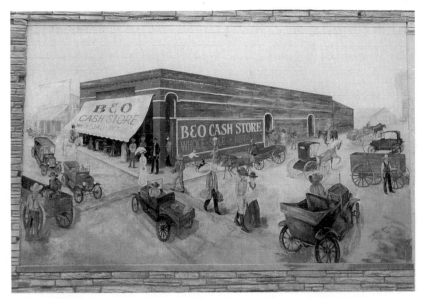

Figure 92. *Visual re-creation: Main Street is given an element of historical drama in this colorful, historically themed mural painted on the side of a commercial building in Temple, Oklahoma. These murals are often commissioned by local historical societies in close cooperation with merchants on Main Street. 1994 photo by the author.*

past (fig. 92). Some murals are more or less photographic reproductions and others exhibit more artistic license, but all such murals juxtapose the "real" current scene with the imagined or vanished scene, often to great effect. Stunning use may be made of black-and-white murals that seem more authentic in that they duplicate the limited technology of film (black or sepia and white) during historic periods; others, in color, present images of towns in the polychromatic intensity that is normally associated with paintings. Whereas the latter may seem less credible historically, they invite the observer into a colorful picture-book world that, like our storybook memories of childhood, has vanished with the passage of time.

Images of places like Main Street are created and perpetuated through a complex process of selection and abstraction. They must be repeated if the image is to be accepted by the public: repeated replication gives credibility to otherwise selected imagery. In the late nineteenth century, as new technology for reproducing photographs in books became widespread and cost-effective, landscape and streetscape engravings became passé. One contemporary observer criticized them, stating, "Inasmuch as engravings are usually cut from sketches, drawn perhaps by enthused artists, perfect satisfaction is not given, but with photographic views, which cannot lie, argument as to truthfulness is unnecessary."[39] We are less naive about photography today, for we recognize that photographers have agendas. This has led historians of photography to a more critical interpretation: "Photographs don't lie, but liars take photographs."[40]

One could expand upon this sentiment by noting that *all* images are selective, that is, are filtered statements about the design and content of streetscape. A person sketching a townscape may select or omit certain elements; even entire buildings present in the real scene may not make it into the final scene. Sometimes, photographers even perform seeming darkroom magic by adding or subtracting, as when a trolley or streetcar line is added to make Main Street appear more progressive,[41] or when something ugly is removed by "dodging" to make the scene more attractive.

These acts may appear fraudulent to objective historians, but we now realize that the seemingly simple process of photographing and thus preserving an actual scene is actually a complex process of selection that works at various levels. Therefore a student of streetscapes should always ask several important questions when encountering a historic photo (or for that matter, *any* photo). The first relates to the agenda of the photographer: *Who* took the picture? The second relates to the content of the scene: *Why* did the photographer point his or her camera in one direction (say, down Main Street) and not another? Although one should always remember that historic photos may have been "cropped" in the process of printing, many historic photos survive virtually intact — and tell us much about the viewpoint or perspective of the photographer. The fact that so many photographers selected a position just off-center on Main Street and photographed both sides of the street is revealing: the photographer evidently thought that this composition accurately depicted the scene, but it did much more. It also revealed the photographer's sense of perspective and the natural order: Main Street was a synergistic composition, more than simply a street flanked by an often matching assemblage of buildings in otherwise empty space. In fact, Main Street is charged with the drama of people and their conveyances moving and interacting. In a manner of speaking, then, the architecture of Main Street forms the bookends that capture the human drama on the street itself.

The process of selection, however, does not stop here. After a photograph is taken and developed, an even more elaborate process begins. What happens to the photograph itself after it is printed and sold? Is it filed away in a drawer or box? In a scrapbook? Or is it published as a postcard, or in a weekly newspaper or magazine? The same types of questions should be asked years later regarding historic photographs: What happens to such photos when they are found by a later generation? Are they simply discarded, unenthusiastically re-filed, or enthusiastically shown to others, perhaps even published? Why do certain photographs (or particular types of scenes, like Main Street itself) re-appear in numerous publications while others languish in boxes or meet their fate by being destroyed?

Clearly, this process of replication (of individual or generic scenes) is one of the key factors in perpetuating images of places like Main Street. The fact that so many photos of either individual buildings, rows of buildings on one side of the street, or the entire more-or-less-symmetrical streetscape are recorded and preserved reveals an implicit validation or acceptance of the commercial activity of the past. Such photos reaffirm this activity at several levels: at the more mundane, they validate the roles of both the merchant and the architect; at another, the collective role of merchants and consumers; and ultimately the collective, nearly cosmological, importance of town platter-architect-merchant and public in the creation of memorable places.

The fact that so many of our perceptions of place in the twentieth century are colored by moving images — including cinema and video — not only complicates the process; it has increased our expectations. When we stroll down Disney's Main Street, we become participants in a much larger drama that is redefining how we perceive place: we are, at one level, simply participants interacting with the actual streetscape, but, because the streetscape itself was designed as a set of sorts, we also become actors in a collective cultural drama focussing on the reenactment and reinterpretation of history. Thus, Disney's Main Street (and, by definition, historic restorations of Main Streets in real towns) puts the observer in a unique position. In the process of consumption and commodification on the one hand, he is a consumer of the landscape, and, on the other, actually becomes one of the elements or objects consumed by others; the process, like film-making itself, forever confuses consumption with object, and commerce with art. That justifies our viewing Main Street in its many

Figure 93. *Main Street in miniature: scale models of Main Street are quite popular among model railroaders, who have had highly detailed models of commercial buildings available since the late 1970s. Modelers purchase individual buildings and combine them into miniature townscapes, as seen in this view of the Main Street of Mineral Wells on the HO scale Texas & New Mexico Railroad. 1994 photo by the author.*

forms as the ultimate success story in American environmental design and social engineering.

As images of our Main Streets become more cherished, they have been duplicated in miniature. By this I refer to more than the fairly common technique, used by theme-park designers, of making a replica of stores and shops slightly smaller than their prototypes. I am referring, rather, to the actual miniaturization of a place so that one can *possess* it at a scale or proportion of, say, 1 to 50 or 1 to 100. Thus, a miniaturized Main Street could be reproduced in about two or three feet of space. Whereas modelling Main Streets was, until fairly recently, a rather tedious task for model railroaders, the introduction of injection-molded plastic and cast-resin models of common Victorian-era Main Street buildings in the late 1970s has ensured that Main Streets are immortalized on thousands of model-railroad layouts (fig. 93). The William K. Walthers Company of Milwaukee, Wisconsin, markets a wide range of Main Street Victorian-era commercial buildings as part of their "cornerstone" series, and at least three other companies have created similar miniature buildings. The accuracy of these buildings is stunning, for almost every detail of their Victorian-era design is reproduced: as an advertisement claims, "now you can recapture the excitement and nostalgia of Main Street on your layout with the 'Main Street USA' collection from Walthers."[42] These Main Street model buildings are available in several popular scales, including HO (1:87) and N scale (1:160). Moreover, Dover Publications markets several "easy-to-build, cut and assemble" assemblages of historic buildings in HO scale, including the early American seaport, frontier town, early New England village, and 1920s Main Street. These popular books feature full-color cardboard-cutout buildings that are easy to assemble. Several Victorian bandstands are, naturally, available in miniature. Significantly, the words "bring back" or "return to" the past are often associated with the miniaturization of Main Street — a testimony of its nostalgic power in late-twentieth-century America. As the sixteenth, and last, axiom of Main Street development, I would note: *The miniaturization of Main Street signifies its acceptance as an integral part of American life and leisure.* By assuming a place in the home, Main Street joins the ranks of dollhouses and miniature trains as an endearing symbol of America's past. Miniaturization is, in a sense, the ultimate in commodification, for we embrace Main Street as our own personal property when we bring it into our homes through a process that parallels the purchase of other home products: model manufacturers replicate and market Main Street, and we purchase it. Taking a lesson from shapers of popular culture like Walt Disney, model railroaders and others who buy these miniatures imagineer them into townscapes. In so doing, they redefine the Main Street of the American past to fit their present emotional needs and future aspirations.

CONCLUSION: REVISITING MAIN STREET

For every historic downtown that has been preserved in murals or miniature, or salvaged or stabilized by efforts like the Main Street Program, however, there are many others that stand forlorn and abandoned (fig. 94). In these communities, the boarded-up downtown area is an indicator that hard economic times have fallen on Main Street. These remind us of the poignant words of Iris Dement's song "Our Town," in which the listener is taken on a nostalgic trip through the small town, including Main Street, "where I bought my first car"; but each phrase ends with the lament that "nothing good ever lasts in our town, our town." In "My Hometown," Bruce Springsteen paints an even more depressing picture, noting that

Figure 94. *A forlorn row of commercial buildings, with some of the stores in ruins, faces the public square in Archer City, Texas. Inspiration for, and location of,* The Last Picture Show, *a novel and film about the declining fortunes of people in a small Texas town, the streetscape is a reminder that the survival of Main Street depends on a strong local economy and the concerted efforts of merchants and residents. 1994 photo by the author.*

"Main Street's closed down," and "no one wants to come down here anymore." Change is sweeping the country, and Springsteen sees his hometown as signifying the end of an era. It is not coincidental that Americans have come to think of change as threatening at exactly the time they have become a history-conscious nation. Because change oftentimes indicates an economic realignment that is a more or less "natural" process of life, the dilemma faced by Main Street may simply be a reflection of the change that has always characterized our turbulent history. When we hope to preserve all Main Streets, we are being decidedly unrealistic about the selection process that makes some enterprises survive and others die.

This study of Main Street confirms that we have transformed our real Main Streets, many of which were linear, into essentially enclosed or nodal spaces. We have done this both psychologically (in that we want to believe American towns in the past were more nodal than they actually were) and physically (in that we have transformed many real towns by creating nodes in them in relatively recent times). Texas writer Joyce Gibson

Roach recently compared her town of Jacksboro, with its courthouse square, to fellow writer Robert Flynn's town of Chillicothe, with its linear Main Street. In *The Bounty of Texas* (1990) Roach chided Flynn by noting that "you simply cannot trust any town that is not built on a square. A square speaks of antiquity, of stability, and the shape of a town's personality." To use the words of William Taft, an architectural history intern with the Indiana Heritage Commission who wrote on courthouse squares, "It's Hip to be Square," because "these squares have served successive generations of Hoosiers as commercial centers, spaces for social and political gatherings, shady parks for summer relaxation."[43] The symbolic connotations are important: it is not only hip to be square in the sense of appreciating central places; it is hip to emphasize their role as historic places, and by extension urge their rediscovery (even their re-creation) in order to preserve or reproduce the sense of community that their prototypes inspire in a culture longing for community.

For many people, Main Street seems to be constant or permanent, but it has changed, and continues to change despite the desire of many to freeze it in time. Our popular culture openly laments the passing of Main Street. On an episode of the television sitcom *Evening Shade* that aired on January 11, 1993, the hundred-year-old mercantile store on Main Street owned by Whit's family is in danger of being torn down. As the cast laments the new, impersonal discount store that will replace the family store on the outskirts of town, one of the townsfolk voices the opinion, "The further we get from Main Street, the worse this town gets." This, of course, is a popular sentiment: at the same time we condemn what is modern (and the future in general), we drive to the edge of town to new stores where prices and selection are better than can be found on Main Street.

Main Street is often preserved as a group of specialized retail stores as our culture romanticizes, preserves, and recreates it in its New England or Victorian Midwestern guises, but it should be realized that Main Street also survives in its modern incarnations, including the shopping mall and the strip shopping center. These strip centers are certainly less attractive to many critics and preservationists than Victorian-era Main Streets, but they also embody the inevitable relationship that exists between the pedestrian, her vehicle, and the merchant. Although these latest incarnations of commercial development — the ubiquitous commercial strips with their Seven-Eleven, Blockbuster Video, WalMart, or Speedy Mart stores — sometimes thrive at the expense of a community's original Main Street, they perform much the same function as the original; they simply and honestly perpetuate the connection between the stationary merchant and the mobile customer. Today, of course, the customer is in an automobile and he will drive from one place to another with great ease. Nevertheless, the customer still patronizes commercial enterprises as an individual in search of both products and services. If he forgoes much unnecessary socializing in the process, that is because time has become an increasingly important element in affecting mobility and shaping our perceptions.[44] These shopping strips, then, are an inevitable expression of the mobility that we have all come to demand, but it would require a radical reshaping of our attitudes toward "architecture" in order for them to be accepted as significant. If we were more objective, we would see them in the same light as, say, Victorian buildings: as statements of their era.

The fact that even the most contemporary of shopping centers and shopping strips now facing America's streets and highways may look to earlier Main Streets for their inspiration is seen in the Williamsburg-inspired Williamsburg Shopping Center in Katy, Texas (fig. 95). The designers of this shopping center chose to emulate late-eighteenth-century colonial architecture, with its substantial gabled firewalls, massive chimneys, and simple gabled dormers. To better perpetuate the colonial-historical theme, gas lamps line the street — actually the parking lot — in front of the stores in this road-oriented shopping center.

Rather than bemoan the loss of Main Street and condemn strip commercial areas, then, one would do well to see them as part of the rich visual variety of the American landscape today — a variety that reflects how much America has changed in the twentieth century. One may take some solace in realizing that, if current preservation trends continue, Americans may find themselves anxiously preserving threatened shopping strips in, say, the year 2050, when these places too become "historic." After all, in the early 1950s, on the eve of Disney's rediscovery of late-Victorian architecture, the buildings of the 1900 era were considered so much obsolete garish rubble by many Americans. Disney helped change that, but a dwindling number of people still prefer demolition and new construction over preservation. In retrospect, then, we might consider ourselves fortunate that we have so many options: preserved historic Main Streets that offer character and charm, shopping centers or malls that offer climate-

Figure 95. *The Williamsburg Shopping Center in Katy, Texas, was constructed in the mid-1980s and emulates late-eighteenth-century colonial architecture. 1994 photo by the author.*

controlled comfort in shopping, and also the automobile-oriented strips that offer shoppers a variety of lower-order goods and services in a hurry.

On revisiting (which is to say, reinterpreting) Main Street, I have presented sixteen basic axioms. These, it is hoped, will help the reader to understand the principles affecting the design of Main Street. They are restated, and slightly reworded, into the themes outlined below. Main Street:

1. Reveals a diversity of origins: If traced to its roots, Main Street architecture is seen to evolve from residential and/or vernacular as well as more formal and public and commercial building forms, and as such represents a dialogue between "high" and "low" culture.
2. Is the sum of individual buildings yielding to grouping: In Main Street development, a series of individual structures, many of them originally residences, become "townscape" by being placed side by side, or end to end, to maximize the use of valuable space in the commercial sections of communities.

3. Showcases architecture as image-builder: The façade of buildings on Main Street become more important than any other elevation because they face the principal thoroughfare. Thus, Main Street puts its best face (or façade) forward.

4. Is a reflection of the economy: If building or remodeling occurs during a period of prosperity, the resulting Main Street architecture will have a relatively uniform appearance in that a popular architectural style will sweep across all of the façades, helping to unify them visually.

5. Shows that materials influence design: The prevalent building material for architectural construction also helps to dictate the actual form that structures will take, because architects and designers actively seek to employ new materials that beautify, or reduce costs.

6. Demonstrates that form follows access: Because people's mobility affects their access to buildings, and because the speed with which they move in turn determines how they view structures and assemblages of buildings, the shape of Main Street architecture is, in part, determined by the prevalent type of transportation.

7. Interprets disaster as opportunity: The developmental and economic forces operative on Main Street *before* a disaster will be continued, and intensified, as a consequence of that disaster, in effect compressing the time in which changes occur, as merchants and builders use the disaster as an opportunity to build in the latest, most popular, styles.

8. Reaffirms location as asset: Even a short Main Street exhibits considerable spatial difference from location to location. The more visible or accessible a property on Main Street, the more valuable it will be as commercial property, and the more elaborate the resulting building will be.

9. Is a reflection of distant and local innovation: Although the most significant innovations in Main Street design occurred in urban areas and spread to the frontier, local decisions that developed on the frontier also affected the design of Main Street.

10. Is more than economic: Main Street is both functional and aesthetic in that design is related to deeply held values about the way space should be arranged and how people should relate to it and to each other.

11. Reflects a shared but hierarchically influenced process of design: Main Street develops as designers conceive and then share an image of how a town should look; this information normally diffuses from larger to smaller places, that is, cities to towns, but it is ultimately dependent on local townsfolk accepting these design treatments.

12. Is a result of editing at numerous levels: The image of Main Street that reaches the public is often selected or edited to depict what the street should look like, rather than a random view of it.

13. Reflects attitudes toward the future and the past: Popular, collectively held interpretations of a community's past affect how its historic structures and other features will be treated. A contempt for the past will translate into the destruction of the reminders of the past, while a romanticizing of it will translate into the preservation of its historic fabric.

14. Is a setting in which social dramas unfold: Main Street is essentially a stage upon which several types of human dramas are performed simultaneously, each character or actor in the drama having a designated role (e.g., consumer, merchant, designer) that is dependent on his or her relationship to the "set."

15. Reflects the social life of a community: Despite its market-driven businesses, Main Street is primarily a social environment in that everyone involved in the process of Main Street development hopes to affect interpersonal behavior through the creation of spaces that concentrate populations and encourage people (merchant and customer) to interact.

16. Is iconically very persistent, being perpetuated through replication and miniaturization: The widespread appearance of Main Street in imagic and miniature form signifies its acceptance as an integral part of American life and leisure.

It is hoped that readers will discover other axioms as they study Main Streets from other perspectives. This study stresses that American Main Streets, like Americans themselves, must be viewed both as individuals and as parts of a larger tapestry that includes a regional and national identity. I have attempted to demonstrate that America's Main Streets — from the early town centers to modern Main Street–inspired shopping centers — are a panoply of rich designs and patterns adopted by individuals in search of identity. If Main Streets are ultimately statements about people's relationships to one another, this explains why an entrepreneur, who, when asked why he built a theatre on the Main Street of Wilmington, Ohio, said he "built it for himself, since he had rather have a monument on Main Street than in the cemetery."[45]

If one lesson stands out from my thirty years of exploring and recording America's Main Streets, it is that they — like all American landscapes — are more than simply buildings arranged in certain patterns: when studied carefully, they offer extremely important insights for students of American culture, architecture, and design. Everywhere on Main Street we see *time* (change or stasis and preservation) and *space* (patterns of local, regional, national, even international traits) interacting. These help individuals create and sustain social networks as they in turn create *place* in America. Although we might be more cautious than the fictional character in the novel *Stations: An Imagined Journey*, who believed that "places are the only things you can trust,"[46] places like Main Street are as concrete a manifestation of American values as are any statements — written or spoken — that we have on record. Main Street is, in fact, one of our most important and persistent statements about America in time and space.

EPILOGUE

This book began with a quote by historian Henry Howe and will end with one that might prompt us to be more patient and understanding as we go about interpreting America's Main Streets. Next to two photos of himself — one photo taken in 1846 when he was a young man of thirty and the other in 1886 as an older man of seventy — the elderly Henry Howe wrote the following words in a personally autographed copy of his *Historical Collections of Ohio*, now in the archives of the Ohio Historical Society. In typically Victorian prose, ninety-two-year-old Howe penned a poignant message that can refer either to life or to the places like Main Street that he so loved:

Time changes us all, and happy that change where justice, truth, and love which can know no change grow in beauty with the passing years.

NOTES

INTRODUCTION

1. Larry Nelson, "Here's Howe: Ohio's Wandering Historian," *Timeline* 3, no. 6 (December 1986–7): 44.

2. See, for example, Henry Howe's histories of individual states, such as Ohio and Virginia, as well as his *Historical Collections of the Great West*.

3. Manon Pavy and Fritz Wagner, "Focusing the Old Downtown on Specialty Retail for Economic Survivals: The Transition of Ponchatoula, Louisiana," *Small Town* 24, no. 3 (November–December 1993): 18.

4. "Welcome to Main Street USA," Walther's advertisement in *Railroad Model Craftsman* 63, no. 5 (October 1993): 55.

5. "Move Your Playroom to Main Street" advertisement, *Family Fun* 3, no. 8 (October 1994): 38.

6. Richard Francaviglia, "Main Street Revisited."

7. See, for example, John Jakle, *The American Small Town: Twentieth Century Place Images*.

8. D. W. Meinig, "Symbolic Landscapes: Models of American Community."

9. The term archetype, as popularized by psychologist Carl Jung, refers to an inherited idea that is derived from earlier times and passed through the unconscious; I also use it in its more commonly understood sense, as prototype or "perfect example."

SECTION 1. TIME AND MAIN STREET

1. James Fenimore Cooper, "American and European Scenery Compared" in Motley F. Deakin, *The Home Book of the Picturesque* (New York: G. P. Putnam, 1852): 65.

2. See, for example, Fred Kniffen, "Folk Housing: Key to Diffusion"; Allen G. Noble, *Wood, Brick, and Stone: The North American Settlement Landscape*; Peirce Lewis, "Common Houses, Cultural Spoor," *Landscape* 19, no. 2 (1975): 1–22; Richard Pillsbury and Andrew Kardos, *A Field Guide to the Folk Architecture of the Northern United States*; and Michael Vlach, ed., *Common Places: Readings in American Vernacular Architecture* (Athens: University of Georgia Press, 1986).

3. Oliver A. Rink, *Holland on the Hudson: An Economic and Social History of Dutch New York* (Ithaca: Cornell University Press, and Cooperstown: New York State Historical Association, 1986).

4. See Terry Jordan, *German Seed in Texas Soil: Immigrant Farmers in Nineteenth Century Texas* (Austin: University of Texas Press, 1975), for a description of how communities developed.

5. See Henry Glassie, *Pattern in the Material Folk Culture of the Eastern United States*; and Kniffen, "Folk Housing, Key to Diffusion."

6. Roger Kennedy, *Greek Revival America* (New York: Stewart, Tabori, and Chang, 1989).

7. Richard Longstreth, *The Buildings of Main Street*.

8. J. B. Jackson, "First Comes the House."

9. Bainbridge Bunting, *Early Architecture in New Mexico* (Albuquerque: University of New Mexico Press, 1976): 8.

10. Robert C. West, "The Flat-Roofed Folk Dwelling in Rural Mexico," *Geoscience and Man* 5 (1974): 111–32.

11. William E. Doolittle, "Culture, History, and Landscape: The Regionalization of Northern Mexico," in *Cultural Adaptation and Ecological Change in Northern Mexico and the American Southwest*, edited by John Peterson (Albuquerque: University of New Mexico Press, forthcoming).

12. James Griffith, *Beliefs and Holy Places: A Spiritual Geography of the Pimería Alta* (Tucson: University of Arizona Press, 1991).

13. Antoinette Lee, "Cast Iron in American Architecture": 102.

14. *Arizona Miner*, September 7, 1864.

15. *Arizona Miner*, September 7, 1867: 3.

16. *Philadelphia Public Ledger*, July 13, 1852.

17. Antoinette Lee, "Cast Iron in American Architecture": 97.

18. *Fayetteville Weekly Democrat*, April 20, 1872.

19. Kent R. Brown, *Fayetteville, a Pictorial History* (Norfolk: Donning Company Publishers, 1982): 25.

20. *Bloomfield Square, Bloomfield, Iowa: A Plan for Preservation, Restoration, and Revitalization*, prepared for the Greater Bloomfield Chamber of Commerce by Wehner, Nowysz, Pattschull, and Pfiffner. Iowa City, Iowa, March 1979: 7–9.

21. Harris Sobin, "From Vigas to Rafters: Architectural Evolution in Florence, Arizona," a chapter in *Florence Townsite, A.T.: A Guide to Territorial Florence, Arizona* (Florence, Ariz.: Industrial Development Authority of the Town of Florence, 1976).

22. *History of Fresno County* (San Francisco: Wallace W. Elliott & Co., 1882).

23. For a typology of false-front styles, see Kingston M. Heath, "False Front Architecture on Montana's Urban Frontier," in *Perspectives in Vernacular Architecture III*, edited by Thomas Carter and Bernard L. Herman (Columbia: University of Missouri Press, 1989).

24. Arthur Hart, "Iron in the Sky: Utah's Sheet Metal Cornices," *Utah Preservation/Restoration — A Magazine for the Preservationist* 1, no. 1 (1979): 9.

25. *Arizona Miner*, September 7, 1867: 3.

26. These boardwalks were constructed to keep pedestrians from becoming mired in the mud while crossing or walking along Main Street, and they are the forerunners of today's stone or cement sidewalks. Where they cross the street, they are called "crosswalks."

27. William Schaumburg, "Placefulness — Part II," *Railroad Model Craftsman*, July 1994: 76.

28. Hildegard Binder Johnson, "Toward a National Landscape."

29. Arthur Hart, "Notes on Sources of Architectural Iron in the West": 42.

30. Ibid.

31. Jay Henry, *Architecture in Texas*: 74–75.

32. Robert Bastian, "Store-Front Remodeling in Small Midwestern Cities."

33. Thomas Hines, *Burnham of Chicago*.

34. Louis Sullivan, *The Autobiography of an Idea* (New York: Dover, 1956 [1924]): 324–25.

35. Meredith Clausen, "Frank Lloyd Wright, Vertical Space and the Chicago School's Quest for Light," *Journal of the Society of Architectural Historians* 44, no. 1 (March 1985): 66–74.

36. Karen J. Weitze, *California's Mission Revival*.

37. Larry Millett, *The Curve of the Arch: The Story of Louis Sullivan's Owatonna Bank* (St. Paul: Minnesota Historical Society Press, 1985): 53.

38. *The Bankers Magazine*, 1912, n.p., as cited in *The Beginning of an Era for the Peoples Savings Bank of Cedar Rapids*, n.p., n.d., 32 pp.

39. James E. Vance, Jr., "Revolution in American Space since 1945, and a Canadian Contrast."

40. Aarne Frobom, "Boilermakers on the Lawn: Small Museums and National Policy," *Trains* 55, no. 3 (March 1985): 74.

41. John Jakle, "The American Gasoline Station 1920 to 1970," *Journal of American Culture* 1, no. 3 (1978): 154–64.

42. Barbara Bailey, *Main Street Northeastern Oregon*.

43. Letter from A. P. May to Mr. McCollum, dated Nov. 24, 1932, in "A Collection of Coalinga's History, Book 1, Pioneers and Old Timers" (loose-leaf book), compiled by Lula Grigsby, Coalinga Public Library, Coalinga, California.

44. Greg Koos and William D. Walter, "Arson, Accidents, and Architecture," *Historic Illinois* 8, no. 1 (June 1985): 1.

45. *Plano, Texas: The Early Years*, compiled by the Book Committee of the Plano Public Library (Wolfe City, Tex.: Henington Publishing Co., 1985): 363.

46. Ibid: 365–66.

47. Vernon B. Schultz, *Southwestern Town: The Story of Willcox, Arizona* (copr. Regents of the Universities and State College of Arizona, 1964): 31.

48. R. Francaviglia, "Xenia Rebuilds: Effects of Predisaster Conditioning on

Postdisaster Redevelopment," *American Institute of Planners Journal* 44, no. 1 (January 1978): 13–24.

49. J. Eugene Haas, Robert W. Kates, and Martyn J. Bowden, *Reconstruction Following Disaster* (Cambridge, Mass.: MIT Press, 1977).

SECTION 2. SPACE AND MAIN STREET

1. Charlie Jacoby, "The Superstore Is Back in Town," *Geographical* 66, no. 6 (June 1994): 22.

2. Lyrics from the popular song "Chevy Van," written by Sammy Johns (1970).

3. Brian K. Roberts, *The Making of the English Village*: 33.

4. Madison Cooper, *Sironia, Texas*: 6.

5. See Christopher Yip, "A Time for Bitter Strength."

6. Ennis (Texas) Railroad and Cultural Heritage Museum brochure, n.d., n.p., distributed by the city in 1993 and 1994.

7. For a description of the Township and Range System in relation to mapping and settlements, see Ronald E. Grim, "Maps of the Township and Range System," in *From Sea Charts to Satellite Images: Interpreting North American History through Maps*, edited by David Buisseret (Chicago: University of Chicago Press, 1990): 89–109.

8. Richard Francaviglia, *Hard Places*.

9. John A. Jakle, *The American Small Town*: 18–19.

10. See John Reps, *Town Planning in Frontier America; The Forgotten Frontier: Urban Planning in the American West before 1890* (Columbia: University of Missouri Press, 1981); *Cities of the American West: A History of Frontier Urban Planning* (Princeton: Princeton University Press, 1979); and *The Making of Urban America*.

11. Thomas Harvey, "The Making of Railroad Towns in Minnesota's Red River Valley" (master's thesis, Pennsylvania State University, 1982).

12. For more information on bird's-eye views, see John Reps, *Views and Viewmakers of Urban America: Lithographs of Towns and Cities in the United States and Canada* (Columbia: University of Missouri Press, 1984); and Gerald Danzer, "Bird's-Eye Views of Towns and Cities," in *From Sea Charts to Satellite Images: Interpreting North American History through Maps* (Chicago: University of Chicago Press, 1990): 143–63.

13. William Pattison, *Beginnings of the American Rectangular Land Survey System, 1784–1800* (Chicago: University of Chicago, Dept. of Geography Research Paper no. 50, 1957).

14. Homer Croy, "County Seat Wars," chap. 9 in *Corn Country* (New York: Duell, Sloane & Pearce, 1947): 55–56.

15. Edward T. Price, "The Central Courthouse Square in the American County Seat." Price discussed the effect that trade and transportation had on the central courthouse square, implying that these factors often strongly shaped the town.

16. Lewis Atherton, *Main Street on the Middle Border*: 29.

17. William D. Middleton, *The Interurban Era* (Milwaukee: Kalmbach Publishing Co., 1961): 140.

18. Helen Santmyer, *Ohio Town*: 3.

19. Richard Francaviglia, "County Seat Centrality as a Regional Trait."

20. Edward T. Price, "The Central Courthouse Square in the American County Seat": 32.

21. I base this statement on observations made during several field trips along the Mississippi River valley in Minnesota, Wisconsin, Iowa, Illinois, and Missouri, as well as on hundreds of topographic maps.

22. Richard Francaviglia, "County Seat Centrality as a Regional Trait."

23. Willard B. Robinson, "The Public Square as a Determinant of Courthouse Form in Texas": 344.

24. Ibid.: 346.

25. *The Barn Builders: Pennsylvania Settlers in Ohio*, a video documentary written, directed, and edited by David Mould (Athens, Ohio: Ohio Landscape Productions, 1989).

26. Gerald Danzer, *Public Places: Exploring Their History*: 1.

27. William Humphrey, *The Ordways*: 4.

28. James O. Breeden, ed., *A Long Ride in Texas: The Explorations of John Leonard Riddell* (College Station: Texas A&M University Press, 1994): 52–53.

29. D. W. Meinig, *Southwest: Three Peoples in Geographical Change*.

30. Fr. Francisco Atanasio Domínguez, *The Missions of New Mexico*, translated by Eleanor B. Adams and Fr. Angélino Chavez (Albuquerque: University of New Mexico Press, 1956): 110.

31. Andrés Tijerina, *Tejanos and Texas under the Mexican Flag, 1821–1836* (College Station: Texas A&M University Press, 1994): 33–34.

32. Frank Waters, *Pumpkin Seed Point* (Chicago: Sage Books — The Swallow Press, 1969): 46–47.

33. Ibid.

34. Hans-Peter Schwöbel, "The Dictatorship of the Right Angle: The Geometrification of Our Realities," *Universitas* 34 (1992): 277.

35. David Lowenthal and Hugh Prince, "The English Landscape," *Geographical Review* 58 (1968): 61–88.

36. Nina Veregge, "Transformation of Spanish Urban Landscapes in the American Southwest, 1821–1900."

37. Ian Barwick, "Establishing That the Spatial Characteristics of Preindustrial Pedestrian Precincts Coincide with the Important Components of Effective Urban Space" (master's thesis, School of Architecture, University of Texas–Arlington, 1994).

38. Rose Wilder, *Old Home Town* (New York: Longmans, Green, 1935).

39. D. W. Meinig, *Southwest: Three Peoples in Geographical Change*.

40. Ellen Threinen, *Architecture and Preservation in Las Vegas: A Study of Six Districts* (Las Vegas: Design Review Board, City of Las Vegas, New Mexico, 1977): 11.

41. See Richard Francaviglia, "Some Comments on the Historic and Geographic Importance of Railroads in Minnesota," *Minnesota History* 43, no. 2 (Summer 1972): 58–62; and John Jakle, *The American Small Town*.

42. Robert Sayre, Introduction to *Historical Railroad Atlas of Iowa*, unpublished manuscript, 1994.

43. William Humphrey, *The Ordways*: 1–2.

44. Diane Glancy, *Firesticks: A Collection of Stories* (Norman: University of Oklahoma Press, 1993): 83–84.

45. Fred Kniffen, "Folk Housing: Key to Diffusion," *Annals AAG* 55, no. 4 (1965): 549–77; D. W. Meinig, *The Shaping of America: A Geographical Perspective* (New Haven: Yale University Press, 1990, 1993).

46. Joseph Wood, "'Build, therefore, your own world.'"

47. John Stilgoe, "The Puritan Townscape: Ideal and Reality."

48. Lewis Atherton, *Main Street on the Middle Border:* 3.

49. Richard Pillsbury, "The Urban Street Pattern as a Culture Indicator."

50. Alfred Wright, "Ohio Town Patterns."

51. Richard Francaviglia, *Hard Places*.

52. Richard Francaviglia, "Mining Town Commercial Vernacular Architecture: The Overhanging Porches of Ohio's Hocking Mining District," *Pioneer America Society Transactions* 13 (1990): 45–51.

53. Steven D. Hoelscher and Robert Ostergren, "Old European Homelands in the American Middle West," *Journal of Cultural Geography* 13, no. 2 (Spring/ Summer 1993): 87–106.

54. Michael Hough, *Out of Place*: 155.

55. Mira Engler, "Drive-Thru History: Theme Towns in Iowa."

56. See Richard Francaviglia, "Elusive Land: Changing Geographic Images of the Southwest," and Marta Weigle, "On Coyotes and Crosses: That Which Is Wild and Wooden of the 20th Century Southwest," in *Essays on the Changing Images of the Southwest* (College Station: Texas A&M University Press, 1994).

57. David Weber, Introduction to *Essays on the Changing Images of the Southwest* (College Station: Texas A&M University Press, 1994): 4.

SECTION 3. IMAGE BUILDING AND MAIN STREET

1. James Barker, "Introduction: Order and Image in the American Small Town."

2. Rod Serling, "The Stop at Willoughby," in *More Stories from the Twilight Zone* (New York: Bantam Books, 1961): 55–56.

3. John Bowen, *America's Living Past* (New York: M&M Books, 1990): 1.

4. The Ohio Historical Society is fortunate to have the original artwork from which many of the lithographs in Henry Howe's books are composed, and so places like Findlay and Fostoria, Ohio, are featured not only in his books but also in the early sketches. Some of them would show some of the early whiteout techniques that were used to enhance the drawings. These streetscape illustrations are marvelous for the detail that they convey, including the way trees were placed on public squares and along the street and protected with boards to keep them from being damaged by wagon wheels or animals.

5. Joseph Wood, "'Build, therefore, your own world.'"

6. James Howard Kunstler, "The Geography of Nowhere: Does Woodstock, Vermont, Represent a Sense of Place in an Unconnected Image?" *Small Town* 24, no. 3 (November–December 1993): 24.

7. Page Smith, *As a City upon a Hill.*

8. Mildred H. Comfort, *Walt Disney, Master of Fantasy*: 145.

9. Ibid.: 141.

10. Robert Jackson, personal communication with author, 1971.

11. "An Interview with Harper Goff," *The "E" Ticket*, no. 14 (Winter 1992–3): 7.

12. Christopher Finch, *The Art of Walt Disney from Mickey Mouse to the Magic Kingdoms.*

13. Jack E. Janzen, "MAIN STREET . . . Walt's Perfect Introduction to Disneyland": 24.

14. Richard Snow, "Disney: Coast to Coast," *American Heritage*, February/March 1987: 22.

15. Richard Francaviglia, "Main Street USA: A Comparison/Contrast."

16. Judith Adams, *The American Amusement Park Industry*: 90.

17. Karal Ann Marling, personal communication with author, January 27, 1995. See also Marling's essay "Disneyland 1955: Just Take the Santa Ana Freeway to the American Dream," *American Art*, Winter/Spring 1991: 168–207.

18. Based on a personal initial meeting with Bert Sklar, Disneyland, Anaheim, California, January 27, 1995, and meetings in Burbank, California, June 26–27, 1995. The author has conducted interviews with the remaining members of the original Disney imagineering team in order to learn more about the sources of their inspiration.

19. Ben Agger, *Gender, Culture and Power: Toward a Post Modern Critical Theory* (Westport, Conn.: Praeger, 1993): 13.

20. John Weiner, "Tall Tales and True," *Nation* 258, no. 4: 134.

21. Paul Goldberger, in Judith Adams, *The American Amusement Park Industry*: 98.

22. Arline Chambers, "The Architecture of Reassurance: Designing the Disney Theme Parks," "Disney Chronology" (unpublished paper), p. 5.

23. Andrew Lainsbury, personal communication with author, July 13, 1995.

24. Letter from David Mumford to Jack and Leon Janzen, November 13, 1992, reproduced in Jack E. Janzen, "Main Street . . . Walt's Perfect Introduction to Disneyland": 30.

25. Richard Francaviglia, "Main Street USA: A Comparison/Contrast."

26. Jack E. Janzen, "Main Street . . . Walt's Perfect Introduction to Disneyland": 26.

27. Such was not always the case, for hippies took over Disneyland briefly in the late 1960s, shocking the nation.

28. Judith Adams, *The American Amusement Park Industry*: 98.

29. Richard Francaviglia, "Main Street Revisited."

30. Jane Holtz Kay, "When You Stimulate a Star," *Landscape Architecture*, June 1990: 54.

31. *New Times*, May 1, 1978: 33.

32. Edward Tauber, "Sociorecreational Shopping," *Human Behavior* 2, no. 4; reproduced in *Intellectual Digest* 4, no. 3 (November 1973): 38.

33. Alan R. H. Baker, "Collective Consciousness and the Last Landscape: National Ideology and the Commune Council of Mesland (Loir-et-Cher) as Landscape Architect during the 19th Century," chapter 12 in *Ideology and Landscape in Historical Perspective*, edited by Alan Baker and Gideon Biger: 255–88.

34. *Medina — The City, The County, The People* (Medina, Ohio: Phoenix Bank, 1970), fold-out section.

35. William Murtagh, *Keeping Time: The History and Theory of Preservation in America* (Pittstown, N. J.: Main Street Press, 1980): 114.

36. Margaret King, personal communication with author, August 12, 1994.

37. Alan D. Haas, "Bringing Back Main Street," *Amtrak Express*, February–March 1991: 53.

38. Richard Francaviglia, "Selling Heritage Landscapes," in *Heritage Landscapes*, edited by Arnie Alanen and Robert Melnick, forthcoming.

39. *Redwood and Lumbering in California Forests* (San Francisco: Edgar Cherry & Co., 1884).

40. Carol Roark, "What's in a Picture? Photographs as a Tool for Understanding Local History," presentation at the *Exploring Community History* Symposium, University of Texas at Arlington, October 15, 1994.

41. Frank Rowsome, *Trolley Car Treasury: A Century of American Streetcars —
Horsecars, Cable Cars, Interurbans, and Trolleys* (New York: Bonanza Books,
1956): 118.

42. "Welcome to Main Street USA," Walthers advertisement in *Railroad
Model Craftsman* 63, no. 5 (October 1993): 55.

43. William Taft, "It's Hip to Be Square," *Indiana Preservationist* no. 4 (July–
August 1989): 6.

44. Ralph Keyes, *Timelock: How Life Got So Hectic & What You Can Do about
It* (New York: Ballantine, 1992).

45. Marcy Hawley, "Murphy's Monument on Main," *Ohio*, December 1988: 79.

46. Michael Flanagan, *Stations: An Imagined Journey* (New York: Pantheon
Books, 1994): 1.

GLOSSARY

adobe. *Unfired brick dried in the sun, commonly used for building in Spain and Latin America.*

Art Deco. *A decorative style stimulated by the Paris Exposition International des Arts Decoratifs et Industrielles Modernes of 1925, widely used in the architecture of the 1930s; characterized by sharp angular or zigzag surface forms and ornaments.*

Art Moderne. *A decorative style popular in the 1940s and 1950s that featured curving or streamlined surfaces.*

balustrade. *A short post or pillar in a series supporting a rail or coping.*

Block Square. *An entire block within a regular rectangular grid that is not built upon (i.e., it is open) and usually serves as a public park.*

canales. *Spanish term for pipes or tubes used to divert water off a flat roof through a parapet wall.*

Central Hall. *A house type featuring a centrally placed door in the façade which leads into a central hallway flanked by rooms such as parlor and living room.*

Chicago Style. *A style of architecture that originated with architects in Chicago in the late nineteenth and early twentieth centuries; it featured the use of steel and larger window openings.*

circle in a square town plan. *(Sometimes called Harrisonburg or Philadelphia style plan.) A town plan in which a circular parcel of land is located centrally through the removal of a corner of four adjacent or contiguous blocks.*

colonnades. *A series of columns set at regular intervals and usually supporting the base of a roof structure. Often seen in the Southwestern United States.*

corbels. *Projecting blocks, usually of stone, supporting a beam or other horizontal members.*

cornice. *In classical architecture, projecting ornamental moulding along the top of a building, wall, arch, etc., finishing or crowning it.*

culture hearth. *A source area in which cultural traits develop, and from which these traits spread.*

daguerreotype. *An early (ca. 1840–50) photograph produced on a silver or silver-covered copperplate.*

European classical. *A detailed, ornamented style of architecture that developed in the Renaissance (1500–1700) and was used for prominent buildings.*

façade. *The exterior face of a building which is the architectural front, sometimes distinguished from the other faces by elaboration of architectural or ornamental details.*

faux. *From the French, signifying false or imitation architectural features and designs.*

Federal Style. *In the U.S., the Classic Revival style, from ca. 1790 to 1830.*

frieze. *1. The middle horizontal member of a classical entablature, above the architrave and below the cornice. 2. A similar decorative band in a stringcourse, or near the top of an interior wall below the cornice. 3. In house construction, a horizontal member connecting the top of siding with the soffit of the cornice.*

gable. *The triangular upper portion of a wall to carry a pitched roof.*

Greek Revival. *Greek as opposed to Roman architecture became known in Europe only about 1750–60. It was at first regarded as primitive and imitated by only a few architects. Its popularity culminated in the United States in the 1820s and 1850s.*

green. *A public open space, usually located in the center of a community.*

hipped roof. *A roof which slopes upward from all four sides of a building, requiring a hip rafter at each corner.*

imbricated. *A pattern involving overlapping in a regular order, as shingling, tiles, etc.*

International Style. *A functional architecture devoid of regional characteristics, created in Western Europe and the U.S. during the early twentieth century and applied throughout the world.*

Italianate. *Of or pertaining to Italian architecture of either the classical or Renaissance periods.*

Lancaster Square. *A square block that is placed at the intersection of two major perpendicular streets, containing a central county courthouse.*

linear. *Of, relating to, resembling, or having a straight line.*

lintel. *A horizontal structural member (such as a beam) over an opening which carries the weight of the wall above it; usually of a strong material such as steel, stone, or wood.*

lithograph. *A print made from a plane surface on which the image to be printed is ink-receptive.*

mandala. *A Hindu or Buddhist graphic symbol of the universe, usually a circle enclosing a square with a deity on each side.*

mansard roof. *A roof having a double slope on all four sides, the lower slope being much steeper.*

material culture. *The physical or tangible objects, such as housing, furniture, and jewelry, of a people.*

Mission Revival Style. *A popular style in the early twentieth century that made liberal use of elements seen in earlier Spanish/Mexican buildings; originally regional, the style spread nationwide by 1920.*

neo-classical revival. *The last phase of European classicism, in the late eighteenth and early nineteenth centuries, characterized by monumentality, strict use of the orders, and sparing application of ornament.*

nucleated. *Having a nucleus; clustered, such as a town developed around a central square.*

obelisk. *A monumental, four-sided stone shaft, usually monolithic and tapering to a pyramidal tip.*

open square. *Any block that is not built up, and usually serving as a public open space.*

oriel. 1. *A bay window corbeled out from the wall of an upper story.* 2. *A bay projecting, inside or out, extending a room.* 3. *A windowed bay or porch at the top of exterior stairs.*

Palladian design. *A revived classic style in architecture based on the works of Andrea Palladio; often used for large, formal buildings but sometimes encountered in vernacular architecture.*

parapet. 1. *A low guarding wall at any point of sudden drop, as at the edge of a terrace, roof, battlement, balcony, etc.* 2. *In an exterior wall, fire wall, or party wall, the part entirely above the roof.*

pediment. 1. *In classical architecture, the triangular gable end of the roof above the horizontal cornice, often filled with sculpture.* 2. *In later work, a surface used ornamentally over doors or windows; usually triangular but sometimes curved.*

Philadelphia Square. *A square block that is placed at the intersection of two perpendicular streets, and is open, that is, contains no public building or courthouse.*

plat. *A map, plan, or chart of a city, town, section, or subdivision, indicating the location and boundaries of individual properties.*

popular culture. *The culture, both material and non-material, of ordinary people; also, the culture of societies having high-tech communications and marketing systems.*

public square. *A rectangular or square block, usually but not always open, and often centrally located in a community.*

ridge pole. *A longitudinal member at the apex of a roof supporting the upper ends of the rafters, and defining the way the roof "runs."*

Romanesque Style. *The style emerging in Western Europe in the early eleventh century, based on Roman and Byzantine elements, characterized by massive articulated wall structures, round arches, and powerful vaults, and lasting until the advent of Gothic architecture in the middle of the twelfth century.*

Roman Revival. *A style that uses architectural and design elements from the Romans. Often involves masonry, arches, and large-scale structures.*

scupper. *An opening in a wall or parapet that allows water to drain from a roof.*

Second Empire style. *The eclectic style of the French Second Empire (1852–70), which became popular in Victorian American architecture.*

Shelbyville Square. *One of the regular rectangular or square blocks of a community that is built up, and* serves as the location of a central county courthouse.

spatial. *Relating to, occupying, or having the character of space.*

splayed entrance. *A sloping, chamfered surface cut into the walls. The term usually refers to the widening of doorways, windows, or other wall openings by slanting the sides.*

Sullivanesque. *Of or pertaining to the architecture of American architect Louis Henri Sullivan (1856–1924), who introduced unique materials and bold compositions in his designs.*

terra cotta. *Hard, unglazed fired clay; used for ornamental work and roof and floor tile.*

turret. *A very small and slender tower, characteristically corbeled from a corner.*

vernacular. *Based on regional forms and materials.*

Victorian architecture. *The Revival and Eclectic architecture in nineteenth-century Great Britain, named after the reign of Queen Victoria (1837–1901); also used for its American counterpart.*

viga beam. *One of the heavy rafters supporting the roof in native Indian and Spanish architecture of the Southwest.*

vignette. *A scene or view that depicts the character of a place or time.*

BIBLIOGRAPHY

Adams, Judith. *The American Amusement Park Industry: A History of Technology and Thrills.* Boston: Twayne Publishers, 1991.

Allen, James B. *The Company Town in the American West.* Norman: University of Oklahoma Press, 1966.

Ambler, Cathy. "Mastering Mud on Main Street: Paving Technology in the Late Nineteenth-Century." *Pioneer America Society Transactions* 17 (1994): 39–47.

Anderson, Sarah. "Wal-Mart's War on Main Street." *The Progressive* 58, no. 11 (November 1994): 19–21.

Anderson, Sherwood. *Hello Towns!* New York: H. Liveright Co., 1929.

Atherton, Lewis. "The Midwestern Country Town: Myth and Reality." *Agricultural History* 26 (July 1952): 73–80.

———. *Main Street on the Middle Border.* Bloomington: Indiana University Press, 1954.

Bailey, Barbara R. *Main Street Northeastern Oregon: The Founding and Development of Small Towns.* Portland: Oregon Historical Society, 1982.

Baker, Alan R. H., and Gideon Biger. *Ideology and Landscape in Historical Perspective: Essays on the Meanings of Some Places in the Past.* Cambridge: Cambridge University Press, 1992.

Barker, James F. "Introduction: Order and Image in the American Small Town." *Southern Quarterly* (Special Issue — The Small Town: Order and Image) 19, no. 1 (Fall 1980).

Basso, Hamilton. *Court House Square.* New York: Scribner's, 1936.

Bastian, Robert W. "Architecture and Class Segregation in Late Nineteenth Century Terre Haute, Indiana." *Geographical Review* 65 (1975): 166–79.

———. "Indiana Folk Architecture: A Lower Midwestern Index." *Pioneer America* 19 (1977): 115–36.

———. "Storefront Remodeling in Small Midwestern Cities, 1890–1940." *Pioneer America Society Transactions* 1 (1978): 1–14.

Blumenson, J., and G. Blumenson. *Identifying American Architecture: A Pictorial Guide to Styles and Terms, 1600–1945.* Nashville: American Association for State and Local History, 1977.

Blumenthal, Albert. *Small Town Stuff.* Chicago: University of Chicago Press, 1932.

Bolton, Kate. "The Great Awakening of the Night: Lighting America's Streets." *Landscape* 23, no. 3 (1979): 41–47.

Brown, Calvin S. "Faulkner's Geography and Topography." *Publications of the Modern Language Association* 77 (December 1962): 652–59.

Brush, John E., and Howard E. Bracey. "Rural Service Centers in Southwestern Wisconsin and Southern England." *Geographical Review* 45, no. 4 (October 1955): 559–69.

Buckley, G. T. "Is Oxford the Original of Jefferson in William Faulkner's Novels?" *Publications of the Modern Language Association* 76 (September 1961): 447–54.

Burghardt, Andrew F. "The Location of River Towns in the Central Lowland of the United States." *Annals, Association of American Geographers* 49, no. 3 (September 1959): 305–23.

Campbell, Thomas, Jr. "Galena, 1820–1830: The Creation of a Mining Boom Town." *Historic Illinois* (June 1985): 8–13.

Cinquino, Michael, Marvin Keller, Carmine Tronolone, and Charles Vandrel, Jr. "Log Roads to Light Rails: The Evolution of Main Street and Transportation in Buffalo, New York." *Northeast Historical Archaeology* 15 (1986): 53–64.

Comfort, Mildred H. *Walt Disney, Master of Fantasy*. New York: T. S. Denison and Co., 1968.

Conzen, Michael P. *The Making of the American Landscape*. Boston: Unwin Hyman, 1990.

Cooper, Madison A. *Sironia, Texas*. Boston: Houghton Mifflin, 1952.

Corey, Paul. *County Seat*. Indianapolis: Bobbs-Merrill, 1941.

Croy, Homer. *West of the Water Tower*. New York: Harper, 1923.

Cruz, Gilberto. *Let There Be Towns: Spanish Municipal Origins in the American Southwest, 1610–1810*. College Station: Texas A&M University Press, 1988.

Danzer, Gerald. *Public Places: Exploring Their History*. Nashville: American Association for State and Local History, 1987.

Davies, Wayne K. D. "The Morphology of Central Places." *Annals AAG* 58, no. 1 (March, 1968): 91–110.

Davis, Charles M. "The Cities and Towns of the High Plains of Michigan," *Geographical Review* 28, no. 4 (October 1928): 664–73.

Debo, Angie. *Prairie City: The Story of an American Community*. New York: A. A. Knopf, 1944.

Dodge, Stanley D. "Bureau and the Princeton Community." *Annals AAG* 22, no. 3 (September 1932): 159–209.

Douglas, Harlan Paul. *The Little Town Especially in Its Rural Relationships*. New York: Macmillan, 1921.

Ekola, Giles G. *Town and Country America*. St. Louis: Concordia Publishing House, 1967.

Engler, Mira. "Drive-Thru History: Theme Towns in Iowa." *Landscape* 32, no. 1 (1993): 8–18.

Finch, Christopher. *The Art of Walt Disney from Mickey Mouse to the Magic Kingdoms*. New York: Harry N. Abrams, 1973.

Fleming, Robert Lee. *Facade Stories*. New York: Cambridge and Hastings House, 1982.

Francaviglia, Richard. "County Seat Centrality as a Regional Trait." *Geographical Survey* 2, no. 2 (April 1973): 1–21.

——. "Main Street Revisited." *Places* 1, no. 3 (October 1974): 7–11.

——. "Main Street U.S.A.: The Creation of a Popular Image." *Landscape* 21, no. 3 (Spring–Summer 1977): 18–22.

——. "Main Street U.S.A.: A Comparison/Contrast of Streetscapes in Disneyland and Walt Disney World." *Journal of Popular Culture* 15, no. 1 (Summer 1981): 141–56.

——. "Bisbee, Arizona: A Mining Town Survives a Decade of Closure." *Small Town* 13, no. 4 (January–February 1983): 4–8.

——. "Reading the Landscape and Other Historical Detective Stories." *Local Historian* (September–October 1988): 7–9.

——. "MAIN STREET: The Origins." *Timeline* 5, no. 6 (December 1988–January 1989): 28–39.

——. "MAIN STREET: The Twentieth Century." *Timeline* 6, no. 1 (February–March 1989): 28–43.

——. *Hard Places: Reading the Landscape of America's Historic Mining Districts*. Iowa City: University of Iowa Press, 1991.

Gerloff, Scott, Tom Lutz, Tom Muriarty, and Clark Schoette. Edited by Libby Hoffman. *National Trust for Historic Preservation: National Main Street Center: Training Program*. Washington, D.C.: National Trust for Historic Preservation, 1981.

Glassie, Henry. *Pattern in the Material Folk Culture of the Eastern United States*. Philadelphia: University of Pennsylvania Press, 1968.

Goldthwait, James W. "A Town That Has Gone Downhill." *Geographical Review* 17, no. 4 (October 1927): 527–52.

Gorby, Richard. "Shopping around Prescott's Plaza — The First Five Years." *The Gazette*, Journal Edition, no. 1 (December 1988). Sharlot Hall Museum, Prescott, Arizona. N. p.

Grills, Russell A. *Cazenovia: The Story of an Upland Community*. Cazenovia, N.Y.: Cazenovia Preservation Foundation, 1977.

Gulliford, Andrew. "Vernacular and Small Town Architecture of Northwest Ohio." *Northwest Ohio Quarterly* 58, no. 4 (Autumn 1986): 107–21.

Gussow, Alan. "A Sense of Place." *Amicus* 1, no. 2 (Fall 1979): 14–7.

Hamlin, Talbot. *Greek Revival Architecture in America*. New York: Oxford University Press, 1944.

Harper, R. Eugene. "Town Development in Early Western Pennsylvania." *Western Pennsylvania Historical Magazine* 71, no. 1 (January 1988): 3–26.

Hart, Arthur. "Notes on Sources of Architectural Iron in the West." In *Festschrift: A Collection of Essays on Architectural History*. Northern Pacific Coast Chapter of the Society of Architectural Historians, 1978.

Harvey, Thomas. "Railroad Towns: Urban Form on the Prairie." *Landscape* 27, no. 3 (1983): 26–35.

Heath, Kingston M. "Defining the Nature of Vernacular." *Material Culture* 6, no. 4 (1986): 47–56.

——. "False-Front Architecture on Montana's Urban Frontier." In *Perspectives in Vernacular Architecture III*, edited by Thomas Carter and Bernard L. Herman. Columbia: University of Missouri Press, 1989.

Heimsath, Clovis. *Pioneer Texas Buildings: A Geometry Lesson*. Austin: University of Texas Press, 1968.

Henry, Jay C. *Architecture in Texas, 1895–1945*. Austin: University of Texas Press, 1993.

Herron, Ima Honaker. *The Small Town in American Literature*. Durham: Duke University Press, 1939.

Hicks, Granville. *Small Town*. New York: Macmillan Co., 1946.

Hines, Thomas S. *Burnham of Chicago: Architect and Planner*. New York: Oxford University Press, 1974.

Hough, Michael. *Out of Place: Restoring Identity to the Regional Landscape*. New Haven: Yale University Press, 1990.

Howe, Henry. *Historical Collections of Ohio*. Cincinnati: Derby, Bradley & Co., 1847. Reprint, 2 vols., Cincinnati: The State of Ohio, 1907.

——. *Historical Collections of the Great West, Containing Narratives of the Most Important and Interesting Events in Western History — to which Is Appended Historical and Descriptive Sketches of Oregon, New Mexico, Texas, Minnesota, Utah, and California*. 2 vols. Cincinnati: Henry Howe, 1853.

Hummon, David M. "Popular Images of the American Small Town." *Landscape* 24, no. 2 (1980): 3–9.

Humphrey, William. *The Ordways*. New York: Alfred A. Knopf, 1964.

Hypes, J. L. "The Future of the Sparsely Populated Rural Towns of Connecticut." *Geographical Review* 26, no. 2 (April 1936): 293–98.

Jackson, J. B. "The Almost Perfect Town." *Landscape* 2, no. 1 (Spring 1952): 2–8.

——. "First Comes the House." *Landscape* 9, no. 2 (Winter 1959–60): 26–32.

Jakle, John. *The American Small Town: Twentieth Century Place Images*. Hamden, Conn.: The Shoe String Press, 1982.

Jakle, John, Robert W. Bastian, and Douglas K. Meyer. *Common Houses in*

America's Small Towns: The Atlantic Seaboard to the Mississippi Valley.
Athens: University of Georgia Press, 1989.

Janzen, Jack E. "Main Street . . . Walt's Perfect Introduction to Disneyland."
The "E" Ticket, no. 14 (Winter 1992–93): 24–33.

Johnson, Hildegard Binder. "Man, Rectangularity and Landscape." In
International Geography 1, sec. 5, *Historical Geography,* edited by W. P.
Adams and F. M. Helleiner, 436–37. Toronto: University of Toronto Press,
1972; for the International Geographical Union.

———. "The United States Land Survey as a Principle of Order." In *Pattern and
Process: Research in Historical Geography,* edited by Ralph E. Ehrenberg,
114–30. Washington, D.C.: Howard University Press, 1975.

———. "Toward a National Landscape." In *The Making of the American
Landscape,* edited by Michael P. Conzen, 123–45. Boston: Unwin Hyman,
1990.

Keister, Kim. "Main Street Makes Good." *Historic Preservation* 42, no. 5
(September–October 1990): 44–50.

Kerr, Elizabeth M. *Yoknapatawpha: Faulkner's "Little Postage Stamp of Native
Soil."* New York: Fordam University Press, 1969.

King, Margaret. "Empires of Popular Culture: McDonald's and Disney." *Journal
of American Culture* 1, no. 2 (Summer 1978): 424–37.

———. "The New American Muse: Notes on the Amusement/Theme Park."
Journal of Popular Culture 15, no. 1 (Summer 1981): 56–62.

———. "Disneyland and Walt Disney World: Traditional Values in Futuristic
Form." *Journal of Popular Culture* 15, no. 1 (Summer 1981): 116–40.

———. "The Theme Park Experience." *The Futurist,* special issue on
"Tomorrow's Museums." World Future Society, November–December 1991:
24–31.

Kniffen, Fred. "Folk Housing: Key to Diffusion." *Annals AAG* 55, no. 4 (1965):
549–77.

Kostof, Spiro. *American by Design: The Street.* 60 min. Washington, D.C.:
Guggenheim Productions and WTTV, 1986. PBS broadcast.

Kowinski, William Severini. *The Malling of America: An Inside Look at the Great
Consumer Paradise.* New York: William Morrow and Company, 1985.

Ladd, Everett Carll. *Ideology in America: Change and Response in a City, a
Suburb, and a Small Town.* Ithaca: Cornell University Press, 1969.

Lane, Rose Wilder. *Old Home Town.* New York: Longmans, Green, 1935.

Larson, Albert J. "The County Courthouses of Florida's Panhandle." *Pioneer
America Society Transactions* 12 (1989): 55–63.

———. "The County Courthouses of Southern Wisconsin." *Pioneer America
Society Transactions* 23, no. 1 (1991): 27–42.

Larson, Paul C., and Susan M. Brown, eds. *The Spirit of H. H. Richardson on the*

Midland Prairies: Regional Transformations of an Architectural Style. Ames: Iowa State University Press, 1988.

Lee, Antoinette J. "Cast Iron in American Architecture: A Synoptic View." In *The Technology of Historical American Buildings: Studies of the Materials, Craft Processes, and the Mechanization of Building Construction*, edited by H. Ward Jandl. Washington, D.C.: Association for Preservation Technology, 1983.

Lewis, Peirce. "Small Town in Pennsylvania." *Annals AAG* 62, no. 2 (June 1972): 323–73.

Lewis, Sinclair. *Main Street*. New York: New American Library, 1961.

Liebs, Chester H. *Main Street to Miracle Mile: American Roadside Architecture*. Boston: Little, Brown and Company, 1986.

Lingeman, Richard. *Small Town America: A Narrative History, 1620–The Present*. New York: G. P. Putnam's Sons, 1980.

Longstreth, Richard. "Compositional Types in American Commercial Architecture: 1800–1950." Washington, D.C.: National Trust for Historic Preservation, 1981.

———. *The Buildings of Main Street: A Guide to American Commercial Architecture*. Washington, D.C.: National Trust for Historic Preservation, 1987.

Lowenthal, David. "The American Scene." *Geographical Review* 58, no. 1 (January 1968): 61–88.

———. *The Past Is a Foreign Country*. New York: Cambridge University Press, 1985.

Lynch, Kevin. *The Image of the City*. Cambridge: MIT Press, 1960.

McAlester, Virginia, and Lee McAlester. *A Field Guide to American Houses*. New York: Alfred Knopf, 1984.

MacDonald, Kent. "The Commercial Strip: From Main Street to Television Road." *Landscape* 28, no. 2 (1985): 12–19.

Martin, Robert L. *The City Moves West: Economic and Industrial Growth in Central West Texas*. Austin: University of Texas Press, 1969.

Meinig, D. W. *Southwest: Three Peoples in Geographical Change, 1600–1970*. New York: Oxford University Press, 1970.

———. "Symbolic Landscapes: Models of American Community." In *The Interpretation of Ordinary Landscapes*, edited by D. W. Meinig. New York: Oxford University Press, 1979.

Mercer, Blaine B. *The American Community*. New York: Random House, 1956.

Morgan, William T. "Strongboxes on Main Street: Prairie-Style Banks." *Landscape* 24, no. 2 (1980): 35–40.

Morrison, Paul C. "A Morphological Study of Worthington, Ohio." *Ohio Journal of Science* 34 (January 1934): 31–45.

Mystic Seaport. Rochester, N.Y.: 30 min. Eastman Kodak Company, 1989. Videocassette.

Nelson, Howard J. "Townscapes of Mexico: An Example of the Regional Variation of Townscapes." *Economic Geography* 39 (1963): 74–83.

Nelson, Lowry. *The Mormon Village: A Pattern and Technique of Land Settlement*. Salt Lake City: University of Utah Press, 1952.

——. *The Minnesota Community: Country and Town in Transition*. Minneapolis: University of Minnesota Press, 1960.

Noble, Allen. *Wood, Brick and Stone: The North American Settlement Landscape*. 3 vols. Amherst: University of Massachusetts Press, 1984.

Noe, Sally. *Greetings from Gallup: Six Decades of Route 66*. Gallup, N.M.: Gallup Downtown Redevelopment Group, 1991.

Nolan, John. *New Towns for Old: Achievements in Civic Improvement in Some American Small Towns and Neighborhoods*. Boston: M. Jones, 1927.

Old Sturbridge Village. Rochester, N.Y.: 30 min. Eastman Kodak Company, 1989. Videocassette.

Oszuscik, Philippe. "Germanic Influence upon the Vernacular Architecture of Davenport, Iowa." *Pioneer America Society Transactions* 10 (1987): 17–27.

Pattison, William D. "Reflections on the American Rectangular Land Survey System." In *Pattern and Process: Research in Historical Geography*, edited by Ralph E. Ehrenberg, 131–38. Washington, D.C.: Howard University Press, 1975.

Pillsbury, Richard. "The Urban Street Pattern as a Culture Indicator: Pennsylvania, 1682–1815." *Annals AAG* 60, no. 3 (September 1970): 428–46.

Pillsbury, Richard, and Andrew Kardos. *A Field Guide to the Folk Architecture of the Northeast United States*. Geography Publication no. 8. Hanover, N.H.: Department of Geography, 1971.

Poster, Corky. "Sombra, Patios, y Macetas: Modernism, Regionalism, and the Elements of Southwestern Architecture." *Journal of the Southwest* 35, no. 4 (Winter 1993): 461–500.

Price, Edward T. "The Central Courthouse Square in the American County Seat." *Geographical Review* 58, no. 1 (January 1968): 29–60.

——. *Dividing the Land: Early American Beginnings of Our Private Property Mosaic*. Geography Research Paper, no. 238. Chicago: University of Chicago Press, 1995.

Rasmussen, Steen Biler. *Towns and Buildings Described in Drawings and Words*. Cambridge: Harvard University Press, 1951.

Reid, Loren. *Hurry Home Wednesday: Growing up in a Small Missouri Town, 1905–1921*. Columbia: University of Missouri Press, 1978.

Relph, E. *Place and Placelessness*. London: Pion, 1976.

Reps, John W. *The Making of Urban America: A History of City Planning in the United States*. Princeton: Princeton University Press, 1965.

——. *Town Planning in Frontier America*. Princeton: Princeton University Press, 1969.

———. "Bonanza Towns: Urban Planning on the Western Mining Frontier." In *Pattern and Process: Research in Historical Geography*, edited by Ralph E. Ehrenberg. Washington, D.C.: Howard University Press, 1975.

Rifkind, Carole. *Main Street: The Face of Urban America*. New York: Harper Colophon Books, 1977.

———. *A Field Guide to American Architecture*. New York: Times Mirror–New American Library, 1981.

Roberts, Brian K. *The Making of the English Village: A Study in Historical Geography*. Essex, Eng.: Longman Scientific & Technical, 1987.

Robinson, Willard B. "The Public Square as a Determinant of Courthouse Form in Texas." *Southwestern Historical Quarterly* 75 (January 1972): 352–54.

Rose, Harold M. "The All-Negro Town: Its Evolution and Function." *Geographical Review* 55, no. 3 (July 1965): 362–81.

Ross, Pat. *Remembering Main Street: An American Album*. New York: Viking/Penguin Books, 1994.

Roueche, Berton. "Forty Flights of Steps." *New Yorker*, July 16, 1973: 32–44.

Santmyer, Helen. *Ohio Town*. Columbus: Ohio State University Press, 1962.

Sasser, Elizabeth Skidmore. *Dugout to Deco: Building in West Texas, 1880–1930*. Lubbock: Texas Tech University Press, 1993.

Schickel, Richard. *The Disney Version: The Life, Times, Art and Commerce of Walt Disney*. New York: Simon and Schuster, 1968.

Schuyler, David. *The New Urban Landscape: The Redefinition of City Form in Nineteenth Century America*. Baltimore: Johns Hopkins University Press, 1986.

Scofield, Edna. "The Origin of Settlement Patterns in Rural New England." *Geographical Review* 28, no. 4 (October 1938): 652–63.

Sculle, Keith. *The Gas Station in America*. Baltimore: Johns Hopkins University Press, 1994.

Smith, Everett G., Jr. *Downtown Change in Three Middle-Sized Cities*. Urbana: University of Illinois, Bureau of Economic & Business Research, 1965.

Smith, Page. *As a City upon a Hill: The Town in American History*. New York: Knopf, 1966.

Solomon, R. J. "Procedures in Townscape Analysis." *Annals AAG* 56, no. 2 (June 1966): 254–68.

Stanislawski, Dan. "The Origin and Spread of the Grid Pattern Town." *Geographical Review* 36, no. 1 (January 1946): 105–20.

Stephens, David T., Alexander T. Bobersky, and Joseph Cencia. "The Yankee Frontier in Northern Ohio: 1796–1850." *Pioneer America Society Transactions* 17 (1984): 1–18.

Stilgoe, John. "The Puritan Townscape: Ideal and Reality." *Landscape* 20, no. 3 (Spring 1976): 3–7.

———. *The Common Landscape of America, 1580 to 1845*. New Haven: Yale University Press, 1982.

———. "Small Town and Urban Edges." *U D Review* 6 (Spring–Summer 1983): 5–7.

Sutton, Robert K. *Americans Interpret the Parthenon: The Progression of Greek Revival Architecture from the East Coast to Oregon, 1800–1860*. Niwot, Colo.: University Press of Colorado, 1992.

Sweet, Fred Oney. "An Iowa County Seat." *Iowa Journal of History and Politics* 38 (October 1940): 339–408.

Torma, Carolyn. "An Attitude toward Landscape: The Kentucky County Seat Plan." Unpublished paper, Kentucky Heritage Commission, Frankfort, Kentucky, ca. 1979.

Trewartha, Glenn T. "Types of Rural Settlement in Colonial America." *Geographical Review* 36, no. 4 (October 1946): 568–96.

"Upper Ashuelot": A History of Keene, New Hampshire. Keene, N.H.: Keene History Committee, 1968.

Upton, Dell. *America's Architectural Roots: Ethnic Groups That Built America*. Washington, D.C.: National Trust for Historic Preservation, 1986.

Upton, Dell, and John M. Vlach. *Common Places: Readings in American Vernacular Architecture*. Athens: University of Georgia Press, 1986.

Vance, James E., Jr. *The Continuing City: Urban Morphology in Western Civilization*. Baltimore: Johns Hopkins University Press, 1990.

———. "Revolution in American Space since 1945, and a Canadian Contrast." Chap. 18 in *North America: The Historical Geography of A Changing Continent*, edited by Robert D. Mitchell and Paul A. Groves, 438–59. Savage, Maryland: Rowman & Littlefield Publishers, 1990.

Vaughan, Thomas, ed., and Virginia Guest Ferriday, associate ed. *Space, Style and Structure: Building in Northwest America*. 2 vols. Portland: Oregon Historical Society, 1974.

Veregge, Nina. "Transformations of Spanish Urban Landscapes in the American Southwest, 1821–1900." *Journal of the Southwest* 35, no. 4 (Winter 1993): 371–460.

Vidich, Arthur J., and Joseph Beusman. *Small Town in Mass Society: Class, Power and Religion in a Rural Community*. Garden City, N.Y.: Doubleday, 1960.

Wallace, Michael. "Mickey Mouse History: Portraying the Past at Disney World." Chap. 7 in *History Museums in the United States: A Critical Assessment*, edited by Warren Leon and Roy Rosenzweig, 158–80. Urbana: University of Illinois Press, 1989.

Walters, William D. "Change and Continuity in the Materials of Downtown Building: 1842–1910." *Pioneer America Society Transactions* 8 (1985): 37–43.

———. "The American Shale Paver: Its Origin, Evolution and Role in Landscape Preservation." *Pioneer America Society Transactions* 10 (1987): 59–65.

Watts, May Theilgaard. *Reading the Landscape*. New York: Macmillan, 1957.

Webb, John. "Basic Concepts in the Analysis of Small Urban Centers of Minnesota." *Annals AAG* 49, no. 1 (March 1959): 55–72.

Webster, Clarence M. *Town Meeting Country*. New York: Duell, Sloane & Pearce, 1945.

Weitze, Karen J. *California's Mission Revival*. Los Angeles: Hennesy and Ingalls, 1984.

Wheeler, Thomas C., ed. *A Vanishing America: The Life and Times of the Small Town*. New York: Holt, Rinehart and Winston, 1964.

Wilhelm, Hubert. *Saltboxes and Schools: The New England Landscape of Ohio — A Documentary to Mark the Bicentennial of the Northwest Ordinance of 1787*. 27 min. Athens, Ohio: Ohio Landscape Productions, 1987. Videocassette.

———. *The Barn Builders: Pennsylvania Settlers in Ohio*. Written, directed, and edited by David Mould. 50 min. Athens, Ohio: Ohio Landscape Productions, 1989. Videocassette.

Withers, Carl. *Plainville, U.S.A.* New York: Columbia University Press, 1945.

Wood, Joseph. "'Build, therefore, your own world': The New England Village as Settlement Ideal." *Annals AAG* 81, no. 1 (March 1991): 32–50.

Wright, Alfred J. "Ohio Town Patterns." *Geographical Review* 27, no. 4 (October 1937): 615–24.

Yip, Christopher. "A Time for Bitter Strength: The Chinese in Locke, California." *Landscape* 22, no. 2 (Spring 1978): 3–13.

Zelinsky, Wilbur. "Classical Town Names in the United States: The Historical Geography of an American Idea." *Geographical Review* 57, no. 4 (October 1967): 463–95.

———. "The Pennsylvania Town: An Overdue Geographical Account." *Geographical Review* 67 (April 1977): 127–47.

———. "Where Every Town Is above Average: Welcoming Signs along America's Highways." *Landscape* 30, no. 1 (1988): 1–10.

———. "On the Superabundance of Signs in Our Landscape — Selections from a Slide Lecture." *Landscape* 31, no. 3 (1992): 30–38.

Ziegler, Arthur P., Jr., and Walter Kidney. *Historic Preservation in Small Towns: A Manual of Practice*. Nashville: American Association for State and Local History, 1980.

INDEX